THE PATH TO PERFECTION

"There was one doctrine of John Wesley's—the doctrine of perfect sanctification—which ought to have led to a great and original ethical development; but the doctrine has not grown; it seems to remain just where John Wesley left it. There has been a want of the genius or the courage to attempt the solution of the immense practical questions which the doctrine suggests. The questions have not been raised—much less solved. To have raised them effectively, indeed, would have been to originate an ethical revolution which would have had a far deeper effect on the thought and life—first of England, and then of the rest of Christendom—than was produced by the Reformation of the sixteenth century."

DR. R. W. DALE (1879).

"Wesley's doctrine of Christian perfection has been inadvertently stigmatized as a theological provincialism of Methodism. ... 'It is the innermost kernel of the Christian ethic of life and is thoroughly rooted and grounded in New Testament teaching and in the teaching of historic Christianity.' ... It is an original and unique synthesis of the Protestant ethic of grace with the Catholic ethic of holiness."

PROFESSOR GEORGE CROFT CELL (1934).

THE
PATH TO PERFECTION

AN EXAMINATION AND RESTATEMENT OF JOHN WESLEY'S DOCTRINE OF CHRISTIAN PERFECTION

By

W. E. SANGSTER

M.A., Ph.D.(Lond.)

Minister of the Central Hall, Westminster

ABINGDON-COKESBURY PRESS
New York • *Nashville*

> **WAR EDITION**
> Complete text. Reduced size in compliance
> with orders of the War Production Board
> for conserving paper and other materials.

10-19-43

First American edition, September, 1943

*Photographically reproduced from the first
British edition (for which type was set
by The Camelot Press, Limited, London
and Southampton) by Marshall & Bruce
Company, Nashville, Tennessee. Bound by
the Parthenon Press, Nashville, Tennessee.*

To

R. NEWTON FLEW

M.A., D.D.

Principal of Wesley House, Cambridge

C. RYDER SMITH

B.A., D.D.

Sometime Professor of Theology in the
University of London

E. S. WATERHOUSE

M.A., D.D., D.LIT.

Principal of Richmond College, Surrey

AMICIS DILECTISSIMIS
ET DOCTRINAE HUIUS DISCIPULIS VESTIGIA
DOMINI HUMILITER SEQUENTIBUS

PREFACE

THIS book has been written during the period in which I forsook my home to share the life of bombed-out people in a public air-raid shelter. That is not intended as a covert apology for any deficiencies in the book. It is hoped that the work will stand without that. It is stated merely for the slight interest it may have for the social student of the future who will wonder how people spent their time underground. When the last incendiary had been put out and the last group of homeless people received and made welcome, I filled the hours of the vigil which had still to be kept by thinking on perfection. If that seems a little mad to some who read this, I can only reply that it was part of the way in which I kept sane.

There is both need and room for a book on this subject. The doctrine of Christian Perfection has been regarded by some scholars as a by-path of theological thought and even as a dangerous cul-de-sac. It is neither.

Nor is it (so far as I am aware) denominational loyalty which has led me to examine the doctrine as taught by John Wesley. Most close students of modern Protestant "holiness movements," whether they accept or reject the teaching, recognise that they stem-down from the founder of Methodism. If this teaching is understood in him, one has the key to the variant forms it has taken in the last two hundred years.

I am not unaware that many who hold this teaching in its traditional form will be dissatisfied with some of my conclusions. If it gives them pleasure that attention has been directed again to a doctrine which is central to their life and thought, it will give them no pleasure that I throw away parts of it which will seem to them as precious as the parts which I retain.

But I can do no other. After much thought, I do not believe them to be true, and I am now convinced that the effort to retain them is part of the explanation of the wide neglect of this doctrine in those branches of the Holy Catholic Church where one would expect this emphasis to fall. To bind up what is for ever gloriously true and securely set in the Scriptures, with things from which a healthy Christian conscience recoils, and which can claim no undisputed warrant in the Book of God, is to hinder the things one most desires to advance.

This is sure. There is an experience of God the Holy Spirit, available for all who will seek it with importunity, which imparts spiritual power far above the level enjoyed by the average Christian: which inspires a caring God-like love different in kind and degree from the affections of normal nature: which communicates to the eager soul the penetrating power of holiness. No book can give this experience. It belongs to the secret intercourse of the soul with God. It lies at the very heart of personal religion. Its wide reception would transform the Church and shake the world.

Yet a book can do something.

Within the covers of this slight volume an effort is made to examine part of the teaching of a man who enjoyed this experience and who passionately sought for more than fifty years to share it with others. Some of his explanations now seem unsatisfactory and even obstructive if overpressed. But my deepest hope is that, jettisoning some of the explanations, I might myself share the experience—and that others might be quickened in the quest for it too. Faith and prayer are the ordained means, and progress may be measured by one's progress in humility.

Several of my friends deserve my thanks. Those to whom this volume is dedicated helped me more than they knew: the Rev. Dr. E. S. Waterhouse, with whom I took my first steps in philosophical thinking and who has been my friend and guide for twenty years; the Rev. Dr. C. Ryder Smith, whose theological lectures remain to me and all who heard them a noble example of how mind and heart "may make one music," and who read my manuscript and made many helpful suggestions. I am least sure of myself where I have dared to differ from him! And the Rev. Dr. R. Newton Flew, to whose considerable volume, *The Idea of Perfection*, I confess a constant indebtedness in footnotes and who has never denied me the privilege of a stimulating talk.

On the biblical section of the book I was helped by correspondence with the Rev. Noel J. Chew, B.A., B.D.; on the theological section by conversation with the Rev. Dr. Harold Roberts; on the psychological section by the Rev. Dr. R. Scott Frayn. None of my friends, however, must be saddled with responsibility for all the views which I express.

My further indebtedness is even harder to put into words: to my wife who has shared so cheerfully our voluntary exile from normal home life for more than two years; to my colleague, the Rev. T. C. Baird, B.A., B.D., who has closely read the book both in manuscript and in proof; to my secretary, Mr. P. E. Found, who, at each stage of the work, and in addition to other heavy duties, has relieved me of every task that he could and been my unfailing helper at all times.

I acknowledge with gratitude the permission of Messrs. Sheed and Ward to quote from *The Spirit of Catholicism*, by Karl Adams; of Messrs. Hodder and Stoughton to quote from Studdert Kennedy's *The Unutterable Beauty*; and of the Epworth Press to quote from the Standard volumes of Wesley's *Journals*, *Letters* and *Sermons*. The frequent citation of Wesley's own words needs, perhaps, no justification. He has a right to be read in his own phrasing. Too many people who have written on Wesley have avoided the labour of going to Wesley himself.

I have preserved the spelling and punctuation of the people I quote even when they are at variance with the standards of to-day.

The book has been approved as a thesis for the Degree of Doctor of Philosophy in the University of London.

W. E. SANGSTER.

THE CENTRAL HALL,
  WESTMINSTER,
    S.W.I.
November, 1942.

ABBREVIATED TITLES

Cell.	. .	George Croft Cell. *The Rediscovery of John Wesley* (1935).
E.B.	. .	*Encyclopædia Britannica* (14th edn.).
E.R.E.	. .	Hastings' *Encyclopædia of Religion and Ethics*.
Fletcher's *Works*		*The Works of the Rev. John Fletcher* (9 vols., 1806–8).
Flew	. .	R. Newton Flew. *The Idea of Perfection in Christian Theology* (1934).
Journal	. .	*John Wesley's Journal*, ed. Curnock (8 vols., 1909–16).
Lee .	. .	Umphrey Lee. *John Wesley and Modern Religion* (1936).
Letters	. .	*John Wesley's Letters*, ed. Telford (8 vols., 1931).
Lives of E.M.P. .		*The Lives of Early Methodist Preachers* (1871).
Piette	. .	Maximin Piette. *John Wesley in the Evolution of Protestantism* (1937).
Plain Account	.	John Wesley. *A Plain Account of Christian Perfection* (n.d.).
Rogers	. .	*Life of Mrs. Hester Ann Rogers* (1840).
Sermons	. .	*John Wesley's Standard Sermons*, ed. Sugden (2 vols., 1921).
Warfield .	.	Benjamin B. Warfield. *Perfectionism* (2 vols., 1931–2).
Works	. .	*John Wesley's Works*, ed. Jackson (14 vols., 3rd edn., 1829–31).

CONTENTS AND SUMMARY

THE PROBLEM

ii

cleansing the heart from sin. The idea of
growth was not excluded from his mind: it
could operate both before and after the sublime moment, but Wesley never claimed this
experience himself. Many of his followers did,
and for some of them there is independent
testimony of their beautiful lives.

THE EXAMINATION

(A) Biblical

Wesley was a keen Bible student all his life,
and he taught nothing which he did not
believe was firmly set in the Scriptures. He
was convinced that the doctrine of Christian
Perfection was in harmony with "the whole
tenor of the New Testament." But he wrote
in pre-higher-critical times and, for the most
part, treats the word of God as uniformly
precious. Much of his *Plain Account* is a
catena of biblical quotations, but he rests
the weight of this doctrine on thirty texts:
ten from Paul, ten from the 1st Epistle of
John, and ten from the rest of the Bible.

The thirty texts, taken from the following
books, are reviewed in the light of present-
day exposition:—Ezekiel, the Synoptics,
Romans, 2 Corinthians, Galatians, Ephesians,
Philippians, 1 Thessalonians, Titus, Hebrews,
St. John, 1 John, and James. The conclusion
is drawn that the passing of two centuries
of biblical scholarship has not undermined
Wesley's position. Textual scrutiny alone
cannot settle this question. The stones are
there. Whether Wesley was right in fashioning them into the superstructure which he
did has yet to be decided.

Wesley defined sin as "a voluntary transgression of a known law." The definition is
felt by many to be too narrow and too shallow
but—with certain differences—it is similar
to the definition of a modern theologian like
Dr. F. R. Tennant. Both held that "sins are
volitions and only volitions can be sins." Both
looked upon the term "unconscious sin" as
a contradiction in terms. The loose use of the
term "unconscious sin" is set out and
illustrated.

It is now possible to analyse Wesley's idea of
perfection. Love is the keynote: perfect love
to God and man. The complete exclusion of
conscious sin is claimed as a glorious by-
product. It happens in a moment as a gift of
God in response to faith and is maintained
from moment to moment by humble dependence on Him. It carries its own assurance with
it but is ascetic in its emphasis and world-
forsaking.

The significance of Wesley's evangelical conversion is a matter of controversy, some
holding that it was a mere flush of feeling, and
others that it was an epoch in his life and in
world history. But, whatever be the truth
about that, he did not derive his passion for
Christian Perfection from that day. His
evangelical conversion affected his concern
about Christian Perfection chiefly in this:
that whereas before May 24th, 1738, he had
toiled for perfection by works, he now

believed that it could only be attained by
faith. Luther urged, "Believe and be saved."
Wesley said, "Believe, be saved and, by faith
also, be entirely sanctified too." Dr. G. Croft
Cell says that Wesley's doctrine is "an
original and unique synthesis of the Protestant ethic of grace with the Catholic ethic of
holiness." The weakness of the synthesis is
set out.

(C) Psychological

Wesley read most of the philosophic treatises
published during his long life but his comments on few of them are full. He refers to
Leibnitz, Locke, Hume, Butler, Berkeley,
Thomas Reid, Hutcheson, Wollaston, Mandeville and Rousseau. The academic psychology
of the age seems not to have stirred his
interest very much. Yet, there was a psychology implied in his teaching on perfection
which forces certain questions upon us. We
must take them in turn.

Life cannot be lived as a succession of discrete
bits. It is not only being: it is becoming.
Whatever will be, *is*. Wesley was aware of
this, but, in his practical approach to the
problem, he stressed the empirical "now."
So does the New Testament, and so do the
saints. We do not find the objections to
Wesley's plea for a "moment-by-moment"
life sustained.

The question whether sin can be eradicated is
still disputed, as in Wesley's day, but is based
on a false psychology. It presupposes that sin

is a *thing*, like a rotten tooth, and not a condition of balance (or unbalance) among our
motives. The question, therefore, must be
refused in that form because the whole
problem is misconceived in its phrasing.
That it was so misconceived is illustrated by
the distress the sanctified suffered over their
dreams.

It is difficult to define the "unconscious" with
any precision but the unconscious cannot sin.
Amoral it may be, but not immoral. A good
deal of established Christian practice presumes
that the Holy Spirit influences the sub-conscious: e.g. some intercessory prayer, part of
the theory of infant baptism, and the effort to
win swift conversions. But, howsoever this
relationship is conceived, it must not be
conceived as the utter overwhelming of the
human personality by omnipotence, for that
would rob it of all moral worth. A suggestion
is made as to how God may respect our personalities and yet exercise a beneficent
influence on the sub-conscious mind.

Witnesses are summoned from Wesley's
earliest followers to state, in their own words,
what happened to them when this high experience came. The characteristic features are all
present. Love is the key. All conscious sin
has gone. It happened in an instant. It brought
its own assurance with it. The element of
asceticism is there. The words are artless and
convincing. Something had happened. But
what?

We cannot believe that the narrators were
deceivers but were they self-deceived? None

of them analyses his mental processes in the sublime moment itself, so two modern witnesses to this same experience are called. The human side becomes clearer. There is a militancy in their faith: they *will* to believe that this complete cleansing has been effected in them, and fight down all doubt as of the devil. The risks they run are obvious, and light is thrown on the rare but recurrent moral casualties of this teaching. Conscience and Satan are sometimes confused. But that God moves out to these desiring souls in some special response to their faith it is hard to disbelieve. Nor is their experience adequately described (and dismissed) as "the peace which comes to any man at the end of toilsome mental effort." It is something other and more.

THE RESTATEMENT

The constructive task begins. We want the answer to the questions: "Can we be free from sin, can we know it, and should we say so?" Wesley was inconsistent in his exposition of this doctrine and any restatement should aim to remove those inconsistencies. "Christian Perfection" is not a good name for the teaching. "Perfect Love" is a better term even though "love" in English is too wide and blurred in meaning, and the difficulties of "perfection" are not removed in using it as an adjective rather than a substantive. But the term is positive and social, and the gains under both those headings are immense.

The demerits of the English word "love" are considerable and some effort must be made to re-mint it. But it has the highest New

Testament warrant and there are greater
objections to the rival words. It avoids the
negative character of "perfection" as commonly used. Love can be stern and is richer
far than "duty." It does not trap its devotees
into holy egoism and, had he held to it,
Wesley's limited definition of sin would have
troubled him less. It would, moreover, have
made clearer the "given-ness" of holiness,
for love has the character of "given-ness" at
any time.

The inward assurance of salvation was a distinctive note in Wesley's teaching and he
carried assurance over (without any apparent
sense of crossing a gulf) to sanctification as
well. People could be positive that they were
cleansed from all sin. He never had this
assurance himself and J. W. Fletcher seems
to be the only outstandingly impressive
instance among the early Methodists who
did. Normally, the people enjoying this high
experience talked not of being cleansed
from all sin but of being "filled with love."
This harmonises with the conclusion of previous chapters. It is a dangerous thing for
anyone to say that they are freed from all sin
because: (*a*) the worth of such a witness
depends on their sensitivity of conscience,
(*b*) it does not harmonise with a "moment-
by-moment" life, and (*c*) it is shaped in
ignorance, for no man knows what is in him.
Pride and presumption so easily attend this
claim.

Dr. R. W. Dale believed that this doctrine
ought to have led "to a great and original
ethical development" but it never provoked

any adequate social concern! It became the
interest only of coteries and conventions.
The influence of Methodism on social conditions has been variously estimated but, at
its best, it was social salvage work. No new
communal planning or constructive social
thinking was borne on this tide of evangelical
religion. People could be passionate in pursuit of personal holiness but fail to see how it
could, or should, affect their commercial life.
Nor did they seriously plan "a new order."
Some lived their life in compartments, and
others, facing the facts, despaired of ever
living a perfect life in an imperfect world.
The problem of a Christian's duty to his
country at war illustrates the difficulty. The
effect of the deeper realisation of the social
nature of the gospel on our thought of
perfection is set out.

The argument of the book is summarised up
to this point and it is conceded that nothing
which has been set out can convince a man
that perfection is possible to mortals on this
earth if he holds firmly, say, to the Westminster Catechism. The question is, therefore, raised again: "Can perfect love exclude all sin?" All conscious sin, it seems,
may go even in a man of sensitive conscience,
and the plea for a little harboured sin, on the
ground that it keeps a mortal humble, is set
aside. The liability of anti-perfectionists to
antinomianism is faced. Accepted hymns and
liturgies of the Church (as well as the Scriptures) are shown to carry the possibility of
mortal perfection in them, and the importance of this doctrine is suggested by the
observation of three common facts: (*a*) the
sub-Christian level of many Church members,

THE PROBLEM

CHAPTER I

THE GENIUS OF JOHN WESLEY

No informed person to-day disputes the greatness of John Wesley, but there is still a wide difference of view as to the *range* of his greatness. Some are content to leave it vague and to describe him, with Augustine Birrell, as "the greatest force of the eighteenth century,"[1] but when the further question is raised "In what did his greatness lie?" there is less agreement of opinion. None now denies his pre-eminence as preacher, organiser and Church leader, and few can be found who will dispute his right to be called a "saint" If the judgment of his own spiritual children be ignored on the supposition that filial piety might bias their judgment, there is no lack of distinguished men of other communions who are eager to testify to the greatness of the founder of Methodism.[2]

Dr. Maximin Piette, the Roman Catholic Professor of History at Brussels, concludes his scholarly work on John Wesley by reminding his readers that Wesley

> "has been compared to St. Benedict as regards his liturgical sense and piety: to St. Dominic for his apostolic zeal: to St. Francis of Assisi for his love of Christ and detachment from the world: to St. Ignatius of Loyola for his genius as an organizer. . . ."[3]

Dr. T. R. Glover, the Public Orator Emeritus of Cambridge, a member of the Baptist Church, places Wesley with Paul, Augustine and Luther to make the four outstanding figures of the evangelical succession.[4] Canon J. H. Overton, the Anglican historian, whose special researches dealt with *The English Church in the Eighteenth Century*, does not hesitate to describe Wesley's

[1] *Miscellanies*, 34.
[2] Bishop Warburton said: "William Law begot Methodism," but the world has long since given the honour to Wesley; cf. Abbey and Overton, *The English Church in the Eighteenth Century*, 61.
[3] Piette, 480.
[4] *The Preaching of Christ*, 16 *ff.*

life as "the busiest and, in some respects, the most important life
in that century."[1]

It is when we turn from Wesley as evangelist, organiser and
Church leader to Wesley as philosopher and theologian that the
wide approval his work excites is challenged, and close students
of his amazingly busy life differ sharply in their estimate of his
intellectual contribution to the theology of the Church and the
thought of his age. Nobody claims that his *chief* service either to
his own generation or subsequent ones was an intellectual
service. There is common agreement that the natural bent of his
mind was practical rather than speculative, and the day can be
fixed when he consciously turned from systematic to pastoral
theology as his main concern. The question shapes itself rather
in this way: Granted that his chief interests and manner of
approach were practical, and that he deliberately chose to challenge the prevailing Deism of his age, not in the manner of Butler
and Warburton (by a philosophical approach to men with his
own educational advantages) but rather by going to the mass of
ignorant and unlettered people with a plain, religious appeal . . .
being the trained and clear thinker that he was, did he, in point
of fact, make any enduring contribution to theological thought
and has he any claim to rank among the intellectual leaders of
the Church? Put that way, the question reveals at once the widely
differing estimates held of Wesley and prepares us for an examination of the doctrine which he came to regard as the chief treasure
of the Methodists and for the propagation of which, he believed,
God had raised them up.

This much is clear. Wesley himself would have set the question
impatiently aside. Having no other concern than to "save souls,"
he would have taken only the slightest interest in the opinion of
subsequent generations of his status as an "intellectual." He did
not share William Law's scorn of scholarship but, in a letter to
the author of the *Serious Call*, dated from London on January 6th,
1756, he stresses the danger of mixing philosophy and religion.
He reminds Law of his own earlier opinion on the point:

"Religion is the most plain, simple thing in the world. It is
only, 'We love Him, because He first loved us.' So far as you
add philosophy to religion, just so far you spoil it."[2]

[1] Overton, *John Wesley* (preface, v).   [2] *Works*, ix, 466.

In the preface to his one hundred and forty-one sermons, he says plainly:

"I abstain from all nice and philosophical speculations; from all perplexed and intricate reasonings; and, as far as possible, from even the show of learning."[1]

The last thing Wesley desired was to offer anything new in doctrine. He believed that everything he taught was in the New Testament and in the authoritative documents of the Church of England. If what he preached *appeared* new, that could be easily explained by its unhappy neglect and could be settled at once by an appeal to the Scriptures. Even his *Notes on the New Testament*, which have been a standard of Methodist doctrine for a century and a half, were largely borrowed.

It is not surprising, therefore, that the judgment of Dr. George Eayrs, who would make Wesley not less distinguished as a thinker than the world esteems him as an evangelist, is not the common one.[2] Vulliamy says, "We cannot give John Wesley a place among the great intellectual reformers of the Church."[3] Piette says, "He had no leanings towards the learned world, but shunned them rather."[4] Overton is sure that it would "be absurd to contend that anything which John Wesley wrote is of the same calibre as the great works of his contemporaries such as Butler. . . ."[5] All these are sympathetic biographers, fully aware of Wesley's freedom both with the ancient and modern languages and of the logical acuteness his polemical writings invariably display. But he was not a great thinker, they say, either as philosopher or theologian. He might have been—but he had read his commission another way. The whole aim of his strenuous life was to tell plain people in plain words the things which belong to their peace.

And here the discussion has rested for some time. That it is being reopened is due, in large part, to the work of Dr. G. Croft Cell. Dr. Cell challenges the general view that Wesley is of slight importance as an intellectual and asserts that he "has made a contribution to theology no less important than his contribution to practical Christianity."[6] He regards him as "a principal founder

---

[1] *Works*, v, ii.
[2] Eayrs, *Wesley: Christian Philosopher and Church Founder*, 16 f.
[3] Vulliamy, *John Wesley*, 359.   [4] Piette, 435.
[5] Overton, *John Wesley*, 170; cf. also Harrison, *Arminianism*, 185.
[6] Cell, viii.

and first conspicuous exemplar of a theology of experience."[1]
Comparing him with Hume and Kant, he suggests that there
can be—

"traced in the work of Wesley on Christian doctrine a revolution in the whole approach to the interpretation of the Gospel
and in the whole method of theology quite comparable in
importance and closely analogous in significance to what his
philosophical contemporaries set themselves to do in their
own field, namely, to substitute experiential thinking for the
purely logical use of the intellect."[2]

These are big claims. How far they can be substantiated in
regard to Christian Perfection it is part of the purpose of this
book to find out.

[1] *Cell*, 347.   [2] *ibid.*, 83 *f.*

CHAPTER II

THE IMPORTANCE AND DATA OF THE DOCTRINE

IT will not be too positively inferred, therefore, that Wesley was negligible as a theologian. Any who derive their impression of his preaching from Horace Walpole[1] and suppose that it was "very ugly enthusiasm" and that the preacher "decried learning" would have this impression immediately corrected by reading the published sermons themselves. Even allowing for the fact that the illustrative matter was omitted on publication, it is clear that the preacher's message was remote from ranting and that every sermon carried its freight of clear, theological thought.

The doctrine which is the main concern of this thesis occupied his mind from the year 1725. He preached on it before the University of Oxford on the first day of 1733, before he was thirty years of age. It remained one of his chief theological preoccupations till he died on March 2nd, 1791. With passing time, his conviction of its importance grew. He regarded it as the "grand depositum"[2] which God had committed to his followers. It involved him in more controversy and odium than anything else he taught. Yet he never wavered. Perfection, as he had defined it, was possible: possible now: possible in an instant. Three months before he died, he wrote to Dr. Adam Clarke concerning this doctrine.

"If we can prove that any of our Local Preachers or Leaders, either directly or indirectly, speak against it, let him be a Local Preacher or Leader no longer. I doubt whether he shall continue in the Society. Because he that can speak thus in our congregations cannot be an honest man."[3]

When the numbers of his followers declined in any locality, he normally traced it to the neglect of this teaching.

"I was surprised to find fifty members fewer than I left in

[1] Walpole, *Letters*, v, 16 (Cunningham edn.).
[2] *Letters*, viii, 238.
[3] November 26th, 1790. *Letters*, viii, 249. But cf. 188, where the same letter is given under date November 26th, 1789, with slight verbal differences.

it last October. One reason is, Christian Perfection has been little insisted on; and wherever this is not done, be the preachers ever so eloquent, there is little increase, either in the number or grace of the hearers."[1]

Most students who have taken in hand a study of modern "holiness movements" have traced their origin to Wesley's teaching. Dr. Warfield says, "It was John Wesley who infected the modern Protestant world with this notion of 'entire instantaneous sanctification.' "[2] The idea of perfection in Christian theology is, as Dr. Flew has already shown, as old as the faith itself, and yet there is some justice in tracing most of its modern expressions in Protestant thought to the founder of Methodism. Few others brought a keener or more patient mind to its exposition. No other reached so large a constituency with it. If this doctrine is understood in the teaching of John Wesley, one has the key to its solution in the varying forms it has taken since.

The data of Wesley's doctrine may be simply set out. Its chief source is his much-revised book, *A Plain Account of Christian Perfection*, but hardly less valuable are the sermons dealing specifically with this theme, and many references in his voluminous *Journals* and *Letters*. His brother's hymns and the books which, on his own statement, turned his mind in this direction and shaped his thought, are also relevant. When these sources are amplified by the writings of his friend and collaborator, John William Fletcher, *The Lives of Early Methodist Preachers*, and the biographical material in the *Arminian Magazine*, his convictions clearly emerge and can be examined. As we come to its closer study, it will seem strangely out of harmony with the theological temper of our times. Dr. Günther Dehn, the eminent Lutheran theologian, lecturing at Oxford in 1935, referred to it as a dangerous error, holding that "Christian Perfection largely consists in recognising that a man *cannot* be perfect";[3] and many other admirers of Wesley look upon this aspect of his teaching as an aberration in an otherwise sober mind.

[1] *Journal*, v, 149.   [2] Warfield, ii, 562; cf. 463.
[3] Dehn, *Man and Revelation*, 212; cf. 194-7.

CHAPTER III

THE DOCTRINE STATED

No small part of Wesley's controversial difficulties with this
doctrine turned upon its name. It is sometimes called
"Sanctification" and sometimes "Entire Sanctification" (though
these are distinct stages in Wesley's theory); sometimes "Christian
Perfection," "Holiness," or "Perfect Love." Wesley preferred
the last term, but his book upon the theme is entitled *A Plain
Account of Christian Perfection*, and each of the names had some
warrant in his writings and some warrant in the Bible.

Yet, whatever authority can be cited for its use, the word
"perfect" is a provoking word. Like the word "law" and the
word "nature," which are variously defined and commonly and
dangerously used without any definition at all, the word "perfect" invites challenge. It was easy and not untruthful for critics
to retort, "Perfection is not for us." Wesley was driven to apply
limits to his illimitable term: to make distinctions, in his own way,
between "blameless" and "faultless," "purity" and "maturity";
the perfection of the stage and the perfection of the end. It will
suffice at this point if we say that the distinctions he draws (which
must be more closely examined) are, at least, real and recognisable
and are not to be lightly dismissed with the suggestion that his
judgments on the intricacies of this doctrine were "obviously
tempered by diplomacy."[1]

He believed and taught this: that, in an instant, and by a simple
act of faith, perfection was "wrought in the soul." It was, indeed,
the second of two distinct stages in the Christian experience of
Salvation as he conceived it: the first consisted of justification and
sanctification; the former being a change in our relations with
God, our pardon and reconciliation; the latter a change in ourselves wrought by the Spirit of God. In the first stage, a new
heart is given to us, so that we now love God and desire to please
Him, and will not *willingly* sin against Him in anything. But
"sinful tempers" remain, and, though they are resisted, and
resisted successfully, they remain.

The second stage, with which we are now chiefly concerned,
is *entire* sanctification, which comes as an immediate gift of God,

[1] J. B. Mozley, *Lectures and Other Theological Papers*, 175.

entirely cleansing the heart from sin and "slaying the dire root and seed" of it. By virtue of this gift, the Christian

". . . loveth the Lord his God with all his heart, and serveth Him with all his strength. He loveth his neighbour (every man) as himself; yea, as Christ loved us. . . . Indeed, his soul is all love, filled with bowels of mercies, kindness, meekness, gentleness, longsuffering. And his life agreeth thereto . . . whatsoever he doeth, either in word or deed, he doeth it all in the name, in the love and power, of the Lord Jesus. In a word, he doeth the will of God on earth, as it is done in heaven. . . ."

"In every thought of our hearts, in every word of our tongues, in every work of our hands, to show forth His praise who hath called us out of darkness into His marvellous light."[1]

"To clear this point a little farther: I know many that love God with all their heart. He is their one desire, their one delight, and they are continually happy in Him. They love their neighbour as themselves. They feel as sincere, fervent, constant a desire for the happiness of every man, good or bad, friend or enemy, as for their own. They rejoice evermore, pray without ceasing, and in everything give thanks. Their souls are continually streaming up to God, in holy joy, prayer, and praise. This is a point of fact; and this is plain, sound, scriptural experience."[2]

Whether this is "a point of fact" and "plain, sound, scriptural experience" is an important part of the enquiry which we are prosecuting now.

Several relevant factors should be noted here. Wesley believed that this perfection was plainly taught in the Bible. It need hardly be stated that his citation of texts did not anticipate the findings of the higher critics, and he is as happy to make his point with a word of national significance from Ezekiel as with a word of deep, personal religion from Paul.[3] But he finds no lack of pertinent references capable of passing the most sensitive expositional test.

---

[1] *Letters*, ii, 281.   [2] *Plain Account*, 90.   [3] *ibid.*, 99.

"Ye shall therefore be perfect as your Father who is in heaven is perfect" (Matt. v. 48).[1]

"Neither pray I for these alone, but for them also who shall believe on Me through their word; that they all may be one; as Thou, Father, art in Me, and I in Thee, that they also may be one in Us; I in them, and Thou in Me, that they may be made perfect in one" (John xvii. 20–3).

"The very God of peace sanctify you wholly; and I pray God, your whole spirit, soul, and body may be preserved blameless unto the coming of our Lord Jesus Christ" (1 Thess. v. 23).[2]

"I am crucified with Christ: nevertheless I live; yet not I, but Christ liveth in me" (Gal. ii. 20), a text which (so Wesley believed) manifestly described a deliverance from inward as well as from outward sin.

"Herein is our love made perfect, that we may have boldness in the day of judgment, because, as He is, so are we *in this world*" (1 John iv. 17).

"God is light, and with Him is no darkness at all. If we walk in the light, as He is in the light, we have fellowship one with another, and the blood of Jesus Christ His Son *cleanseth* us from all sin" (1 John i. 7).

"If we confess our sins, He is faithful and just to forgive us our sins, and to cleanse us from all unrighteousness" (1 John i. 9).

Stressing the present tense of the word "cleanse," insisting that the promise concerned "now" and not a distant time succeeding death, on which some of his opponents took their stand, and ignoring the fact that most of his texts were garnered from one epistle (the First Epistle of John), Wesley contended that no close student of the New Testament could deny that the doctrine had emphatic scriptural warrant. Working over the same ground in more detail, his friend and colleague, John William Fletcher, in his *Last Check to Antinomianism*,[3] showed how much more

---

[1] *Plain Account*, 132.   [2] *ibid.*, 43.
[3] Fletcher's *Works*, vi, sections iv–x.

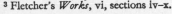

extensive were the biblical references than Wesley had paused to set out.

Wesley's definition of sin is important. In the judgment of some scholars, the variant reactions to his doctrine turn largely on the view taken of this definition.[1] Wesley held that sin was a "wilful transgression of a known law," a definition entirely in line with the view of a modern theologian like Dr. F. R. Tennant.[2] Dr. Flew contends that the word has "too long a history behind it for such a limitation to be possible. Indeed, the narrower sense is not even desirable. Our worst sins are often those of which we are unconscious. . . ."[3] But, at this stage, it will be enough to say that it was only in the sense in which he clearly defined sin that Wesley believed we could be free of it, and that a definition of sin which equated it with sinfulness he would resolutely have set aside.

Nor must our summary of Wesley's doctrine leave any doubt about his insistence that growth, both before and after the momentous instant, was part of the process of perfection. Its instantaneous character did not preclude the idea of development. He clarifies his meaning by an analogy drawn both from physical birth and death. A man may be said to be dying a long time but there is an instant in which he dies. There is growth in the womb before birth: there is clearly growth after: but the actual birth is normally a matter of minutes. So—as he understood it—is the birth of perfect love in the soul. A growth precedes it, longer or shorter with different individuals: an infinite development lies before it after birth—but the birth itself could be noted on a calendar and almost timed by a watch. That some who had passed through this experience could not date it did not disprove their experience, but this was clearly regarded as exceptional. Their entirely sanctified condition could still be submitted to ethical tests.

A man perfected in the sense for which Wesley contended was still liable to infirmity, ignorance and mistake, but he was not now guilty of sin. His heart being full of love to God, "every evil temper is destroyed: and every thought, and word, and work springs from, and is conducted to the end by, the pure love of God and our neighbour."[4]

Believing that this possibility was held before the Christian in

---

[1] Bett, *The Spirit of Methodism*, 158 (footnote).
[2] Tennant, *The Concept of Sin*, 101 *f.*, 205, 245.   [3] Flew, 332 *f.*
[4] Simon, *John Wesley, the Master Builder*, 152.

the New Testament, Wesley believed also that the possibility
was fulfilled in multitudes of his followers. He tested hundreds
who claimed this perfect love and approved their claim. He never
"claimed" it himself. Chadwick is clearly wrong in his reiterated
assertion that Wesley did so.[1] Dr. Curtis, while recognising that
Wesley never overtly announced his possession of it, thinks that
he did enjoy the experience and that the sublime moment can be
shown in his *Journal*.[2]

But that only deepens the mystery. Urging this upon all his
preachers and people, making it the test doctrine of spiritual
health, including it with two other central doctrines as the basis
of union which he hoped at one time to effect with the evangelical
clergy of the Church of England,[3] contending for it publicly and
privately from 1733 till he died in 1791 . . . , he is scrupulously
careful never to claim it himself. Indeed, he *disclaims* it. Replying
to an attack by Dr. William Dodd on this very point, he says
plainly, "I tell you flat I have not attained the character I draw."[4]
Dr. Bett thinks that "the peculiar publicity" of his life made
him hesitate.

"There must have been in his life from day to day a thousand
insignificant and innocent words and actions which, distorted
and exaggerated, might have been alleged by his enemies
against the high profession of perfect love, had he made it.
He knew this, and was careful not to give the world any
unnecessary occasion to blaspheme."[5]

Dr. Flew finds it an "insoluble question" and just wonders
whether he had some "half-unconscious suspicion that avowal
would be perilous to the health of his soul."[6]
But there was no lack of those who did claim it and whose
artless narratives bear the unmistakable stamp of sincerity in
their witness to something wonderful that had happened to them.
Nor do their own accounts lack corroboration from critical
witnesses with unusual opportunity to detect a spurious claim.
When Dr. J. B. Mozley considered Wesley's doctrine at Oxford
in 1874, he laid it down that if perfection were possible it could
not be authenticated by an instance of "absolute matchless rarity,"

[1] Chadwick, *The Call to Christian Perfection*, 44, 77.
[2] Curtis, *Christian Faith*, 375 f. [December 24th, 1744].
[3] Simon, *John Wesley, the Master Builder*, 152.
[4] *Letters*, v, 43.
[5] Bett, *The Spirit of Methodism*, 161 f.   [6] Flew, 330.

but "may be expected to come out in a certain number of cases"
and that "these instances would not be wholly wanting in
number."[1] Wesley contended that they were not wanting in
number.

He met whole "societies" composed of people enjoying the
experience. Sparse as the material has become since, it was almost
voluminous in the early days of the eighteenth century revival of
religion. In a hundred instances that might be given, perhaps one
classic case would serve as example. John William Fletcher, the
Vicar of Madeley, adoringly announced his reception of this gift
on August 24th, 1781, at a house in Park Row, Leeds. He said,
stressing and enlarging the claim at length, "I am freed from
sin."[2] The critic who would brush the whole thing impatiently
aside as bordering on the blasphemous should know that it is
credibly reported that Voltaire, when challenged to produce a
character as perfect as that of Christ, at once mentioned Fletcher
of Madeley,[3] and that Wesley, preaching Fletcher's funeral
sermon, took as his text: "Mark the perfect man."

---

[1] J. B. Mozley, *Lectures and Other Theological Papers*, 164.
[2] Rogers, 225.
[3] *E.B.*, ix, 373. Abbey and Overton, *The English Church in the Eighteenth Century*,
113.

THE EXAMINATION

(A) Biblical

CHAPTER IV

WESLEY'S APPROACH TO THE BIBLE

THE Book of Psalms opens with a eulogy of the man whose "delight is in the law of the Lord" and who meditates in that law "day and night." If we enlarge the meaning of the word "law" in this connection to cover the whole of the Bible, John Wesley fully qualifies for the praise the Psalmist gives. Bible study was a habit formed in him in childhood and a daily—and almost hourly—occupation to the end of his long life.

It was the basis of all his work in teaching and preaching. He sought the truth on any aspect of the Christian faith, first, by an intensive and prayerful study of the Bible, then by an examination of the experience of devout people and, finally, by a comparison of what others had written on the subject both in ancient and modern times. In the general Preface to his *Works*,[1] he puts it like this:

> "In this edition, I present to serious and candid men, my last and maturest thoughts: agreeable, I hope, to Scripture, Reason, and Christian Antiquity."

Always the Scriptures were first. He offered no teaching until he had convinced himself that its foundations were well set in the Book of God.

Nowhere is this more plainly set out than in the famous passage in which he proclaims himself *homo unius libri*. It appears in the Preface to his *Sermons* in the year 1746.[2]

> "To candid, reasonable men, I am not afraid to lay open what have been the inmost thoughts of my heart. I have thought, I am a creature of a day, passing through life as an arrow through the air. I am a spirit come from God, and

---

[1] *Works* (1771), par. 4; cf. also vol. xiii, 272.   [2] Par. 5.

C   33

returning to God: just hovering over the great gulf; till a few moments hence, I am no more seen; I drop into an unchangeable eternity! I want to know one thing—the way to heaven; how to land safe on that happy shore. God Himself has condescended to teach the way; for this very end He came from heaven. He hath written it down in a book. O give me that book! At any price, give me the book of God! I have it: here is knowledge enough for me. Let me be *homo unius libri*. Here then I am, far from the busy ways of men. I sit down alone: only God is here. In His presence I open, I read His book; for this end, to find the way to heaven. Is there a doubt concerning the meaning of what I read? Does anything appear dark or intricate? I lift up my heart to the Father of Lights: 'Lord, is it not Thy word, "If any man lack wisdom, let him ask of God"? Thou "givest liberally, and upbraidest not." Thou hast said, "If any be willing to do Thy will, he shall know." I am willing to do, let me know, Thy will.' I then search after and consider parallel passages of Scripture, 'comparing spiritual things with spiritual.' I meditate thereon with all the attention and earnestness of which my mind is capable. If any doubt still remains, I consult those who are experienced in the things of God; and then the writings whereby, being dead, they yet speak. And what I thus learn, that I teach."

Wesley's desire to know but one thing, "the way to heaven," falls a little strangely on the ear to-day, but none who reads this moving passage and remembers what an omnivorous reader he was will miss the meaning of his claim to be "a man of one book." The Bible was not the first of books to him: it was in a category by itself and its authority was decisive. If he was mistaken in the belief that a doctrine he taught was in the Bible, it was a mistake made only after much textual scrutiny and the deepest thought.

The doctrine of Christian Perfection was no exception to the general rule. Wesley was convinced that it was in the Scriptures. He says:—

"What is there here which any man of understanding, who believes the Bible, can object to? What can he deny, without flatly contradicting the Scripture? What retrench, without taking from the word of God?"[1]

[1] *Plain Account*, 10.

"In conformity, therefore, both to the doctrine of St. John, and the whole tenor of the New Testament, we fix this con- clusion: A Christian is so far perfect as not to commit sin."[1]

Particularly did he resent his critics' references to it as "Mr. Wesley's doctrine" as though it were an invention of his own.

"They wanted, they sought, occasion against me; there they found what they sought. 'This is Mr. Wesley's doctrine! He preaches perfection!' He does: yet this is not his doctrine any more than it is yours, or any one's else, that is a minister of Christ. For it is His doctrine, peculiarly, emphatically His! it is the doctrine of Jesus Christ. Those are His words, not mine: Ἔσεσθε οὖν ὑμεῖς τέλειοι ὥσπερ ὁ πατὴρ ὑμῶν ὁ ἐν τοῖς οὐρανοῖς τέλειός ἐστι. 'Ye shall therefore be perfect as your Father Who is in heaven is perfect.' And who says ye shall not; or, at least, not till your soul is separated from the body? It is the doctrine of St. Paul, the doctrine of St. James, of St. Peter, and St. John; and no otherwise Mr. Wesley's than as it is the doctrine of every one who preaches the pure and the whole gospel. I tell you, as plain as I can speak, where and when I found this. I found it in the oracles of God, in the Old and the New Testament; when I read them with no other view or desire but to save my own soul."[2]

Nevertheless, he wrote in pre-higher-critical times. If the anonymous publication in Brussels in 1753 by Jean Astruc of *Conjectures on the Original Documents which Moses Appears to Have Employed for the Composition of the Book of Genesis* may be taken as a starting-point for the modern critical study of the Bible, it may be noted that Astruc was an older contemporary of Wesley, but there is no evidence that Wesley had any knowledge of this little book by the French physician, and three-quarters of a century was to pass away after Wesley's death before the publication of *Essays and Reviews* (1860), *The Colenso Controversy* (1863), and the opening of the case against Robertson Smith (1876), were to make the challenge of the new learning widely known among religious men in Britain.

Consequently, Wesley moves with freedom over all parts of the Bible in his search for evidence that perfection is possible for

---

[1] *Plain Account*, 22. [2] *ibid.*, 132.

the devout on this terrestrial plane, though he draws, as will be seen, most of his evidence from the New Testament. He is unhindered by any questions of date or authorship. He recognises a broad and important distinction between the years prior to the coming of Christ and those which succeeded it,[1] and his denunciation of the imprecatory Psalms is well known;[2] but, for the most part, Ezekiel[3] will serve as well as Matthew, and Zechariah[4] as well as Paul. The Word of God is uniformly precious: if one part seems more illuminating than another, the explanation is to be sought in one's need, apprehension, or present interest, and not in the Scripture itself.

In his *Plain Account*—the main source of our knowledge of Wesley's mind on this doctrine—he quotes the Bible one hundred and ninety-five times: twenty-three times from the Old Testament and one hundred and seventy-two from the New.[5] Some of his pages are little more than a catena of quotations. He seems to have lived in the Scriptures so long that Bible phrasing has become second nature to him, and he swims from one citation to another with effortless ease. Ignoring the repetitive use he makes of certain texts, he quotes the Synoptic Gospels twenty-nine times, Paul seventy-four times and the Johannine writings thirty-four times. The most quoted book is the First Epistle of John, from which he culls twenty texts, some of which he repeats frequently. After the First Epistle of John, Matthew and Romans are cited most, with eighteen varied quotations each.

But not all his quotations are concerned with the marrow of this doctrine nor receive his serious exposition. He may be said to rest the weight of his conviction on some thirty different texts, ten from Paul, ten from the First Epistle of John and ten from the rest of the Bible. The close examination of this textual authority must engage our attention now.

---

[1] *Plain Account*, 20. *Letters* iv, 11.   [2] *Works*, xiv, 317. *Journal*, vii, 18.
[3] *Plain Account*, 41.   [4] *ibid.*, 20.

[5] In this analysis I have counted a second or third use of a text as though it were the same quotation. Including repetitions, the figures are: Old Testament twenty-four, New Testament, two hundred and twenty-four.

CHAPTER V

THE TEXTS ON WHICH HE BUILT

(i) ONLY one of the thirty passages on which Wesley chiefly relies for this doctrine is taken from the Old Testament. It is Ezek. xxxvi. 25, 26, 29:

"And I will sprinkle clean water upon you, and ye shall be clean: from all your filthiness, and from all your idols, will I cleanse you. A new heart also will I give you, and a new spirit will I put within you: and I will take away the stony heart out of your flesh, and I will give you an heart of flesh. And I will save you from all your uncleannesses."

Four times in his *Plain Account* Wesley sustains his argument with this passage, quoted in whole or in part,[1] and it is the theme of the long hymn by Charles entitled "The Promise of Sanctification" with which the little volume concludes.

Dr. Perkins has distinguished six Hebrew words used in the Old Testament to express the idea of perfection—though not, in every case, the idea of ethical perfection.[2] None is used here. The inability of certain writers in the Old Testament clearly to distinguish between ritual and moral impurity has often received comment, but, in this passage, Ezekiel rightly takes the two together. It is from all their "filthiness" and their "idols" that God promises to cleanse them—and the two are not as unrelated as some modern readers would think: the foul practices associated with some of the ancient idolatrous worship were dreadful indeed.[3] But it is dubious whether this passage provides Wesley with support for that idea of burning ethical purity which lies at the heart of his doctrine of Christian Perfection.

But it should be noted in passing that the rabbis strongly held that all the commandments of God were *capable* of fulfilment by men, and that Judaism lends no support to the idea that sin is really necessary.

---

[1] *Plain Account*, 34, 39, 41, 99.
[2] Perkins, *The Doctrine of Christian or Evangelical Perfection*, 32–5.
[3] Lofthouse, *Ezekiel* (The Century Bible), 37.

(ii) Three texts only are culled from the Synoptic Gospels: all from Matthew—Matthew v. 8, 48, vi. 10.

The major question of whether or not God's commands imply human capacity to fulfil them, and whether the recurrence of the imperative and subjunctive moods in Wesley's key-texts is deeply significant, is a problem we must examine later. But it meets us at the outset. There can be no question at all as to what Wesley's answer would have been to any critic who disapproved this citation of a beatitude in support of his doctrine: "Blessed are the pure in heart; for they shall see God." He would have asserted that nothing could be plainer than that the implied exhortation to purity in heart carried its own possibility with it. Only those so purified could see God, and Wesley, as we shall see later, having no belief in purgatory, held that purity of heart must be given here.

Matt. v. 48 is a "key" text with Wesley in every sense of the word. "Ye therefore shall be perfect, as your heavenly Father is perfect." We have seen that he sets it down in the *Plain Account* both in Greek and in English, and he would have regarded the doubt cast on its authenticity in recent years as a shock to his scriptural foundations.

Questions have been raised about the text from several sides. Wellhausen[1] and other scholars[2] have argued that Luke's phrasing is nearer the original (Luke vi. 36) in its use of οἰκτίρμονες rather than τέλειοι. "Merciful," it is said, is the simpler, more natural word. Only Matthew, among the evangelists, uses the word τέλειος at all.

Appeal has been made to the Aramaic, but the appeal (except in Dr. Torrey's view) has not settled the point. Dr. Moffatt retains the word "perfect" holding, it would seem, that the Aramaic original *can* mean "perfect";[3] but Dr. Torrey, making the same appeal, rejects the translation "perfect" as impossible. He says:

" 'Be therefore *perfect*' etc. would be mere nonsense, even if it were not wholly unprepared for in this context. Nothing leads up to the idea of perfection—to say nothing of equalling the perfection of God Himself! In this paragraph, vv. 43–47, the disciples are taught that they must show kindness *to all men*; just as their heavenly Father makes no exception."[4]

---

[1] Wellhausen, *Das Evangelium Matthaei*, 24, 98.

[2] M'Neile, *The Gospel According to St. Matthew*, 73; cf. Manson in *The Mission and Message of Jesus*, 347.

[3] Moffatt, *An Introduction to the Literature of the New Testament*, 196.

[4] Torrey, *The Four Gospels*, 291.

The mistranslation, as Dr. Torrey sees it, turns on a wrong vocalisation of the Aramaic: because "the disciple is exhorted to be 'all-including' (*gāmar*) in his good will toward men, not to be 'perfect' (*gĕmīr*)."[1] The point is still in dispute but it cannot yet be said that textual scrutiny has proved the case for taking it out. Dr. Vincent Taylor thinks it possible that Luke vi. 36 and Matt. v. 48 are different sayings.[2]

A phrase from the Lord's Prayer completes Wesley's use of the Synoptic Gospels to prove his teaching: "Thy Kingdom come. Thy will be done, as in heaven, so on earth." So obvious does the exposition of this word seem to Wesley that he limits himself to rhetorical questions in commenting on it. "And is it not done perfectly in heaven? If so, has He not taught us to pray for perfection on earth? Does He not then design to give it?"[3]

(iii) We turn to Paul. Taking the ten texts from Paul, on which Wesley chiefly builds, in the order in which they appear in the New Testament, we start with Rom. ii. 29 and a phrase beloved of Wesley, "circumcision is of the heart." It was on this text that he preached before the University in St. Mary's, Oxford, on January 1st, 1733. It is No. XIII in the *Standard Sermons*. He defines this "circumcision of the heart" as "a right state of soul, a mind and spirit renewed after the image of Him that created it" (par. 3). Preached more than five years before his evangelical conversion (but not published until 1748), the sermon (despite an addition made necessary by his experience on May 24th, 1738) still has a certain immaturity. The influence of William Law is marked throughout, and in section ii, par. 7, Wesley appears to argue that entire sanctification can be achieved by "a constant and continued course of general self-denial," a view which he came afterwards to repudiate. But the explanation is in the date. This was in 1733 when he still laboured for salvation by works.[4]

It can hardly be argued that the text as it stands carries further the case for Christian Perfection. So acute a commentator as Dr. C. H. Dodd is content to note the "inward purity"[5] which is here demanded without feeling any constraint to raise the issue of entire sanctification.

The other text from Romans on which Wesley builds is Rom.

---

[1] Torrey, *Our Translated Gospels*, 92 f., 96.
[2] Vincent Taylor, *Forgiveness and Reconciliation*, 186.
[3] *Plain Account*, 74.   [4] But see Lee, 180.
[5] Dodd, *The Epistle of Paul to the Romans*, 42.

xii. 1. "I beseech you therefore, brethren, by the mercies of God, to present your bodies a living sacrifice, holy, acceptable to God, which is your reasonable service."

Theologians who are convinced that men are polluted through and through, and believe with Hooker that the best thing they ever did had something in it to be forgiven, must take account of this: that all through the Word of God these exhortations to holiness appear. They are not sporadic, occasional or tempered by doubt concerning God's ability to do this thing in us. Underlying them all is the confidence that God can do something more with our sins than forgive them. Wesley would have said in his own way that "God's commands are enablings" and that, by grace, it *is* possible for Christ to present us "holy, acceptable to God."

He uses the word "holy" always in the sense of ethical perfection, and I can trace no awareness in Wesley's writings that this meaning of the word has come into it with the passing of time. The origin and nature of the numinous (for which Otto in *The Idea of the Holy* went in quest), and its psychological basis in some non-rational fact of religious experience ("something for which there is only one appropriate expression, *mysterium tremendum*"),[1] never, it needs hardly to be said, excited the interest of John Wesley. Nor can I trace any explicaton in his writings of the three ideas which intertwine in the Judaistic use of ἅγιοι and contribute the major part of the meaning of that word in the New Testament.[2] "Holy," with Wesley, meant ethical perfection, and where he met the term in the Old Testament, or the New, he understood it that way.

Two texts are garnered from 2 Corinthians, one (2 Cor. iii. 17 *f*) exulting in a process in which "we are being transformed into the same likeness as Himself," and the other (2 Cor. vii. 1) an exhortation to "cleanse ourselves from all defilement of flesh and spirit, perfecting holiness in the fear of God." It is probable that in the former (as in Rom. viii. 29 and Phil. iii. 21) Paul's analogy owes something to the current ideas of the mystery-religions which taught transformation by the vision of God, but with this basic difference, that whereas with the mystery-religions it was some "quasi-magical transmutation of essence,"[3] with Paul it was a glorious, moral and spiritual transformation "passing

[1] Otto, *The Idea of the Holy*, 12.
[2] Flew, *Jesus and His Church*, 141 *ff*.
[3] Kennedy, *St. Paul and the Mystery-Religions*, 183.

from one glory to another" as God works out His will to make us holy. In citing this text, Wesley draws out the full force of the durative present.[1]

The force of the latter text is, of course, in no way weakened in this connection in that it appears to belong to some other part of Paul's correspondence with the Corinthian Church. Some particular kind of pagan uncleanness is almost certainly in the Apostle's mind, and it is from this that he demands decisive separation. In Moffatt's translation "perfecting holiness in the fear of God" (A.V. and R.V.) becomes "let us be fully consecrated by reverence for God."

From Galatians Wesley cites ii. 20, "I am crucified with Christ; yet I live: and yet no longer I, but Christ liveth in me," words which, in Wesley's view, "manifestly describe a deliverance from inward as well as from outward sin."[2] He interprets "I live not" to mean that the evil nature is destroyed, and "Christ liveth in me" to affirm Paul's possession of "all that is holy, just and good."

It is doubtful if this exposition would command general support to-day. Most commentators would feel that Wesley had overpressed the metaphor, and taken an aspiration as an achievement. To interpret this text as a claim by Paul that all sin had been destroyed in him and nothing left but what is "holy, just and good" would seem to them a very unnatural handling of the text, and out of harmony with other sayings of the Apostle.

Not that Paul's epistles contain many—if any—expressions of a deep sense of sin after his conversion. The ineradicable pollution of our nature on which some theologians insist finds but little support in the letters of the Apostle. The vivid description of his divided mind, in Rom. vii. (and who can doubt that it is auto-biographical?), is almost certainly a pre-conversion experience, "It would stultify his whole argument if he now confessed that, at the moment of writing, he was a miserable wretch, a prisoner to sin's law."[3] The only other evidence adduced is contained in Rom. xiii. 12 and 1 Cor. xi. 31 f., which is so indecisive as merely to emphasise how slight the evidence is.

On the other hand, those expositors who set out to prove that Paul was consciously sinless, are in no stronger position. The words on which they chiefly rely (1 Cor. iv. 3 f., 1 Thess. ii. 10) carry no such complete claim in them.

[1] *Plain Account*, 26. [2] *ibid.*, 23.

[3] Dodd, *The Epistle of Paul to the Romans*, 108. Whyte, *Bible Characters* (3rd series), 112. Barth takes the contrary view, *Epistle to the Romans*, 270.

The truth is surely here. Paul had a dual idea of perfection in mind: a perfection absolute, celestial and seen as some distant goal to which he pressed (Phil. iii. 12 *ff.*) and a perfection relative, terrestrial and capable of achievement by all who receive the gift of new life in Christ (Eph. iv. 12 *f.*, Col. i. 28, iii. 14). Only—so it seems to the writer—as this distinction is kept in mind, can coherence be found on this theme in the Pauline writings.

From the Epistle to the Ephesians Wesley takes two texts: the solemn prayer concluding Chapter III and especially vv. 14–19, and Paul's belief that Christ will present the Church to Himself a glorious Church, not having spot or wrinkle or any such thing; but that it should be holy and without blemish (v. 27). To any scholar commenting on the first text—as does Dr. Armitage Robinson[1]—that the phrase "which passeth knowledge" proves that "it is indeed beyond attainment," Wesley would have replied that the inference was not legitimate. Much concerning sanctification, he would have argued, "passeth knowledge" (in the sense that it passed explanation) but he would not have conceded that it passed experience. The second text was used by Wesley to answer the question, "Is there any clear Scripture *promise* . . . that God will save us from *all sin*?" And this is part of his answer as taken from the New Testament and "laid down in the plainest terms."[2] That the fulfilment of the promise belonged to the future must have seemed as obvious to Wesley as to his critics, but the idea that its fulfilment could only be in some sharp separation from the Church militant he would not have allowed.

From Philippians he stresses only iii. 15. He quotes the Epistle in his *Plain Account* ten times but, not unnaturally for his purpose, the stress falls on iii. 15. The word is τέλειος again, and to Wesley it was a plain statement that perfection was possible on this earth and that Paul numbered himself among the perfect. "Let us therefore, as many as be perfect, be thus minded." Moffatt translates the word in this context as "mature," justifying his preference with a quotation from Epictetus.[3]

The difficulty, as is well known, is made all the harder because Paul has already said in v. 12, "Not that I have already obtained, or am already made perfect. . . ." The apparent contradiction has never been completely cleared up. Wesley is content to say that

---

[1] J. A. Robinson, *St. Paul's Epistle to the Ephesians*, 86.
[2] *Plain Account*, 42 *f.*   [3] *Expositor*, November, 1016, 347 *f.*

Paul employs the word in two senses.[1] Moffatt, as we have seen, translates the term as "mature" in v. 15 and retains "perfect" in v. 12. Lightfoot holds that the use of the term in v. 15 is ironical but most recent commentators fail to find the irony.[2] It may seem an over-simplification of the question, and a conclusion reached by ignoring the textual difficulty to revert to Wesley's naïve comment and simply affirm that the Apostle is using the word in two different senses. But is this really contradicted by the best that modern scholarship can say? And how else can the Apostle's established reputation as a deep and clear thinker be defended? And may we not find further warrant here for a conclusion already reached on other grounds that he has a dual idea of perfection—a perfection absolute and celestial: a perfection relative and terrestrial as well?

In the Epistles to the Thessalonians, Wesley makes much of one text only, 1 Thess. v. 23. Again, this is a prayer—an optative, expressing wish. "And the God of peace Himself sanctify you wholly; and may your spirit and soul and body be preserved entire, without blame at the coming of our Lord Jesus Christ."

From the Pastoral Epistles he builds again on but one passage (Titus ii. 11–14) and stresses, what seems so plain to him, that the command is "not given to the dead but to the living"[3] and that here on earth God can and will "redeem us from all iniquity, and purify unto Himself a people for His own possession, zealous of good works."

The doubts which have been entertained for more than a century concerning the authenticity of the Pastoral Epistles never clouded the mind of John Wesley, and do not seriously affect this review of his scriptural evidence. If it be true—as seems probable—that the letters contain genuine fragments of Paul's writings worked over by some disciple who knew his master's mind, it needs only to be noted that the passage Wesley cites is commonly held to be genuine and "among the priceless treasures of Scripture."[4]

So we conclude our brief survey of Wesley's ten texts taken from Paul. Some objection will be felt that he approached his task in this manner at all, lifting a text here and there and not

---

[1] *Plain Account*, 26.

[2] e.g. Michael, *The Epistle of Paul to the Philippians*, 164.

[3] *Plain Account*, 44.

[4] Horton, *The Pastoral Epistles* (The Century Bible), 4. For a less confident appraisal of it, cf. P. N. Harrison, *The Problem of the Pastoral Epistles*, Appendix iv, etc.

rather conducting a broad survey of the Apostle's teaching and elucidating perfection (if that be possible) as one of the leading Pauline ideas. But that is to ignore two points—first, the general approach to biblical theology in the eighteenth century, which invariably proceeded on the basis of "proof-texts," and, secondly, the conviction which Wesley had that this teaching was in conformity with "the whole tenor of the New Testament."[1]

Certainly, he has not adduced all the evidence from Paul that he might in support of his theme. He does not stress the Apostle's great doctrine of the indwelling of Christ in the heart of the believer, nor the believer's "permanent address" as being ἐν Χριστῷ; he does not underline the fact that Paul nowhere speaks of sin as being necessary in the heart of the believer, nor does he link the doctrine enough (as Paul does) with the Cross and the Holy Spirit. He sees that perfect love is the secret and power of it all, but he is far from complete in the citation of texts, even according to the standards his own method imposed. If one instance of this may be given, it is of interest to notice, even though it can only be accidental, that he nowhere in his *Plain Account* quotes Rom. vi., in verse after verse of which (e.g. 2, 6, 9–11, 14, 22) the glorious possibility of freedom from sin is held out to the believer. Nor does he discuss whether "bondage to sin" and the "dominion" of sin imply a suzerainty from which the believer may escape without escaping from sin altogether.

(iv) The Epistle to the Hebrews must engage our attention now. Three of Wesley's foundation texts are quarried here: Heb. vi. 1, vii. 25, x. 14.

Wesley uses the phrase "go on unto perfection" as evidence of a dual stage of Christian growth.[2] The exhortation is clearly addressed, he reasons, to justified persons and yet they are urged to "go on unto perfection." [The word is τέλειος again, and Moffatt again prefers "mature."] It is the text of Wesley's Sermon LXXVI, though the sermon, while it is a spirited statement of Wesley's teaching, adds nothing new to our understanding of his doctrine. It is, in fact, a "pre-text" here, rather than a text: a "motto," as Dr. Whitehead called the text he used for Wesley's funeral sermon.[3] There is no exposition.

But it is upon Heb. vii. 25 that Wesley—and most subsequent

---

[1] *Plain Account*, 22.   [2] *ibid.*, 128.
[3] Whitehead's *Funeral Sermon on John Wesley* (edit. 1791), 1.

exponents of this teaching—put the stress. Taking εἰς τὸ παντελὲς with σώζειν they have found here a plain promise that Christ "saveth to the uttermost,"[1] and echoes of this phrase are constantly found in the language beloved of holiness sects: "uttermost Saviour," "full salvation," etc.

It is, however, seriously to be doubted whether, in the light of modern scholarship, this translation can be maintained as indicating the meaning that was most prominent in the author's mind. It is true that in the only other instance in the New Testament where παντελὲς is used (Luke xiii. 11) the sense of extent is prominent, but the word, which is common in the literature of the time, has normally a *temporal* sense, and a temporal sense seems most in harmony with the argument here. The author of the Epistle is contrasting the priesthoods—the Levitical priesthood and the priesthood of Christ. Levitical priests, being men, serve but for a time. Death puts a term to their service. But Christ "abideth for ever." Most naturally, therefore, as it seems to the writer, Moffatt makes his point, and Heb. vii. 25 runs on: "Hence for all time, He is able to save those who approach God through Him." But Westcott keeps to the translation beloved of Wesley, and Dr. T. H. Robinson thinks that both meanings are there, and both are intended.[2]

We come to Heb. x. 14. Wesley uses this text when he is grappling with the difficult phrase "sinless perfection"[3] but he seems vaguely aware that it does not aid the argument. Indeed, the ablest theologians who have taken in hand a sympathetic interpretation of this doctrine frankly admit that there is no promise here of a relative perfection attainable on this earth.[4] The author is concerned to stress the completeness of Christ's sacrifice and its utter efficacy for the faithful in all generations. Nor can the closest scrutiny of the text sustain the meaning Wesley had most in mind. Dr. J. H. Moulton, commenting on the force of the present participle here, calls it "another ambiguous case,"[5] and concerning these same timeless present participles he says, "grammar speaks to exegesis here with no decisive voice."

It would seem, therefore, that Wesley's citations from the

[1] *Plain Account*, 18.
[2] T. H. Robinson, *The Epistle to the Hebrews*, 103; cf. also Vincent Taylor *Forgiveness and Reconciliation*, 224.
[3] *Plain Account*, 88 f.
[4] Pope, *A Compendium of Christian Theology*, iii, 57. Flew, 74.
[5] Moulton, *A Grammar of New Testament Greek* (vol. i, "Prolegomena"), 127.

Epistle to the Hebrews do not materially strengthen his case, and this would be in line with the expectation of most informed students of perfection who have examined the epistle.

But with this proviso! There is an increasing weight of scholarly opinion that the author of this Epistle was deeply influenced by the Platonic Theory of Ideas, and Dr. Flew has argued that it is just there—in his doctrine of two worlds—that we must seek his teaching on perfection.[1] It cannot be denied that, for certain sins, the author allows no second repentance: but this does not require that he denies the possibility of perfection for those who press on. Is perfection only in the realm of the eternal? Are we to say quite simply that this powerful and independent thinker looks upon sin as a necessity in this present life?

The answer would appear to be this. Full perfection, as he sees it, does belong to the eternal realm (xii. 28) but the underlying spiritualised Platonism in his teaching points to more than a hope on earth. The divorce between the "here" and the "hereafter" is half resolved. "The world to come is really present."[2] It may belong to any interpretation of Platonism to insist that pluralities of phenomena are "transient, mutable and imperfect" but that is to consider them only in comparison with the unities which are eternal, immutable and perfect. If, for the purposes of our enquiry, we think in terms of relative perfection for those new-made in Christ, we may hazard the guess that further study will not find us falsely interpreting the Epistle to the Hebrews.

(v) With the exception of a single text in James, the Johannine writings provide Wesley with the rest of his scriptural warrant. Two texts are taken from the Gospel of St. John and no less than ten from the First Epistle.

In John viii. 34 *ff.* it is laid down that "everyone that committeth sin is the bondservant of sin," and the promise is given that the Son "shall make you free." Wesley enlarges on this.[3] He says (detecting, one must assume, some allusion to national pride in the context) that the Son will make those who are born of God free from "that great root of sin and bitterness, pride." "Free," it will be observed, means *completely* free to Wesley. It is entire emancipation. When handling the words of Scripture, his disposition is always to give as sharp an edge to every term as it will bear. If sin is said to be "destroyed," it is *destroyed*. If the sinner is described as "free," Wesley holds that *no*

---

[1] Flew, 75 *f.*   [2] *ibid.*, 90.   [3] *Plain Account*, 26.

shackle remains upon him. When the commentators of the eighteenth century said, in opposition to Wesley's teaching (what so many commentators say to-day), that this freedom from sin on which Johannine theology puts so marked a stress is a freedom *in principle* and does not mean that every taint has gone, Wesley replied that that was denying the plain word of Scripture and casting some aspersion on the Son who had promised to do this wonderful thing. Beyond that point the controversy never seemed to go. Or, if it proceeded at all, it forsook exegesis and fell back upon experience. Wesley was asked if he had ever seen a perfect Christian, someone really free from sin. He replied that, in the sense in which he used the word, he had seen hundreds . . . and then the controversy was apt to turn in weary circles of ill defined terms.

The great high-priestly prayer of our Lord provides Wesley with the other passage he takes from the Gospel of John. It is John xvii. 20–5. It has special preciousness to him because it is a prayer of the Lord. He believed with his brother Charles,

> Jesus, Thou canst not pray in vain

and he added his own fervent

> "Amen" to what my Lord doth say!

It needs hardly to be stated that Wesley's approach to the problem of the Fourth Gospel was quite uncritical. He was neither helped nor hindered by the thought of an inspired evangelist expounding an Hebraic message to a Greco-Roman world. For him John xvii was a verbatim prayer of his Saviour, that the believer might be united to the Father and to Him, and that the devout might thus be "perfected into one."

Life—one of the dominant notes of the whole Gospel—is the dominant note here too: the life, which finds its Source in the Father and its deep Well in the Son, imparting life to all believers. And because it is the life of God, there can be in it no admixture of evil. It is the perfect gift of perfect life. So Wesley believed. And it is not without interest to notice that Dr. E. F. Scott says of this same passage:

> "The Fourth Gospel may be said to culminate in this magnificent conception of God Himself eternally present in

the believer, through Christ who unites us with Himself as He
is united with God."[1]

A full third of the texts on which Wesley chiefly relies for his
doctrine of Christian Perfection are taken from the First Epistle
of John.

Not unnaturally, for his purpose, some of them receive more
emphasis than others.

> "And this is the message which we have heard from Him,
> and announce unto you, that God is light, and in Him is no
> darkness at all . . . but if we walk in the light, as He is in the
> light, we have fellowship one with another, and the blood of
> Jesus His Son cleanseth us from all sin" (1 John i. 5, 7).

> "If we say that we have no sin, we deceive ourselves, and
> the truth is not in us. If we confess our sins, He is faithful and
> righteous to forgive us our sins, and to cleanse us from all
> unrighteousness" (1 John i. 8, 9).

> "He that saith he abideth in Him ought himself also to walk
> even as He walked" (1 John ii. 6).

> "And everyone that hath this hope set on Him purifieth
> himself, even as He is pure . . . he that doeth sin is of the devil;
> for the devil sinneth from the beginning. To this end was the
> Son of God manifested, that He might destroy the works of
> the devil. Whosoever is begotten of God doeth no sin, because
> His seed abideth in Him: and he cannot sin, because he is
> begotten of God . . . whosoever doeth not righteousness is not
> of God" (1 John iii. 3, 8–10).

In a sermon on this theme which Wesley published in 1741 after
a conversation with Dr. Gibson (then Bishop of London) he is
at pains in setting out this scriptural evidence to stress the present
tense of the verbs.

> "Now, it is evident the apostle here speaks of a deliverance
> wrought in this world. For he saith not, The blood of Christ
> *will* cleanse (at the hour of death, or in the day of judgment),
> but it '*cleanseth*,' at the present time, us living Christians 'from
> all sin.' And it is equally evident, that if any sin remain, we are
> not cleansed from all sin. If *any* unrighteousness remain in the
> soul, it is not cleansed from all unrighteousness."[2]

[1] Scott, *The Fourth Gospel: Its Purpose and Theology*, 319.   [2] *Plain Account*, 24.

The great note of the Johannine theology is Eternal Life—an Eternal Life which is mysteriously and gloriously a present possession. Devout souls in all ages, unenlightened by any modern scholarship but enlightened by the Spirit of God, have scrutinised the Holy Page and fixed with delight on those present tenses:

"He that believeth on the Son *hath* eternal life" (John iii. 36).

"He that heareth my word and believeth Him that sent Me *hath* eternal life, and cometh not into judgment but hath passed out of death into life" (John v. 24).

"He that believeth *hath* eternal life" (John vi. 47).

"These things have I written unto you, that ye may know that ye *have* eternal life" (1 John v. 13).

On those same present tenses, especially when they were concerned with hearts cleansed from all sin, Wesley seized with the eagerness of one before whose eyes a new range of precious promises appeared, and for whom, at last, faith was all but lost in sight. "Not 'will cleanse,'" he cried, "but *cleanses*. Now!!" Convinced that the sub-Christian level of many believers could be explained by their ignorance of God's promises in regard to sin, and that the sanctifying work of the Holy Spirit was being hindered by a consequent lack of faith, he ran to them with eager feet to offer this greater gift of God. Holiness was not merely imputed but imparted. God could do more than forgive sin; He could destroy it. Asked for his scriptural authority, he was never more ready to proffer any part of it than he was ready to proffer what he found in the First Epistle of John.

But his opponents were not slow to point out an apparent contradiction in his own most valued source. They drew his attention to other phrases in the same epistle:

"If we say that we have no sin, we deceive ourselves, and the truth is not in us" (1 John i. 8).

"If we say that we have not sinned, we make Him a liar, and His word is not in us" (1 John i. 10).

He had not overlooked them. He was too close a Bible student for that. He does not discuss the probability of some contemporary and heretical sect proclaiming that they never had sinned and needed not the cleansing of Christ. He takes these texts to

D

refer to those days and years in the lives of all men which preceded
the triumph of God's sanctifying power upon them and—of those
days—admits their unchallengeable truth.

> "If we say we have not sinned [in time past], we make Him
> a liar . . . but *now* He cleanses us 'from all unrighteousness'
> that we may 'go and sin no more.' "[1]

From that position he did not move through the years. When
his opponents, stressing the utter pollution of human nature,
insisted that there was sin in everything that everybody did, he
usually left the controversy to his lieutenants but bent his own
strength to raising up a spiritual community of people who would
authenticate, in their own lives, the promise of God and the
teaching of the Apostle. He believed that the argument could
best be rebutted that way.

Dr. Flew, who finds it impossible to accept the usual interpretation proffered by those who oppose Wesley's teaching of
the passages in the First Epistle of John on which Wesley chiefly
relies (i.e. "that the freedom from sin is given ideally . . . while
the man himself still goes on sinning"), makes the suggestion that
John's letter would be understood by the community to which it
was addressed because "a considerable number in the community
. . . had passed through the experience of deliverance from habits
of sinning."[2] He believes that the rise of Methodism provided a
"notable analogy" with these amazing moral transformations of
the early Church and that the repugnance the teaching invokes in
some quarters gathers its strength from the fact that too often
the Christian community is accepting (and excusing) a lower level
of life than God ever intended that it should live. The moral tone
of the professing Church varies from generation to generation.
Historians talk of some ages as "ages of faith": there are others
when, by common consent, there is "no open vision." There are
periods too, in the world's history, when the power of God seems
outpoured in unlimited measure and spiritual miracles are
wrought on all sides. In such a time neglected doctrines are
rediscovered and parts of the New Testament, otherwise inexplicable, authenticate themselves. There are not a few who

---

[1] *Plain Account*, 22; cf. Brooke, *A Critical and Exegetical Commentary on the
Johannine Epistles*, 16, who holds that the limitation of the meaning to sins committed
before men became Christians is not justified by the words of the writer.

[2] Flew, 111 *f*. But cf. also Moody, *The Mind of the Early Converts*, 21, 32 *f*., 234,
for evidence of the ease with which converts from paganism think of "sinlessness."

think that the eighteenth century was such a period in England and that the chief instrument of it was "a man sent from God whose name was John."

(vi) There remains only a text from the Epistle of James.

"And let patience have its perfect work, that ye may be perfect and entire, lacking in nothing" (Jas. i. 4).

The word is τέλειος again, almost a favourite word with James (i. 17, 25; iii. 2. Notice also ii. 22). Moffatt prefers "finished" in this context. The view taken of τέλειος elsewhere will largely determine the interpretation placed upon it here.

Elsewhere, Wesley devotes space to the Epistle of James, not in direct support of the doctrine of Christian Perfection, but to meet the challenge of another text which the letter includes.[1]

"For in many things we all stumble" (Jas. iii. 2). He labours, not carrying complete conviction, to prove that this text is not opposed to his main thesis, and points out that the writer cannot mean "all" to be entirely inclusive because, in the same verse, he distinguishes some who *are* perfect. Wesley concludes that "we" in this connection is in the nature of a figure of speech and refers not to the apostles, nor true believers, but to the teachers distinguished in the previous verse who shall "receive the greater condemnation."

As we conclude our survey of Wesley's scriptural warrant, a dozen questions leap to the mind. Has he made out his case? Is the doctrine well set in the Scriptures? Has modern scholarship materially affected the problem, or is the exegetical question the same in substance as it was in the eighteenth century? Did he find the doctrine in the Bible, or carry preconceived ideas to it? Would any mature and thoughtful reader studying the New Testament for the first time recognise this teaching on perfection as an integral part of the message—or learn of it later with no little surprise?

Our enquiry is, as yet, too incomplete to give a categorical answer to all those questions. But this can be said with confidence. The passing of two centuries, and all the solid biblical scholarship which has been crowded into them, have not in themselves rendered Wesley's position untenable. In short,

---

[1] *Plain Account,* 21.

grammar, and the closest textual scrutiny undertaken in its light, have not determined the issue either way. The theological presuppositions which subtly affect exegesis have more to do with decisions on this matter than the biblical student might care to concede. As we have surveyed Wesley's textual foundations, we have noticed the shadows of dubiety cast by scholarship on a translation, or interpretation, here and there, but, for the most part, the stones stand. Whether he was right in fashioning the superstructure upon them which he did has yet to be decided.

But this is clear. A modern scholar like Dr. Flew can conduct an independent survey of the biblical evidence for this doctrine, and find it more extensive in certain directions than Wesley supposed, while Dr. Vincent Taylor, writing still more recently and with particular heed to New Testament exegesis, says: "Beyond doubt the New Testament teaches the absolute necessity of ethical and spiritual perfection. . . . It would, indeed, be difficult to find any important doctrinal theme which is more broadly based or more urgently presented."[1] The considered conclusion of these scholars is that the New Testament plainly teaches that the Christian need not sin.

So Wesley believed and taught. If he had left it there, his life would have been more tranquil, but he borrowed the words of his favourite Epistle and said, "A Christian is so far perfect as not to commit sin."[2] When, in addition, he declared that he knew hundreds of whom this was true, the fires of controversy immediately flared up.

Many said that such teaching was heresy and out of harmony with the Scriptures. To all these Wesley stoutly answered: "If I am a heretic, I became such by reading the Bible."[3]

---

[1] Taylor, *Forgiveness and Reconciliation*, 189 *f*.
[2] *Plain Account*, 22.   [3] *Letters*, iv, 216.

CHAPTER VI

IS THERE A CLUE IN THE GRAMMAR?

Towards the close of the last chapter we said that "grammar, and the closest textual scrutiny undertaken in its light, have not determined the issue either way," but it will be remembered that a not unimportant question involving grammar has already been deferred. We can approach it best by a quotation from Dr. W. F. Lofthouse.

Commenting on Charles Wesley's hymns on Christian Perfection (still the most accessible and used exposition of Methodist teaching on this theme), Dr. Lofthouse says:

". . . perfection is a matter of divine command or human longing, rather than of attainment. Here Charles Wesley is at one with the language of the New Testament, and more especially of Paul, who, when he speaks of perfection, almost always will be found to be using the imperative or the subjunctive moods, or the future tense, but never the present or the perfect. . . . John Wesley, indeed, does not appear to notice this characteristic."[1]

It cannot fairly be said that John Wesley does not *notice* this. He does not *stress* it. But he both notices and remarks that the New Testament teaching on perfection is often expressed in *prayers* and *commands* which, he insists, "are equivalent to the strongest assertions."[2] Elsewhere, he enquires rhetorically, "Has God anywhere in Scripture commanded us more than He has promised to us?"[3]

What are the facts? Is it true that, in the thirty texts which we have distinguished as Wesley's scriptural basis for the doctrine, the imperative and subjunctive moods preponderate, and the future tense is most commonly used? And, if it is true, what inference can justly be drawn from those facts?

As to the facts. In the thirty texts we have passed in review, we find that the subjunctive mood implying possibility is used

---

[1] *The London Quarterly and Holborn Review*, April, 1934, 184.
[2] *Plain Account*, 43.   [3] *ibid.*, 73.

eleven times; the imperative mood expressing command (or demand) is used three times; the optative mood expressing wish is used once, and the future tense is used three times also. The present and perfect tenses appear ten and three times respectively: the aorist twice. We do not find, in the texts which Wesley selected, as wide a disproportion as might be expected between Paul's use of the present and perfect, and John's use of them. Indeed, four of Wesley's Pauline texts speak in the present tense, though three of the four (Rom. ii. 29; 2 Cor. iii. 18; Gal. ii. 20) would not seem to some critics to give a very firm exegetical foundation for the doctrine.[1]

What inference is to be drawn from this? It is clearly not to be dismissed as accidental. Conversely, its importance must not be exaggerated.

It will aid us to a sound conclusion if we recognise on both sides the limits of legitimate inference and mark out, as it were, the Scylla and Charybdis of our course.

(i) We cannot say, on the ground of grammar, that Scripture teaches that perfection is unattainable on earth. It is not a just inference from the grammatical form to suggest that it is "only an ideal" in the New Testament: that the exalted standard is set before us without either expectation or possibility of our achievement, and that we have dealt seriously with the solemn admonitions of Scripture if we put them in the same category as the proverbial impossibility of "hitching your wagon to a star."

To suggest that God lays commands on mortals which are utterly incapable of fulfilment is to make nonsense of the moral passion of the New Testament and to reflect adversely on the holy character of God. How else can God—or man—lay a charge on others except in the imperative mood? Nor need it be inferred, because the future tense is used, that it must necessarily be the distant future long after death.

And who is bold enough to put a limit to what grace can do with human nature here on earth? Dare any man say that God has never perfected a child of His, while in this mortal body—no saint in the cloister, or humble and obscure servant toiling in the busy press of normal life? No absolute and philosophic perfection is pleaded for either by Wesley or those who have followed him in this teaching, but the true, if relative, perfection of a perfect bud which has not burst into a perfect flower.

[1] For the purposes of this analysis I have taken in each of the texts what seemed to me to be the "key" verbs, and not always one verb only from each text.

Our examination is still far from complete, but it is pertinent to point out at this stage to those who believe that there is a clue in the grammar that neither moods nor tenses are capable of uttering the last word.

(ii) On the other hand, it is important that those who maintain this doctrine should give due weight to the fact that no New Testament writer announces in plain words: "I am perfect" or "I am freed from all sin."

This will be disputed in some quarters. It will be argued that Paul makes the claim by implication in Phil. iii. 15 and that John could hardly write as he does in 1 John i. 7 unless he too had been "cleansed from all sin." But can either statement be called pellucidly clear and quite unequivocal?

We hazard the guess, even at this early stage of our examination of Wesley's doctrine, that we shall be forced to make terms with this obdurate fact before we end. Wesley bound up his conviction of God's sanctifying power with the believer's awareness that the work had been done. He not only taught that Christians could be cleansed from all sin but normally would *know* it, and were in honour bound to testify to it. If it be true—and it *is* true—that nothing he taught involved him in more odium than the doctrine of Christian Perfection, it is true also that nothing in the doctrine of Christian Perfection involved him in more odium than his instruction to his followers to announce that the work had been done. It exposed him to the most terrible charges of charlatanry and he could sustain it with no unchallengeable authority from the Bible.

Nor is it so integral a part of the doctrine that the doctrine cannot stand without its inclusion. Wesley never claimed to be perfect himself and it seems never to have struck him as odd that none of the nine or ten writers of the New Testament unambiguously affirmed that the miracle had been wrought in him.

We must turn now from the Bible to the hymn-book. The step is not as long as may be thought at first. Hymns were one of the chief means the Wesleys used for teaching their people the Bible. John claims in the Preface to the hymn-book of 1780 that it is "a little body of experimental and practical divinity" and by far the larger part of Charles' sacred verse is a poetical commentary on the Scriptures. Dr. Rattenbury says that Charles Wesley's hymns contain "the Bible in solution" and can be described as "needle-worked or woven-patterned fabrics" from Scripture. He says also that "a skilful man, if the Bible were lost, might extract much of it from Wesley's hymns."[1] Taking a direct stride, therefore, from the Bible to the hymn-book, we can test how close John Wesley kept to his scriptural authority when, chiefly by the genius of his brother, the teaching was turned into song.

[1] Rattenbury, *The Evangelical Doctrines of Charles Wesley's Hymns*, 48 f.

CHAPTER VII

THE TEACHING IS TURNED INTO SONG

Hymns have always occupied a large place in Methodism. The revival of religion in the eighteenth century was cradled in song, and it was an immense gain to the Movement that one of its leaders should be a poet of no mean order. Canon Overton does not hesitate to call Charles Wesley "the great hymn-writer of all ages."[1]

But though the hymns were Charles', they may be said to express in their wholeness, and as finally approved and published, the mind of John even more than the mind of Charles. The elder brother "censored" them. His annotations on the hymns are always clear, quite often trenchant, and sometimes caustic.[2] When he finally approved he did so whole-heartedly, but his enthusiastic commendations always waited on a careful judgment. What he could not approve found no place in the chief of all editions—the "large hymn-book" published in 1780.

The brothers did not always see eye to eye either on Church polity or on every aspect of their message. They did not see— especially during the sixth decade of the century—eye to eye in regard to Christian Perfection. Charles came to think of

"sanctification as a gradual work wrought out through discipline, and not finally achieved until death. He never, indeed, gave up the conviction of his early ministry that the state of entire sanctification is attained by simple faith and therefore might conceivably be realized long before death—a view which John consistently held. But as time went on he realized more vividly the exceeding sinfulness of sin, and its deep penetration into human nature. In the buffetings of life he learned to know himself better and to discern the subtle workings of the old man in actions which seemed to be good. So his natural caution led him to hesitate to declare that he had gained perfection's height."[3]

[1] Overton, *Julian's Dictionary of Hymnology*, 1257.

[2] Some of them are given in *The Poetical Works of John and Charles Wesley* (Osborn vols. ix, x).

[3] Wiseman, *Charles Wesley: Evangelist and Poet*, 167 *f*.

It was this change in his thinking that was most reflected in a collection of hymns he published in Bristol in 1762. They were in two volumes entitled *Short Hymns on Selected Passages of Scripture*. They were not submitted to John's approving—or disapproving—eye. In the Preface, Charles refers specifically to the doctrine of Christian Perfection which, he says, "several of the hymns are intended to prove, and several to guard, . . . I durst not publish the one without the other."[1]

Not unnaturally, the publication of these little volumes caused John some acute concern. The leaders of Methodism were speaking with two voices. It would confuse the simple, to say the least, if John taught one kind of Christian Perfection and Charles another. He wrote, therefore, with some warmth to his younger brother disapproving the want of frankness he had displayed and dwelling particularly on his change of view in regard to Christian Perfection. He says:

"One word more, concerning setting perfection too high. *That perfection* which I believe, I can boldly preach, because I think I see five hundred witnesses of it. Of *that perfection* which you preach, you do not even think you see any witness at all. Why, then you must have far more courage than me, or you could not persist in preaching it. . . . I cordially assent . . . that there is *no such perfection* here as *you* describe—at least, I never met with an instance of it; and I doubt I never shall. Therefore I still think to set perfection *so high* is effectually to renounce it."[2]

The weakness of this reply will not be lost on anyone. John Wesley was forced to stratify perfection and even to put in a plea that perfection be not set too high! It was this admission which later exposed him to the gibe that "one may be a perfect Christian without being a perfect man."[3]

It is not surprising that the hymns which Charles included in these two "unblessed" volumes, and included specifically to *guard* the doctrine, were not in favour with John when he published his definitive edition of the hymn-book in 1780. Most readers would feel that nothing much was lost. These hymns are very short, somewhat sombre, and many of them not in the poet's best vein as verse. But it is important to remember their existence as the background to the statement that the hymns of

---

[1] Par. 2.   [2] *Letters* v, 20; cf. also 39–41, 93.   [3] Warfield, 528.

Charles Wesley on Christian Perfection, as commonly known, reflect, by judicious omission and occasional alteration,[1] the rounded opinions of John Wesley even more than those of their author. And with that warning in mind, we can turn to a consideration of the hymns dealing with our subject in a volume which many beside the Methodists have been willing to acclaim as the first great hymn-book in the English tongue.

It was published in 1780 and was meant to supersede the many smaller collections the Wesleys had already given to their people. It was not intended to be a book for every need of public worship; there were no hymns for the Lord's Supper, for the great festivals or for a funeral. It was meant to meet the need of a "society" within the Church which was in deadly earnest about religion. If the word may be pardoned of a man who looked upon pride as a deadly sin, John Wesley was very proud of this book. He says in the Preface:

> "As but a small part of these Hymns is of my own composing [the vast majority, of course, were Charles'], I do not think it inconsistent with modesty to declare, that I am persuaded, no such Hymn-Book as this, has yet been published in the English Language. In what other publication of the kind, have you so distinct and full an account of Scriptural Christianity? Such a declaration of the heights and depths of Religion, speculative and practical? So strong cautions against the most plausible errors; particularly those that are now most prevalent? And so clear directions for making your calling and election sure; for perfecting holiness in the fear of God?"[2]

"For perfecting holiness in the fear of God!" Always the emphasis was there. The section dealing with our theme is significantly the longest in the book. It is called, "For Believers Groaning for Full Redemption" (not a very happy title for a section of a hymn-book, though borrowed, of course, from Rom. viii. 26), and includes seventy-five hymns, thirty-five of which (in whole or in part) still find a place in the Methodist Hymn-Book of to-day.[3] In the first editions of the book of 1780 about a third of the hymns in this section were separately entitled "For Believers Brought to the Birth." The term "new birth" is sometimes used by the Wesleys for justification and sometimes for Christian Perfection.[4]

---

[1] Rattenbury, *The Evangelical Doctrines of Charles Wesley's Hymns*, 64 f., 316 f.
[2] Par. 5.   [3] Published in 1933.
[4] Rattenbury, *The Evangelical Doctrines of Charles Wesley's Hymns*, 308 f.

Hymns are not a very exact means of expounding theology. They belong to the language of devotion and their composers exercise at least a little of the licence freely allowed to poets. But it is conceded that, for the most part, "the people called Methodists" have learned their theology from their hymns,[1] and it may be doubted whether the mind of John Wesley on Christian Perfection could really be understood if we ignored them.

In our analysis of the hymns of holiness, the number is given from the hymn-book of 1780 but an asterisk precedes the lines which still appear in the book of 1933.

It is a *complete* deliverance from sin which is here taught. Dr. Sugden's comment that Wesley thought of sin as "a *thing* which has to be taken out of a man, like a cancer or a rotten tooth"[2] is a fair and pertinent comment if the emphasis is put upon the cancer rather than the rotten tooth. The hymns suggest that sin is knit into our nature, rather than cupped into it. The word "inbred" is frequently used.[3]

> *Shew me, as my soul can bear,
> The depth of *inbred* sin.   (348)
>
> Forgive and make my nature whole:
> My *inbred* malady remove.   (353)
>
> Bid my *inbred* sin depart,
> And I Thy utmost word shall prove.   (357)
>
> Soon the Lamb of God shall take
> My *inbred* sin away.   (372)
>
> Break off the yoke of *inbred* sin,
> And fully set my spirit free.   (377)
>
> Speak the second time, "Be clean!"
> Take away my *inbred* sin.   (386)

But inbred or not, it is a complete deliverance that is taught. The words "all," "every," "ever," "no more," "perfect," "spotless," "sanctify" are not merely used but pressed into the emphatic place.

> Able Thou art from sin to save,
> From *all* indwelling sin.   (346)

---

[1] *Sermons*, ii, 342.   [2] *ibid.*, ii, 459 (footnote).   [3] The italics are mine throughout.

*And *all* my sins consume!   (351)

*From *all* iniquity, from *all*,
   He shall my soul redeem!   (394)

Come, Saviour, come, and make me whole;
   Entirely *all* my sins remove.   (396)

*An end of *all* my troubles make,
   An end of *all* my sin.   (398)

Seize on our sins, and burn up *all*,
   Nor leave the least remains behind.   (400)

Cleanse me now from *every* sin.   (340)

*Unless Thou purge my *every* stain,
   Thy suffering and my faith are vain.   (364)

*For *ever* cease from sin.   (331)

"I have now obtain'd the power,
   Born of God, to sin *no more*."   (388)

Be Christ in me, and I in Him,
   Till *perfect* we are made in one.   (341)

*And *perfect* me in love.   (344)

*Hallow Thy great and glorious name,
   And *perfect* holiness in me.   (380)

*Finish then Thy new creation,
   Pure and *spotless* let us be.   (374)

*And *sanctify* the whole.   (351)

It is, moreover, a "here and now" deliverance.

I, even I, shall see His face;
   I shall be holy *here*.   (393)

*Be it according to Thy word!
   This moment let it be!   (352)

Now let me gain perfection's height:
   Now let me into nothing fall.   (381)

Now, Saviour, *now* the power bestow
And let me cease from sin!   (391)

*In all the confidence of hope
I claim the blessing *now!*   (405)

If we enquire the means of this amazing change, we find that it is all attributed to the power of God by faith.

My *faith* shall bring the power.   (333)

According to our *faith* in Thee
Let it to us be done.   (378)

*I cannot wash my heart,
But by *believing* Thee. . . .   (398)

And the power of God works in co-operation with faith to the destruction of sin. How sin is dealt with is expressed by such words as "slay," "scatter," "mortify," "extirpate," "consume," "erase," "wash," "root-out," "dry-up."

Slay the dire root and seed of sin!   (332)

Slay me, and I in Thee shall trust.   (352)

**Scatter* the last remains of sin.   (338)

My old affections *mortify*,
Nail to the cross my will;
Daily and hourly bid me die,
Or altogether kill.   (352)

Enter my soul, *extirpate* sin,
Cast out the cursed seed.   (352)

*Hasten the joyful day,
Which shall my sins *consume*.   (356)

The original offence
Out of my soul *erase*.   (356)

And *wash* my nature white as snow.   (385)

Rooting out the seeds of sin.   (387)

Dry corruption's fountain *up*,
Cut off the entail of sin.   (344)

It is hard to resist the idea, as one broods on the hymns, that all this is effected, not within a relationship of persons, but by a stroke of omnipotence.[1] Charles Wesley asks for:

> A heart that *cannot* faithless prove.   (332)

He says:

> When I feel [Christ] fixt within,
> I shall have *no power* to sin.   (345)

> *Confound, *o'erpower* me, by Thy grace.   (381)

Indeed, Fletcher challenged Wesley on this point, dissenting from another line included in the 1780 book but which put this view more directly still:

> Take away the pow'r of sinning.   (374)

Fletcher pertinently enquires in a footnote, "Can God take away the power of sinning without taking away our power of free obedience?"[2]

But when sin is radically dealt with, holiness or perfect love is either "shed abroad" in the heart or "stamped" upon it.

> *Jesus, Thine all-victorious love
> *Shed* in my heart *abroad*.   (351)

> *Stampt* with real holiness,
> And fill'd with perfect love.   (357)

> And *stamp* Thine image on my heart.   (383)

And the devout soul is either described as now enjoying the life of the angels or restored to the innocence of Eden.

> Till of my *Eden* repossest,   (334)
> From every sin I cease.

> To real holiness *restor'd*.   (358)

> Restor'd to our unsinning state,
> To love's sweet paradise.   (378)

---

[1] cf. Scougal, *The Life of God in the Soul of Man* (edit. 1702), 56. "Though there must intervene a stroke of omnipotence to effectuate this mighty change in our souls, yet we ought to do what we can to fit and prepare ourselves."

[2] Fletcher's *Works*, vi, 393.

To Thy perfect love *restor'd*,
O let me sin no more! (390)

The life of *angels* live. (333)

When Thou the work of faith hast wrought,
I shall be pure within;
Nor sin in deed, or word, or thought;
For *angels* never sin. (347)

And let our final quotation from the hymns be one in which, perhaps, the angelic nature is not so prominent but in which the controversy underlying this doctrine is carried into the enemy's camp. In the third edition of the book of 1780 this verse appears:

Let others hug their chains,
For sin and Satan plead,
And say, from sin's remains
They never can be freed:
Rejoice in hope, rejoice with me,
We shall from *all* our sins be free. (336)

(B) Theological

CHAPTER VIII

WESLEY'S THEOLOGICAL PRESUPPOSITIONS

CONVINCED as Wesley was that the doctrine of Christian Perfection was well set in the Scriptures, it would be absurd to suggest that he read those Scriptures with a quite unbiased mind. However open a man may try to be in his thinking, he cannot escape the influences which have shaped him and, if his mind has reached maturity, more forces have worked upon him than he can easily recall.

The study of the New Testament was not, therefore, the only influence which constrained Wesley's mind in framing this doctrine. Certain theological presuppositions played a not unimportant part.

This becomes clear the moment we ask the elementary question, "Why was he so anxious to get people holy?"—the simple answer being that he wanted to get them to heaven. That was, as we have noted, his own chief design: to find the way to heaven. He became *homo unius libri* for that very thing: to find the way to heaven. And the two chief convictions which governed his thinking in this regard were these: first, that none without holiness could see God and, secondly, that there was no opportunity for a sinner to be saved from his sin on the other side of death. If, then, sinners were to get to heaven, it was imperative that sin be destroyed and holiness imparted this side of the grave.

That none could see God without holiness was axiomatic with Wesley. Was it not plainly set down in Hebrews xii.14? Whatever else should cause controversy, surely there could be no controversy about that. He raised the matter at the Conference of 1747 "as several persons were present who did not believe the doctrine of perfection" and he asked the question, "How much is allowed by our brethren who differ from us with regard to entire sanctification?"

On this point there was no dissension. They all agreed "that every one must be entirely sanctified in the article of death."[1]

[1] *Plain Account*, 40.

In his dispute with the Rev. Thomas Church he stresses the same point: "All writers whom I have ever seen till now (the Romish themselves not excepted) agree that we must be 'fully cleansed from all sin' before we can enter into glory."[1]

Yet Wesley had no belief in purgatory. The life after death was not divided for him, as for Roman Catholics, into hell, purgatory and heaven. He believed in hell and heaven, and in "the intermediate state." The intermediate state he sometimes called "paradise," and conceived it as a kind of antechamber of heaven where souls in full and enriched consciousness of fellowship with God dwelt between death and the resurrection.[2] But the intermediate state was not to be confused with purgatory. A modern Roman theologian says:

"Experience teaches us that the great majority of the pious faithful who leave this life have not attained that sublime ideal of being perfect 'as your heavenly Father is perfect' which our Lord puts before us. . . . Now, if we do not suppose that those who die thus without a perfect act of love are purified from their faults and prepared for the Vision of God without any act of theirs and so to speak in a purely magical way by a direct interposition of God's mercy . . . then there must be after death some possibility of a purification of the soul."[3]

Wesley would have none of that. Paradise, but not purgatory. He says:

"In paradise the souls of good men rest from their labours and are with Christ from death to the resurrection. This bears no resemblance at all to the Popish purgatory, wherein wicked men are supposed to be tormented in purging fire till they are sufficiently purified to have a place in heaven. But we believe (as did the ancient Church) that none suffer after death but those who suffer eternally. We believe that we are to be *here* saved from sin and enabled to love God with all our heart."[4]

We are to part with sin *here*. That was the emphasis. If sin did not end here it would remain for ever. Writing to James Hervey, in comment on *Theron and Aspasio*, Wesley says, "If sin remains in

---

[1] *Letters*, ii, 226.
[3] Adam, *The Spirit of Catholicism*, 101 *ff.*
[2] *ibid.*,vi, 214.
[4] *Letters*, vii, 168.

us till the day of judgement, it will remain for ever."[1] When
Elizabeth Hardy enquires, "Is it fit or necessary in the nature
of things that a soul should be saved from all sin before it enters
into glory?" Wesley replies:

> "It is. And so it is written, 'No unclean thing shall enter
> into it.' Therefore, whatever degrees of holiness they did or
> did not attain in the preceding parts of life, neither Jews nor
> heathens any more than Christians ever did or ever will enter
> into the New Jerusalem unless they are cleansed from all sin
> before they enter into eternity."[2]

To the same effect writes Fletcher, "The graces of repentance,
faith, hope, and Christian charity . . . must be perfected *here* or
never."[3]

It will be clear that, in this emphasis, Wesley was in the direct
line of Reformation theology. The Reformers denied purgatory.[4]
Tetzel and his scandalous sale of indulgences had been publicly
condemned by Luther in his thesis of October, 1517. The questionable practice of vending at a price remission of the temporal
punishment of sin had become abominable beyond belief in being
sometimes interpreted as a licence to commit it. When, therefore,
the reformed theology was promulgated, the indulgence system,
together with its creedal basis, was tossed aside, and in the limbo
of things thus lost was purgatory.

The Westminster Confession puts it thus:

> "The bodies of men after death, return to the dust, and see
> corruption: but their souls (which neither die nor sleep)
> having an immortal subsistence, immediately return to God
> who gave them: the souls of the righteous being then made
> perfect in holiness, are received into the highest heavens,
> where they behold the face of God in light and glory, waiting
> for the full redemption of their bodies: and the souls of the
> wicked are cast into hell, where they remain in torments and
> utter darkness, reserved to the judgment of the great day.
> Besides these two places, for souls separated from their bodies,
> the Scripture acknowledgeth none" (xxxii. 1, 1669 edit.).

---

[1] *Letters*, iii, 380.   [2] *ibid.*, iv, 11; cf. iii, 213.   [3] Fletcher's *Works*, vi, 254.
[4] The great precursor of the Reformation did not. See Workman, *John Wyclif:
A Study of the English Medieval Church*, ii, 18 f.

It follows, therefore, that there was no difference of view between Wesley and the main stream of Protestant theology in his century, in denying any future probation for sinners in the life beyond death. The only difference was here: that while Wesley's Calvinistic contemporaries asserted that complete cleansing came in the moment of death by a stroke of divine power, Wesley believed that the same complete cleansing could be ante-dated by five, ten or twenty years. "Why not?" he reasoned. "*You* believe that sin can be radically dealt with *in articulo mortis*: why not now?"

Fletcher argues similarly:

"If our opponents allow that faith and love may be made perfect two or three minutes before death, they give up the point. Death is no longer absolutely necessary to the destruction of unbelief and sin: for if the evil heart of unbelief departing from the living God may be taken away, and the completely honest and good heart given two or three minutes before death; we desire to know why this change may not take place two or three hours—two or three weeks—two or three years before that awful moment?"[1]

Later, stressing the same point, he warns his opponents that "heaven is no purgatory"[2] and that "death, far from introducing imperfect Christians into the state of Christian Perfection, will take them out of the very possibility of ever attaining it."[3]

Nor is it easy to see, on the premises that were common to both sets of controversialists, how Wesley and Fletcher could be rebutted. Neither side thought very clearly of the relationship of God and the individual soul as a relationship of persons. Both thought of sin as a *thing* which could be ripped out by an act of omnipotence. The Calvinist's "death-purgatory" had half-conceded in principle the point which Wesley desired to make. It was not a controversy about whether God *could* or *would* deal with sin this way, or yet *how*. Between these two teams of heated disputants it was merely a question of *when*. Both were agreed that it must be in this life, and Wesley was only peculiar in insisting that it need not be delayed till the moment of leaving it.

Purgatory—without the name, and with some revision of the idea—has been creeping back into modern Protestant theology. Baron von Hügel, it seems, was speaking for more than the

---

[1] Fletcher's *Works*, vi, 249.   [2] *ibid.*, 250.   [3] *ibid.*, 254.

members of his own communion when he said to his niece,
"Purgatory and Hell may be refined, but they must be there. The
majority of souls can't go straight to Heaven."[1]

The name is still scorned among Protestants and it is not
thought of only as penal and disciplinary, as with Roman theologians, but it is now generally allowed that something precious
was lost to Protestantism when all idea of progress was eliminated
from the life after death. Dr. A. E. Garvie pleads for this idea of
eternal progress and says:

> "This is not the doctrine of purgatory, nor of an inter-
> mediate state between death and resurrection; but a recognition
> that even for believers there will be continuity of experience
> and character; and progress toward that which we cannot
> now even imagine."[2]

He cherishes the hope that God will pursue with His grace even
those who die impenitent.

The late Canon Streeter put in a similar plea for progress after
death but also desired that it be not confused with the doctrine of
purgatory as understood in the Roman Church. Yet the word
"purgatory," as he was ready to concede, "is often used in its
ancient mediaeval sense to denote a state of real progress and
moral purification. There is much to be said for a revival of such
an idea."[3] Mr. Emmet is not less emphatic. Talking of those in
whom there is "the faintest spark of the divine life in the soul,"
he says, "We dare not abandon the hope of progress and forgiveness after death for such a soul."[4] Mr. A. Clutton-Brock only
dislikes the word "purgatory" because the idea of "enriching"
is much more important, he holds, than purging,[5] while Dr. J. H.
Leckie affirms that "the idea of a continued ministry of grace in
the state between death and judgment is supported not only by
the direct statement of St. Peter, but by a great mass of indirect
New Testament evidence."[6]

So something of the concept of purgatory has worked itself
back into Protestant thought. Not the name, and certainly not
the seven sharply divided ledges of Dante's mountain *Purgatorio*,
but the idea of discipline, of grace still vouchsafed, of enrichment,
and of progress.

[1] von Hügel, *Letters to a Niece*, xxxv.   [2] Garvie, *The Christian Faith*, 225 f.
[3] Streeter, *Immortality*, 139 f.   [4] *ibid.*, 216.
[5] *ibid.*, 234; cf. 236 f.   [6] Leckie, *The World to Come and Final Destiny*, 95.

But in the Protestant thinking of the eighteenth century, this would have been rank heresy. Sin had to be dealt with while breath remained in the mortal body, and precisely what John Wesley meant by sin when he expounded Christian Perfection must occupy our mind next.

CHAPTER IX

HIS IDEA OF SIN

WESLEY is quite clear in his definition of sin. He calls it "a voluntary transgression of a known law."[1] To this definition he holds firmly through all the movement of his argument and the view of Christian Perfection for which he contends can only be understood in its light.

He is at no little pains to point out that this perfection may include infirmities, ignorance and mistakes.[2] He believes that it could live with a heaviness of imagination, a certain crudity of manners, and a gullibility of mind. He admits freely that a man who is full of love to his fellows will be all the easier to impose upon. Yet none of these things, on his definition, can properly be classified as *sins*. They are not "voluntary transgressions of a known law."

But the question immediately arises: is this an adequate definition of sin? Is it sharp enough, and wide enough, and grave enough? Will it cover every instance of evil properly to be included in this simple, awful term?

Sin is not easy to define. Dr. F. R. Tennant took the theme in hand, he says, because it was plain to him that the ordinary concept of sin "is somewhat amorphous: it lacks the sharp edges and clear-cut angles of the perfect crystal,"[3] and most recent writers on the same subject, while differing from the definition on which Dr. Tennant fixed, agree with him in the urgent need of a clearer statement and a more chiselled meaning.[4]

It will not be without interest if we linger a little on Dr. Tennant's view. He has the distinction among British theologians of being the first to direct attention to this topic during the present century and to have pressed for a clearer definition of sin than was current when the century began. It is of special interest in prosecuting the present enquiry to note that his search for a clear concept of sin brought him at the last to a definition substantially the same as Wesley's. He works the theme out in detail,

---

[1] *Plain Account*, 53.   [2] *ibid.*, 50.

[3] Tennant, *The Concept of Sin*, 2.

[4] Orchard, *Modern Theories of Sin*, 94 *ff*. Moxon, *The Doctrine of Sin*, 204 *ff*. Bicknell, *The Christian Idea of Sin and Original Sin*, 30 *ff*.

giving reasons why inherited dispositions, mental ability, the capacity—or lack of it—for sound judgment,[1] and many other gifts—or impediments—are no subject for ethical comment, and reaches a conclusion in harmony with the founder of Methodism. If he rejects Wesley's phrasing because of ambiguity in the words "transgression" and "law" as commonly used, he rejects, at this point, nothing which Wesley included and takes in nothing which Wesley fenced out. "Sin," he says, "must connote only transgression of a moral law by a moral agent."[2] He says again, "Sins are volitions, and only volitions can be sins."[3] "Unconscious sin" he contends "is a contradiction in terms."[4]

It will not be inferred from this that Dr. Tennant takes Wesley's view of sin in its entirety. That is remotely far from the truth. It is part of his argument that there is no such thing as original sin, and John Wesley never wavered in his belief in original sin. Wesley says, "Sin is entailed upon me, not by immediate generation, but by my first parent. 'In Adam all died; by the disobedience of one, all men were made sinners'; all men, without exception, who were in his loins when he ate the forbidden fruit."[5]

It is in their definition of present actual sin that these two theologians—with most of two centuries between them—come into unexpected harmony, making a clear distinction between sin and sinfulness, and retaining this otherwise blurred word for the transgression of moral law by a moral agent. Wesley nowhere uses the term "unconscious sin" but, when discussing perfection, his definition requires him to reject it as heartily as did Dr. Tennant.

And this brings us to a question of major importance. Is there such a thing as "unconscious sin"? Can there be? Are Wesley and Tennant right here that unconsciousness cancels out the sin, or are we to say with Dr. Flew, "Our worst sins are often those of which we are unconscious. The stress on the consciousness and deliberate intention of the agent is the most formidable defect in Wesley's doctrine of the ideal."[6] And with Dr. Orchard, "Sin without sense of sin is still sin, and, indeed, deeper sin just because we are unconscious of it."[7]

---

[1] Tennant, *The Concept of Sin*, 60 ff.   [2] *ibid.*, 98.
[3] *ibid.*, 205.   [4] *ibid.*, 101.
[5] *Plain Account*, 59.   [6] Flew, 333.
[7] Orchard, *Modern Theories of Sin*, 3. This definition is given as "the ideal point of view."

Now, it will be clear to any reflective thinker that the term "unconscious" is often loosely used, particularly in connection with this subject.[1] Sometimes it is used of sins which really are unconscious, but quite as frequently of sins which are subconscious, and which, in part at least, are plainly objects of moral judgment. The word "unconscious," if we are to have clear distinctions at all, cannot fittingly be used of sins which trouble the conscience even a little, and which a disturbed mind is afraid to examine with care because of a dim awareness that the matter will not bear examination.

The loose use of the terms "conscious" and "unconscious" in regard to sin may be illustrated from Dr. R. E. D. Clark, who says that the distinction corresponds "roughly" to the distinction made by F. W. Newman between "provoked" and "unprovoked" sins. His whole examination of the subject proceeds on this "rough" identification. But it is *too* rough by far. "Provoked sins are those which are committed after a struggle, or in a moment of passion, while unprovoked sins are those which are done thoughtlessly and without temptation."[2] He illustrates the difference by contrasting a child who strikes his nurse in a fit of temper and one who strikes the nurse in no temper at all. Illustrations taken from childhood are always complicated by questions concerning the degree of moral immaturity in the child, but if this is to pass as an illustration of "unconscious sin" most people will think that it is ill-described.

In a subject hard to discuss because of blurred terms, some sharpness of definition must be insisted upon even at the risk of appearing pedantic. And there is nothing pedantic or, at the present point of discussion, nothing foolishly tautologous, in saying that unconscious *is* unconscious. Men, at a certain stage of moral development, do things with a conscience void of offence towards God and man which they come afterwards to regard as wrong, but which could not have been called, in the strict sense, a sin when they did it, because they did not know it was sin, and had no means of discovering its true nature.

In the second decade of this century, a strange figure appeared on the Ivory Coast of West Africa who came to be known as Prophet Harris. A member of the Grebo section of the Kroo tribe, this half-literate man, with a very imperfect knowledge of

[1] The word "unwitting" is a little less liable to misunderstanding.
[2] Clark, *Conscious and Unconscious Sin*, 3.

Christianity but a great passion for the conversion of his fellow-Africans, passed through the French Ivory Coast and into British Apollonia, gathering immense numbers of converts wherever he went. Fifty thousand is the smallest estimate. It may have been double that number. Without the aid of a single white missionary, this astonishing man passed through the bush with a wooden cross, a Bible, a bowl of water and a calabash, and changed the entire character of a vast area. When, years afterwards, pioneer missionaries entered the region it was to discover a great uninstructed host of poor people calling themselves Christians but waiting to be taught the Lord's Prayer and a simple creed.[1]

Not unnaturally, immense interest was aroused in this astonishing man who had then disappeared, but when he was finally traced he proved as zealous as ever for his faith and still preaching in his own neighbourhood. It was found also that he was a polygamist.

Harris, it seems, had no sense of guilt in being a polygamist. It had been the custom of his tribe from time immemorial. Such imperfect knowledge as he had of the Bible had left him in no doubt that the peerless patriarchs of the Hebrews were polygamists too. It appears to have been a stunning revelation to him to learn that he was living in sin, and there is the highest authority for saying that what is truly unconscious is overlooked by God.[2] Is such an act to be called "sin" in circumstances like these? Is the character of the word to be determined by the awful purity of God, outsoaring the mounting thought of His ripest saint, or is it to be determined by the honest awareness of the simple believer himself, patiently receiving the best instruction for his conscience that he can get, and gladly respecting its admonitions?

Wesley had made up his mind about that. He would have said, with Dr. Tennant, "Unconscious sin is a contradiction in terms." He would have said also, "Sin may be defined as moral imperfection for which an agent is, in God's sight, accountable."[3]

It is hard to resist the inference that if the terms "conscious" and "unconscious" had been strictly used much that has proved controversial would have been seen to present no acute problem of theory at all. Voluntary transgression of a known moral law would have been clearly seen as sin, and there would have been far less readiness to place the same awful term on a deed which a man could not possibly know to be evil. Meanwhile, the real

---

[1] F. D. Walker, *The Story of the Ivory Coast*, 11–18, 81 *f.*
[2] Acts xvii. 30.   [3] Tennant, *The Concept of Sin*, 245.

problem was being ignored. Between deliberate, actual sin, and the unconscious failing of a Prophet Harris, there is a whole area calling for ethical and psychological enquiry.

Jeremiah said that "the heart is deceitful above all things" and "desperately sick," and there is no man with a modicum of ability at introspection but has marvelled at the artful stratagems and rationalisations of his own mind. He sees that sin ensnares him in subtle ways. He notices how selfishness can masquerade on the stage of his *own* mind as generosity, or sacrifice, or service. He observes that an evil thought which, on its first appearance in the mind, brings a shock of surprise and a sense of shame, can become so frequent a caller that it insinuates itself into the very citadel of the heart, gets fingered and entertained, suggests more pros than cons and, having awakened and warmed desire, nourishes a fatal sophistry which moves at the last so rapidly that the hour comes when the same thought, which once brought a sense of awful shame, glides into the mind not only easily but wearing a white robe and a halo. So sin succeeds. At the last stage, its sinful character has almost become "unconscious," but it can never be classified as "unconscious" in the sense in which we are using the term here. Conscience has been half-willingly perverted and the man has become an accomplice in his own deceit.

Introspection—even the simplest—reveals other contortions of the thought too. There is often a subconscious shunning by the mind of a certain topic because of a lurking awareness that all is not well at that point and a man is unwilling to face the ordeal of ethical or spiritual examination. "Compensation" is often paid by a divided heart to an unquiet conscience, and people will fling themselves zealously into some social service, or give without stint to some charitable cause, to escape the inward accusation of gross failure in some other area of their life. *Roués* are among the most generous subscribers to "rescue homes."

When one adds to these deceits the curious play upon words with which a craving mind will excuse itself to an honest conscience, and the eager espousal some men make of determinism (not because they are constrained by the evidence but because they are pulled over by clamorous desire and want to convince themselves that their shabby conduct was inevitable), it is clear that the students of sin had not really focussed their problem while they held to the ill-defined terms "conscious" and "unconscious" and neglected the wide area which lay between.

Plain sin and plain innocence—in so far as they are ever plain—present no theoretical problem. But the broad borderlands bristle with problems. How shall we estimate the degree of guilty neglect?—or assess responsibility for that half-induced blindness?—or measure the pull of inherited disposition and early environment?—or (allowing due weight for ignorance) decide how much a man is accountable for his ignorance when knowledge was at hand? Or, if we abandon the whole possibility of judgment on these matters (as Tennant does)[1] because they are clearly beyond our mortal capacity, is it not possible to say something helpful to a pilgrim who essays the path to perfection by which he may understand the twistings of his own mind and the disguises of his own desires, and be less prone to self-deceit?

Wesley and Fletcher both attempted so much in counsel to their followers, who claimed to have attained: Wesley in certain "Advices" which he published as a separate tract in the year 1762 under the title *Cautions and Directions Given to The Greatest Professors in the Methodist Societies*, and Fletcher in section xx of his *Last Check to Antinomianism*. He calls it *An Address to Perfect Christians*. Both contain some pertinent admonition, and Fletcher's is quite searching. But neither gets far beneath the surface nor anticipates the findings of modern psychology. That they do not go in search of the "unconscious motive" is not surprising, but they are barely suspicious that it is there.[2]

So Wesley's definition of sin remains—limited perhaps—but chiselled, sharp, and quite unblurred. It is, in the nature of the case, one of the most determinative influences on his finished view of perfection. Sin is not necessarily an *act*. He was too close a student of the New Testament to miss the inwardness of sin but, in Wesley's view, it always included volition: there was a willing identification of the self with the idea. He attempted no definition of sinfulness. He defined *a sin*. "Racial," "corporate," or "unconscious" sin would all have been to Wesley a misuse of the word. Sin, he held, was "a voluntary transgression of a known law."

[1] Tennant, *The Concept of Sin*, 82.
[2] But cf. Fletcher's *Address to Such as Enquire, What Must We Do to be Saved?* (edit. 1835), 13.

CHAPTER X

HIS IDEA OF PERFECTION

IT is now possible for us to attempt the task which has beckoned us from the moment we set out on this path. What exactly was Wesley's idea of perfection? How did he conceive the Christian ideal for this present life?

(i) In the sixty years that he was thinking and writing on this subject, he defined it variously but most often in terms of love. He says it is—

"loving God with all our heart and serving Him with all our strength. Nor did I ever say or mean any *more* by perfection than *thus* loving and serving God."[1]

He says again:

"Entire Sanctification, or Christian Perfection, is neither more nor less than pure love—love expelling sin and governing both the heart and life of a child of God."[2]

Yet again he says:

"I advise you frequently to read and meditate upon the thirteenth chapter of the First Epistle to the Corinthians. There is the true picture of Christian perfection! Let us copy after it with all our might."[3]

When his followers became confused on the point, it was to love that he called them back. To Lawrence Coughlan he writes:

"You never learned, either from my conversation or preaching or writings, that 'holiness consisted in a flow of joy.' I constantly told you quite the contrary: I told you it was love; the love of God and our neighbour; the image of God stamped on the heart; the life of God in the soul of man; the mind that was in Christ, enabling us to walk as Christ also walked."[4]

Consequently, his favourite term for this debated doctrine was Perfect Love, and it is hard to resist the inference that if

---

[1] *Letters*, iii, 168.　　　　[2] *ibid.*, v, 223.
[3] *ibid.*, vii, 120.　　　　[4] *ibid.*, v, 101.

Wesley had kept consistently to this name he would have avoided
at least some of the ire that his teaching aroused. Unhappily for
him (as the quotations given above make clear), he used other
terms also to describe it. He called it Holiness, Entire Sanctification, and Christian Perfection. Despite his confessed preference
for the term Perfect Love, he entitled his book upon the subject
A Plain Account of Christian Perfection, and around the word
"Perfection" he had to fight many a wordy contest. It provoked
the astonishment and anger of his opponents, and it was sometimes pitifully prostituted by his followers. Sore beset at one time
by the vast misrepresentation of what he taught, he wrote to his
brother Charles, "I am at my wits' end,"[1] and exactly a month
later he wrote to him again:

> "Shall we go on in asserting perfection against all the world?
> Or shall we quietly let it drop? We really must do one or the
> other; and, I apprehend, the sooner the better."[2]

But this was only a mood—even though it lasted a month.
The great little man took a firmer grip of his pen and battled on.
It is, perhaps, all the more surprising that he encumbered
himself with so difficult a term as "Perfection" when he was
frankly not fond of it. He wrote to Dr. William Dodd:

> "I have no particular fondness for the term. It seldom occurs
> either in my preaching or writings. It is my opponents who
> thrust it upon me continually, and ask me what I mean by it."[3]

But that was not the real reason. He used it more frequently
than he realised. The real reason is here: the term was *scriptural*
and Wesley was passionately attached to the language of Scripture. When the wife of General Maitland, who owed much to
Wesley both personally and through her mother, wrote to him on
this subject, she said:

> "Would it not be safer to call it a high state of grace than
> perfection?"

Wesley replies:

> "As to the word, it is scriptural; therefore neither you nor
> I can in conscience object against it, unless we would send the
> Holy Ghost to school and teach Him to speak who made the
> tongue."[4]

[1] *Letters*, v. 88.   [2] *ibid.*, v, 93.   [3] *ibid.*, iii, 167.   [4] *ibid.* iv, 212; cf. iii, 168.

Then he went on to explain again that he had never contended for "absolute and infallible perfection" and only for that degree of freedom from sin which his definition of sin required.

So the difficulty remained. The doctrine bore a name which challenged notice and provoked opposition wherever it was heard. Wesley must have grown weary of defining his term to every new batch of opponents bent upon caricaturing it, and every new band of followers foolish enough to cheapen it. The one called him a devil[1] and the others called themselves angels.[2] Finally, he was jockeyed into the odd position, not only of stratifying perfection, but of pleading that perfection be "not set too high." As we have seen, he wrote in these terms to Charles. To Dr. William Dodd he said, "If I set the mark too high, I drive men into needless fears."[3] He warns Peggy Dale that if she places perfection too high "none will ever attain,"[4] and he tells Miss J. C. March that the same mistake is "the ready way to drive it out of the world."[5]

In his *Plain Account* he is just as explicit. Perfection is not to be put higher than the Bible puts it,[6] which would almost seem, from some expressions in Wesley, not to be a dizzy height. At least, the *Cautions* published in 1762, and particularly intended for those who had reached (in his use of the words) "perfection's height," warn against pride, enthusiasm,[7] antinomianism, sins of omission, schism, and carelessness in such outward things as dress. The very warnings themselves, the necessity for them and the character of them, all bear out the impression that perfection has not been set "too high." The perfect, it seems, are distressingly familiar with the same elementary temptations as those who make no such claim.

Yet it must be borne in mind all the time, and placed first in any analysis of Wesley's idea of perfection, that the stress fell upon love. The first thing about perfection was positive: it was loving God with all our heart and serving Him with all our strength. It was not love as a mere emotion but love as an attitude, almost as a state of mind and certainly as a set will: it was robust, objective, and sometimes stern. To equate this love with mere

---

[1] Bishop Lavington, *The Enthusiasm of Methodists and Papists Compared.* Introduction, xxvi. Toplady's *Works*, i, 194.

[2] *Letters*, iv, 192.   [3] *ibid.*, iii, 168.   [4] *ibid.*, v, 9.

[5] *ibid.*, vi, 88.   [6] *Plain Account*, 54, 61.

[7] In the eighteenth century meaning of "fanaticism." For the meaning of this word two centuries ago cf. Lee, 37, 234.

feeling does Wesley far less than justice. He repeatedly insists that it is not this. To Thomas Olivers he says:

"Barely to feel no sin, or to feel constant peace, joy, and love, will not prove the point."[1]

To Mrs. Bennis he writes:

"A will steadily and uniformly devoted to God is essential to a state of sanctification, but not an uniformity of joy or peace or happy communion with God."[2]

In sympathising with Mrs. Barton in the loss of her child, he adds this:

"Rapturous joy, such as is frequently given in the beginning of justification or of entire sanctification, is a great blessing; but it seldom continues long before it subsides into calm, peaceful love."[3]

Always he came back to that: the essence of perfection was love.

(ii) But this love had certain immense negative consequences. In the sense in which he had defined sin, this love expelled sin from the heart and life of those who received it. They did not commit sin. Sometimes, he says, they *cannot* commit sin,[4] but, in the great majority of instances in which he uses this expression, he is, of course, not denying their capacity but only stressing the steadiness of a will "uniformly devoted to God."

As we have seen, Dr. Warfield is right in insisting that "only *recognised* sins are sins" to Wesley,[5] but it is still an immense assertion to affirm that, whenever a man is *aware* of the press of temptation upon him, his will always turns to the good. So Wesley taught, and, as he told the Countess of Huntingdon, a thousand witnesses leapt up to confirm his word.[6]

Yet it is not surprising that his mind oscillated concerning the term "sinless perfection." In the sense in which he had defined "sin" and "perfection" he meant it, and sometimes he did not hesitate to say so.[7] But on other occasions—weary, I imagine, of defining, and re-defining, difficult terms which had fairly sharp edges in his own mind but a somewhat different connotation in the minds of other people—he repudiated the term, while,[8] in his *Plain Account*, he frankly sat on the fence. He says:

[1] *Letters*, iii, 212.   [2] *ibid.*, vi, 68.   [3] *ibid.*, vi, 269.
[4] *ibid.*, iii, 213.   [5] Warfield, ii, 591.   [6] *Letters*, v, 259.
[7] *ibid*, ii, 226.   [8] *ibid.*, ii, 280.

"It is not worth disputing about. . . . I do not contend for the term *sinless*, though I do not object against it."[1]

Once, indeed, he both repudiates the term and reaffirms it in the same letter,[2] but that is because he permits himself for a moment to define perfection in the manner of his opponents. At times, undoubtedly, he was confused by the clamour about him, and to hold a man to the strict test of exact and consistent definition in a voluminous correspondence spread over sixty years is a test unfairly severe. The marvel is that, in the matter of consistency, he passes it so well. Certainly, anyone who collected all his references on the point in sermons, journals, letters and pamphlets would have to say that on Wesley's definitions of "sin" and "perfection" he was fully committed to the phrase "sinless perfection." He did not over-use it because it was so liable to misinterpretation, but if the terms be chiselled to mean what he meant by them, the phrase stands. A Christian is, for Wesley, so far perfect as not to commit sin.[3]

Nor can we leave this aspect of the matter without raising the problem of Wesley's attitude to the question, still hotly contested among modern schools of holiness teaching, as to whether, in the life of those who enjoy this high experience, sin is eradicated or suppressed. That the question is still theoretically alive can be shown by many of the little books on this topic with which the path of the student of perfection is bestrewn. Agreeing among themselves that "the Christian is so far perfect as not to commit sin," their writers differ as to whether the sin is rooted out or held down.

The Rev. Prebendary Webb-Peploe, speaking at the Keswick Convention in 1895, said:

"When I read such words as dear John Wesley's, 'The evil root, the carnal mind, is destroyed in me; sin subsists no longer,' I can only marvel that any human being, with the teaching of the Holy Ghost upon the Word of God, can thus deceive himself, or attempt to deceive others. It is, I think, a miracle of blindness that we can study God's word, and imagine that any man can be free from sin experimentally while here in the mortal body."[4]

---

[1] *Plain Account*, 88, 136.　　[2] *Letters*, iv, 213.
[3] *Plain Account*, 19, 22.　　[4] Reader Harris, *Is Sin a Necessity?*, 11.

F

On the other hand, in Samuel Chadwick's *The Call to Christian Perfection*, published posthumously in 1936, "eradication" of sin is stoutly held to be possible and "subjugation" described as something less than the Christian may legitimately expect. [1]

The controversy is not new. It runs back—as so much else on this subject runs back—to Wesley, though the words of the battle cry were not in his day "eradication" *versus* "suppression," but "extinction" *versus* "suspension." The substance of the dispute was the same.

And, though he had but little taste for the controversy, Wesley belonged to the "extinction" school. He does, indeed, say in writing to Mrs. Maitland, "Whether sin is *suspended* or *extinguished*, I will not dispute." [2] But, when driven to it, he *did* dispute, and came down definitely for extinction. To those who feel that this was an astonishing conclusion, and entirely out of harmony with the Bible, it ought to be said that it was Wesley's attachment to an actual word here and there in the Scripture which led him to it. To Joseph Benson he writes:

> "Are not the love of God and our neighbour good tempers? And, so far as these reign in the soul, are not the opposite tempers, worldly-mindedness, malice, cruelty, revengefulness, destroyed? . . . I use the word 'destroyed' because St. Paul does; 'suspended' I cannot find in my Bible." [3]

The reference would appear to be to Rom. vi. 6 and to the word καταργηθῇ. On the whole καταργέω in the New Testament (with two exceptions, Luke xiii. 7, Heb. ii. 14, used only by Paul) means to render ineffectual and almost to abolish. Wesley does no obvious violence to the original word in pressing for "destroyed." But the use of ἵνα with the subjunctive clause does not allow us to read it as a statement that the goal has been reached but rather that the goal is in clear view. Strangely enough, Rom. vi. 6 is a text which Wesley nowhere quotes in his *Plain Account*.

(iii) Now, as we have seen from the hymns, the infusion of love into the soul of the believer and the consequent expulsion of sin, is a gift of God in answer to faith, and happens in a moment. To those unacquainted with Wesley's teaching, it may seem to savour more of magic than religion, and Wesley might

---

[1] Chadwick, *The Call to Christian Perfection*, 46.
[2] *Letters*, iv, 213.   [3] *ibid.*, v, 203 f.

not have resented the word. He never ceased himself to regard it as a miracle of grace. It was not the fruit of effort nor begotten by toil. It was a work of God mightily performed in a moment in a truly believing heart.

It is customary with those who give this kind of holiness teaching to-day to connect it with the Holy Ghost. It is often called a "Second Blessing" to distinguish it from justification, and is frequently described as being "filled with the Spirit." The loose and inaccurate translation in the Authorised Version of Acts xix. 2 is taken to prove that there is a necessary interval between the disciple's first coming to Christ and his reception of the Holy Ghost,[1] and Christians are urged to "press on to Pentecost."

Now, Wesley uses the phrase "Second Blessing" more than once, but he has some hesitation in making it a specific work of the Holy Ghost, lest—so it would seem—the impression was given that the Holy Ghost had not been already active at an earlier stage. That the phrase "Second Blessing" is his, it is not hard to show. To Jane Salkeld he says:

"Exhort all the little ones that believe to make haste and not delay the time of receiving the second blessing."[2]

To Ann Bolton he writes:

"Certainly till persons experience something of the second awakening, till they are feelingly convinced of inbred sin so as earnestly to groan for deliverance from it, we need not speak to them of *present* sanctification."[3]

Testing Hetty Roe as to whether or not she has received this gift, he asks:

"Do you feel your own *will* quite given up to God, so that you have no repugnance to His will in anything? Do you find no stirrings of pride? no remains of vanity? no desire of praise or fear of dispraise? Do you enjoy an uninterrupted sense of the loving presence of God? "

Then he adds:

"What a difference between the *first* love and the *pure* love!"[4]

[1] Brice, *Pentecost*, 12 f. [2] *Letters*, v, 333.
[3] *ibid.*, vi, 144 f. [4] *ibid.*, vi, 217.

Yet this Second Blessing is not, in Wesley's thought, well described as "receiving the Holy Ghost." To Joseph Benson he writes:

"With all zeal and diligence confirm the brethren, (1) in holding fast that whereto they have attained—namely, the remission of all their sins by faith in a bleeding Lord; (2) in expecting a second change, whereby they shall be saved from all sin and perfected in love.

If they like to call this 'receiving the Holy Ghost,' they may: only the phrase in that sense is not scriptural and not quite proper; for they all 'received the Holy Ghost' when they were justified. God then 'sent forth the Spirit of His Son into their hearts, crying, Abba, Father.' "[1]

But Wesley held that when the Second Blessing came, it came in a moment. Sometimes using the analogy of birth (when he wanted to stress the new life in Christ) and sometimes using the analogy of death (when he wanted to stress the destruction of our carnal nature), Wesley insisted that there was a growth before and a growth after but both birth and death in this high life of the spirit are—as with the flesh—the great matter of a moment. It could be dated and, indeed, marked upon a clock. It could be *now*! To Miss Ritchie (who was with Wesley when he died and whose account of his death is so often quoted) he writes, on January 19th, 1782:

"Entire salvation from inbred sin can hardly ever be insisted upon, either in preaching or prayer, without a particular blessing. Honest Isaac Brown firmly believes this doctrine, that we are to be saved from all sin in this life. But I wish, when opportunity serves, you would encourage him (1) to preach Christian perfection, constantly, strongly, and explicitly; (2) explicitly to assert and prove that it may be received *now*; and (3) (which indeed is implied therein) that it is to be received by simple faith."[2]

To Arthur Keene he writes:

"A gradual work of grace constantly precedes the instantaneous work both of justification and sanctification. But the work itself (of sanctification as well as justification) is un-

[1] *Letters*, v, 215.　　　　[2] *ibid.*, vii, 102 f. My italics.

doubtedly instantaneous. As after a gradual conviction of the guilt and power of sin you was justified in a moment, so after a gradually increasing conviction of inbred sin you will be sanctified in a moment. And who knows how soon? Why not *now*?"[1]

To George Gibbon (another of his preachers) he writes:

"It is our duty strongly and explicitly to exhort the believers to go on to perfection, and encourage them to expect perfect love by simple faith, and consequently to expect it *now*."[2]

To Sarah Rutter, who carried responsibility in the Society at St. Neots (Hunts.), he says:

"Gradual sanctification may increase from the time you are justified; but full deliverance from sin, I believe, is always instantaneous—at least, I never yet knew an exception."[3]

He will not allow that this great change can possibly be the fruit of efforts or "works." He says—writing to Hester Roe—of those who oppose his teaching:

"All who thus object are really seeking sanctification by works. If it be by works, then certainly these will need time in order to the doing of these works. But if it is by faith, it is plain a moment is as a thousand years."[4]

Yet, though this great change is the work of a moment, it is not in Wesley's clearest thought, the work of one moment for ever. He rejected the Calvinist doctrine of the Perseverance of the Saints. Christian Perfection could be lost—and received again. To "Sister" Bennis he writes:

"Some years since, I was inclined to think that one who had once enjoyed and lost the pure love of God must never look to enjoy it again till they were just stepping into eternity. But experience has taught us better things. We have now numerous instances of those who had cast away that unspeakable blessing and now enjoy it in a larger measure than ever."[5]

It is, in fact, a moment-by-moment life. That is why Wesley

[1] *Letters*, vii, 222. My italics.   [2] *ibid.*, vii, 267; cf. *Plain Account*, 49.
[3] *ibid.*, viii, 190.   [4] *ibid.*, vii, 98.
[5] *ibid.*, v, 138.

came to dislike talking of a *state* of sanctification[1] because that hinted at a permanent achievement secured by the faith of one moment. The faith of the moment received the perfect love of the moment and that moment's deliverance from sin. It was *now*, and then *now*, and again *now*, and these *"nows"* become, as the disciple grows "in grace and faith, a . . . continuous chain."[2] That is why Wesley is concerned to impress upon his followers the need to expect the gift of love *every* moment.

He urges Samuel Bardsley to stress this in his preaching and *"every* moment to expect full salvation."[3] He writes to John Mason to the same effect. He must "press all the believers to go on to perfection and to expect deliverance from sin *every* moment."[4] It would be hard to exaggerate the importance of this if Wesley's teaching is to be understood. His doctrine is caricatured if it is suggested that the height of faith in one moment secured perfection for a lifetime. The person enjoying this high experience lived without strain, but "moment by moment," and "moment by moment" the love was received.

(iv) This blessing, moreover, carried its own awareness with it. The believer was almost always conscious that some great thing had been wrought in his soul. Indeed, Wesley usually enquired for this very thing as when he asked Elizabeth Baker:

"Have you ever received a clear, direct witness that you was saved from inbred sin? At what time? In what manner?"[5]

He had laid it down in a letter to Thomas Olivers:

"One fruit given at the same instant (at least usually) is a direct, positive testimony of the Spirit that the work is done, that they cannot fall away, that they cannot sin."[6]

Ar.d to Miss J. C. March he says:

"There cannot be a lasting, steady enjoyment of pure love without the direct testimony of the Spirit concerning it."[7]

It would be less than fair to Wesley to suggest that this was nothing more than a *feeling*, and a feeling that people would be

---

[1] *Letters*, v, 265.
[2] *Sermons*, ii, 460 (footnote).
[3] *Letters*, v, 290.
[4] *ibid.*, vi, 66, cf. Rogers, 46. (My italics.)
[5] *ibid.*, viii, 181.
[6] *ibid.*, iii, 213.
[7] *ibid.*, vi, 88.

prone to have in the degree of their pride and insensitivity of conscience. There were ethical tests also by which a man might judge whether or not this great gift had been granted to him. If sin had been mortified in him and the assurance of renewal had been given, Wesley believed it was impossible for a man to be self-deceived. He put it like this:

"If a man be deeply and fully convinced, after justification, of inbred sin; if he then experience a gradual mortification of sin, and afterwards an entire renewal in the image of God; if to this change, immensely greater than that wrought before he was justified, be added a clear, direct witness of the renewal; I judge it is as impossible this man should be deceived therein, as that God should lie. And if one whom I know to be a man of veracity testify these things to me, I ought not, without some sufficient reason, to reject his testimony."[1]

Wesley's credulity has often been discussed. His brother Charles once said: "My brother was, I think, born for the benefit of knaves." John knew of this opinion of Charles, and more than once answered it. To Samuel Furly he says:

"When my brother has told me ten times, 'You are credulous,' I have asked, 'Show me the instances.' He could not do it. No, nor any man else. Indeed, jealousy and suspiciousness I defy and abhor, as I do hell-fire. But I believe nothing, great or small, without such kind of proof as the nature of the thing allows."[2]

Credulous in the common sense Wesley was not. To say that he believed in ghosts[3] and witchcraft[4] hardly bears on the present subject. There is not much evidence that he was *easily* imposed upon by mendicants, though his generous heart always leaned towards putting the best construction on the tales they told. The test questions he applied to those of his followers who claimed the gift of perfect love are such as would be shaped by a man not unaware of the devious twistings of the human heart, and they were pressed home with the sharpness and plainness that marked all his commerce with his fellow-men.

[1] *Works*, xi, 402.
[2] *Letters*, viii, 272; cf. Hampson's *Life of Wesley*, ii, 138.
[3] *Journal*, v, 265–275; *Letters*, vii, 139.   [4] *Letters*, vii, 300.

His weakness—if weakness it was—lay here. It was a shadow cast by his own great virtue. He loved truth. He had been taught to respect truth and reason from his childhood. His father once said, "I think Jackie would not attend to the most pressing necessities of nature unless he could give a reason for it." Logic was never a mere discipline to him: it was a delight. And the rigorous tests he brought to his personal self-examinations he always supposed had been applied by others when they looked into their own heart and life.

In the absence, therefore, of any plain, ethical contradiction in a man or woman's life, he believed them when they claimed the gift of perfect love and passed his simple but searching catechism. If they felt in harmony with God's will in everything, were quite unconscious of pride, were living independently of the praise and blame of men, and enjoying an uninterrupted sense of the presence of God . . . who was he to deny that God had done the miracle the New Testament had said that He could do? It would have seemed egregious vanity to Wesley to persuade himself that he brought a sterner introspective test to himself than his followers brought to themselves. He accepted their testimony and gave the glory to God. When Fletcher of Madeley humbly announced his possession of the blessing, Wesley did not join him in making the same claim, but he looked on adoringly at all that God could do with sinful human nature and, as the first biographer of that saintly man, he would have heartily concurred in the judgment of a later and closer student of the same holy life who said of Fletcher, "He was more than Christian, he was Christlike."[1]

But the claimants of perfection were not all Fletchers and, as Wesley himself admitted, some who professed it "made the very name of Perfection stink in the nostrils."[2]

(v) It has been made abundantly clear that this life of love, with its moment-by-moment deliverance from conscious sin, was, in Wesley's view, attainable in this life, and yet there are senses in which it seems to have been conceived *apart* from this life.

The point is important and needs elaboration.

The ideal was not individualistic. Fellowship was the very web of life in the Methodist Societies and it was in Class and

[1] Abbey and Overton, *The English Church in the Eighteenth Century*, 113.
[2] *Letters*, v, 38.

Band Meeting that the members incited one another to reach out for the gift of perfect love. Any candidate for admission to a "Band Society" was asked, among other questions, "Do you desire to be told your faults? Do you desire to be told all your faults, and that plain and home?" And the point of this rigorous questioning was just here. Such questions, it was hoped, would reveal "the depth of inbred sin," and inspire the soul not fully sanctified to press on to perfection.

The ideal was for this life: it was not individualistic . . . and yet, strangely enough, it was not of this world. In some ways the aspiring souls forsook the life around them. They took to heart— as evangelical religion has often taken to heart—the Johannine injunction "Love not the world" and retreated into a mental monastery. In a sense they refused the world. "This earth," they cried, "is not our place." Wesley's overt purpose in becoming *homo unius libri*, as we have seen, was to "find the way to heaven." The world of living, planning, working men was always half-limited in its interest to the first Methodists by the condition of their souls. The beauty of nature made no great appeal. That is one of the few reasons which make Hervey's turgid *Meditations Among the Tombs* still a volume of slight interest. He is almost distinctive among the evangelical writers of the period in that he noticed this lovely world. Wesley's *Journal* rolls on its nobly monotonous way with barely a reference to the beauty that must have greeted his eye a thousand times when, reading on horseback, as he did so often, he looked up from the printed page.

Some historians have said that the leaders of the Evangelical Revival of the eighteenth century had no interest in the *bodies* of men—but it is not hard to rebut this criticism. They had the deepest interest in men's bodies. They fostered a hundred philanthropies—orphanages, hospitals, dispensaries, homes for the aged poor, loan societies and many kindred works of mercy. They fought slavery, smuggling, intemperance, the evil conditions in our prisons, and every form of vice which they recognised as such. It is true that it was mostly social salvage work— even with the great Lord Shaftesbury, who gladly traced his inspiration to John Wesley.[1] But to complain that these men were not communally constructive, and had no great Christian sociology, is to lose all time-sense and accuse them for not being born a century or two later than they were.

The truth we are reaching for is deeper than this. The early

[1] Bready, *Lord Shaftesbury and Social-Industrial Progress*, 389.

Evangelicals had not seen God's purpose in this world *as* this world. They looked upon it as a school, or place of pilgrimage, or (more explicitly than Keats meant) "the vale of Soul-making"[1] which had no other meaning or interest than its influence on their eternal destiny. They could not have sung with any inwardness the hymn of a later generation:

> Thine is the loom, the forge, the mart,
> The wealth of land and sea,
> The worlds of science and of art,
> Revealed and ruled by Thee.

All through the study of Christian Perfection, as they conceived it, this divorce appears. Work and worship do not belong together. The early hymn-books, so rich in other ways, do not contain a single identifying hymn of man's toil and man's prayer,[2] though God could be served in daily toil and idleness was a grave sin. One segment of life was jealously guarded as "sacred" and the rest ran the risk of being half-despised as secular. Even when a man was necessarily occupied with the things of this life, they were not expected to hold attention by themselves but the reverent eye would "spiritualise" them, and discover hidden moral meanings.

Charles Simeon called on Fletcher of Madeley one day towards the end of 1784. Simeon was twenty-five years of age, a Fellow of King's College, Cambridge, and already giving promise of his subsequent career. He had been drawn by the reputation of Fletcher's sanctity.

During his brief visit, he went with Fletcher for a walk and they slipped into the iron-works. Simeon was much impressed with the ability of Fletcher to turn everything to "spiritual profit." To a man hammering on an anvil he remarked, "O, pray to God, that He may hammer that hard heart of yours!" To another, heating a bar of iron, he said, "Ah! thus it is that God tries His children in the furnace of affliction." To a third, in the act of drawing a furnace, he whispered, "See, Thomas, if *you* can make such a furnace as that, think what a furnace God can make for ungodly souls!"[3]

---

[1] *The Letters of John Keats*, 326 (Forman Edn.).

[2] Two apparent exceptions will occur to the close reader: "Servant of all, to toil for man" (313) and "Forth in Thy name, O Lord, I go" (315), but even these fine hymns are not real exceptions. God can be found in work, and work can be a sacrifice to Him, but the work, *as work*, was of no concern to the Almighty. But cf. Rattenbury, *The Evangelical Doctrines of Charles Wesley's Hymns*, 275 *ff*.

[3] *Christian Miscellany*, 1848, 326.

Iron, as iron, did not matter. The world's work was only building sand castles: the tide of time would smooth it out. The health of the soul was not simply the *first* thing: it was the *only* thing. And to attain ebullience of soul-health one had to pursue holiness and live in a world within the world.

They sang with lustiness:

> Not in the tombs we pine to dwell,
> Not in the dark monastic cell,
> By vows and grates confin'd.[1]

And yet, because aspiring souls have always found it easier to escape the world than to subdue the world, it was into a mental monastic cell that the feet of these Protestant pilgrims finally came, by vows, if not by grates, confined. Against pleasures they were particularly on guard. They eschewed games,[2] dancing,[3] the theatre,[4] novels,[5] art,[6] smart clothes,[7] spirits, snuff and tobacco,[8] and all conversation not spiritually "profitable."[9] Nor is it hard, in some ways, to understand why. Most of these "pleasures" were as closely knit with sin as horse-racing is now. Wesley himself was never completely incarcerated, inasmuch as he went to a concert occasionally in the eventide of his life, and displayed the deepest interest in such varied things as medicine and mathematics, logic and electricity. He actually left a Shakespeare annotated in his own hand. But an effort was made to cover these "delinquencies." One of his successors at the Chapel in City Road, John Pawson, burned the Shakespeare as a thing "which tended not to edification."

We may now summarise our conclusions on Wesley's idea of perfection. It is indwelling love, banishing all conscious sin, received by faith in an instant, and maintained from moment to moment by humble dependence on God. It is aware of itself, attainable in this life, and yet ascetically detached from the normal life of men.

In what sense was this teaching original with John Wesley? If

---

[1] Hymn 512, v. 4 (1780 Edn.).   [2] *Works*, viii, 251.
[3] *Letters*, vii, 227 *f.* But cf. vi, 47; Rogers 17.
[4] *Works*, vii, 34; viii, 354.
[5] There was some excuse; cf. Andrew Lang, "The Evolution of Literary Decency" (*Blackwood's Magazine*, March 1900, 368). But cf. also *Letters*, vii, 228.
[6] *Journal*, v, 69, 444.   [7] Rogers, 23.
[8] *Letters*, v, 133.   [9] Rogers, 212.

it was original in expression, did he take it direct from the New Testament, or is it another illustration of his undeniable eclecticism? Are those scholars right who believe, with Dr. G. C. Cell, that this doctrine is no "provincialism of the Wesleyan Reformation" but "an original and unique synthesis of the Protestant ethic of grace with the Catholic ethic of holiness"?[1]

Commenting on this opinion, Dr. Umphrey Lee, who differs from Dr. Cell on many points of Wesley interpretation, says, "This is a wise and just observation."[2]

To decide whether or not this is "a wise and just observation" and if, indeed, we have here another of Wesley's syntheses of Protestant and Catholic doctrine is our next immediate task.

[1] Cell, 347.   [2] Lee, 190.

CHAPTER XI

IS THE DOCTRINE A SYNTHESIS?

FOR some years students of Wesley have disputed about the degree of importance that should be attached to his experience of a warmed heart on May 24th, 1738. Traditional Methodist teaching has placed the greatest stress upon it. For two centuries it has been described by his own followers as the hour of his conversion and, in their estimation, by far the most important day in his spiritual pilgrimage. Loyal to the Empire as British Methodists unquestionably are, the national celebrations now associated with May 24th have no power to oust from their memory and affections the older and greater event with which this day is piously connected.

Yet its primacy in Wesley's unfolding career has been seriously challenged of recent years, and challenged both within and without the family of "people called Methodists." Some of the confusion has resulted from varied definitions of the word "conversion" and doubts are even expressed as to whether the word means anything at all. All are agreed that Wesley made no *volte-face* on that day from a life of blatant sin to one of impressive goodness. Whatever happened, it was an event in the life of a man disciplined in virtue and constantly on the stretch for the highest. But was it an hour supremely important, and without which Wesley's great work would never have been done?—or was it incidental both in his life, and in his own subsequent thought, and magnified into a legend only by the theological bias of those who came after him?

A thorough examination of this question would be a deviation from our main purpose in this monograph, but it is of some help in our chief task to notice how his conversion is linked with his great concern for Christian Perfection. Dr. Piette, distorting the "official Wesleyan legend," suggests that Wesley's early denominational biographers had pictured him prior to 1738 as a great sinner. But for this stricture on those first biographers, as Dr. Rattenbury has shown, there is only the very slightest warrant.[1] Even if, as in the judgment of a Roman Catholic theologian like

---

[1] Rattenbury, *The Conversion of the Wesleys*, 106. Whitehead remarked in Wesley's funeral sermon, "His character was moral from early youth" (1791 Edn.), 5.

Dr. Piette, they grossly exaggerated the importance of that visit to Aldersgate Street, it was not because they were so ill-informed about their founder as to forget that he was disciplined in virtue "from his youth up." Dr. Piette believes that Wesley's true conversion should be dated in 1725, when, as a young man at Oxford, he resolved to give his whole life to God. May 24th, 1738, he would dismiss as a mere flush of feeling.[1]

Mr. Dimond would explain this much debated experience rather as a mystical than an evangelical conversion because "the distinctive mark of this class is the transition from an ordinary religious life to various stages of religious experience which can be described as mystical."[2]

Dr. Umphrey Lee is still more emphatic that the importance of May 24th has been exaggerated. He stresses the sparse references to the experience through all the subsequent volumes of Wesley's *Journal*, and stresses also certain corrections Wesley made in what he had already set down concerning it. He notices too his lowness of spirit and inward uncertainty as revealed in the *Journal* on days subsequent to May 24th, 1738 (e.g. October 14th, 1738—January 4th, 1739), and still more in his letter to Charles on June 27th, 1766; finally, he emphasises Wesley's failure to make any reference to the day on such important occasions as the opening of City Road Chapel, when he was reviewing the growth of Methodism, and in his *Short History of the People Called Methodists* written in 1781. "There can be no doubt," he concludes, "that Wesley changed his mind about the Aldersgate experience."[3]

On the other hand, Dr. Bett sustains the traditional view of Wesley's conversion, strongly urging that Lecky's description of it as "an epoch in English history" is fully substantiated by the facts,[4] and this same interpretation is made with force, and great fullness of quotation from Wesley's own writings, by Dr. G. C. Cell. He shows that Wesley's immense effectiveness as a preacher, his "offensiveness" to the formal and official religion of the day, and even his double system of chronology (*Anno Domini* and *anno meae conversionis*) all point to the paramount importance of May 24th, 1738, and of Wesley's own awareness of its importance.[5]

---

[1] Piette, 305–9.   [2] Dimond, *The Psychology of the Methodist Revival*, 88–103, 180.
[3] Lee, 89 *f.*, 100, 102.
[4] Bett, *The Spirit of Methodism*, 33 *ff.*
[5] Cell, 57, 162, 171, 177, 183, 185 *f.*, etc., cf. Rattenbury, *The Conversion of the Wesleys*, 31–8.

But whatever Wesley gained on that memorable day, it has never been argued—and it *could* not be argued—that he then received his first impetus to Christian Perfection. That he gained something at that time of immense importance in his quest after holiness, it is the aim of this chapter to make clear, but it was not the first incitement to its pursuit. As we have already noticed, he begins his *Plain Account* by explaining how this concern was first imparted to him:

> "In the year 1725, being in the twenty-third year of my age, I met with Bishop Taylor's *Rules and Exercises of Holy Living and Dying*. In reading several parts of this book, I was exceedingly affected: that part in particular which relates to purity of intention. Instantly I resolved to dedicate all my life to God. . . .
>
> • "In the year 1726 I met with Kempis's *Christian Pattern*. The nature and extent of inward religion, the religion of the heart, now appeared to me in a stronger light than ever it had done before. . . .
>
> "A year or two after, Mr. Law's *Christian Perfection* and *Serious Call* were put into my hands. These convinced me more than ever of the absolute impossibility of being half a Christian. And I determined, through His grace (the absolute necessity of which I was deeply sensible of) to be all devoted to God—to give Him all my soul, my body and my substance."[1]

Clearly, therefore, his longings after holiness and his resolute aim to attain it antedate his evangelical conversion by at least thirteen years.

The books that most influenced Wesley on this subject belong to his Catholic inheritance. Taylor was at one time Chaplain to Laud. The *Imitation* came out of a monk's cell. Law was a Non-juror.

Nor are we left in any doubt as to the means the youthful Wesley will employ to attain his end. The way is the way of iron discipline and rigid self-denial. He will buffet the body. He will hold the flesh under. He will be merciless with every vagrant feeling and every idle thought. Under the influence of Taylor, he labels idleness a gross sin, and, while still a youth, he parts company with leisure for ever. He starts from his bed at four every morning and gives his first hour to prayer: from all the

---

[1] *Plain Account*, 5 f.

hours which follow through the day he takes a further five minutes from each that he may have continued conversation with God. Yet all these five minutes are but "extras" in the rigid scheme of his devotions.

And what he practises he makes the substance of his preaching. In the sermon he preached before the University of Oxford on January 1st, 1733, he says:

"Vain hope! that a child of Adam should ever expect to see the Kingdom of Christ and of God without striving, without *agonizing*, first 'to enter in at the strait gate'; that one who was 'conceived and born in sin' and whose 'inward parts are very wickedness,' should once entertain a thought of being 'purified as his Lord is pure,' unless he tread in His steps and 'take up his cross daily,' unless he 'cut off his right-hand' and 'pluck out the right eye, and cast it from him'; that he should ever dream of shaking off his old opinions, passions, tempers, of being 'sanctified throughout in spirit, soul, and body' without a constant and continued course of general self-denial!"[1]

He lived on the barest pittance taken from his Fellowship money and gave the rest gladly and stealthily to charity.

When he sailed for America in 1735 as a minister to the colonists and a missionary to the Indians, he declined even such simple variety in food as ocean travel then made possible and, on a self-imposed regimen of rice, biscuits and water, this passionate pilgrim of perfection crossed the wild Atlantic and began his life on the edge of beyond.[2] Unaware of it himself, he was repeating the experiences and travails and failures of his three great predecessors in the Evangelical Succession. Paul had out-Phariseed the Pharisees. Augustine, back in Tagaste, had still need to talk of "the groans of my heart, and the floods of mine eyes."[3] Luther, as a monk, wearied his confessors with his constant attendance, practised every form of scourging and maceration that he knew and then invented new ones, yet still cried, "My sin: my sin: my sin!" Wesley was bent upon holiness and, as yet, he knew no way thither but the way of sacrifice, self-denial and asceticism.

And he failed! He failed in his work and in his interior life! He came back from America with a cry in his heart: "I went to

[1] *Sermons*, i, 277 *f*.   [2] *Journal*, i, 111.   [3] *Confessions*, Book x, par. 60.

America, to convert the Indians; but oh, who shall convert me?"[1]

Years after, he concluded that even then he had the faith of a servant though not of a son, but, whether his judgment at the time is more to be respected, or the judgment of his *Journal* annotations which belong to his later years, this, at least, is not in dispute: the trustees of the colony could hardly look upon him as an effective minister and his own conscience sharply condemned him when he lifted his eyes to the serene peak of holiness which, nearly thirteen years before, he had essayed to climb. Years afterwards, commenting on this effort to win holiness by works, he said, "I was (fundamentally) a Papist and knew it not."[2]

Then came May 24th, 1738, and all the heart-searchings and Scripture study and earnest conversations which led up to it. It is impossible to think that a trained theologian like Wesley was unacquainted with the doctrine of Justification by Faith before Peter Böhler explained it to him.[3] But it can have been little more than a lump of academic lumber in a mind which contested its plain inferences so stubbornly. But when slowly, and half unwillingly, his mind was first convinced, and then his heart so wondrously warmed, and the personal assurance given to him which led him to cry, "I felt I did trust in Christ, Christ alone for salvation; and an assurance was given me that He had taken away *my* sins, even *mine*, and saved *me* from the law of sin and death . . ."[4] then the primacy of *faith* really burst upon him and the great revival of religion was born. Nothing, so it seems to the writer, can really rob this day of its immense significance in the life of John Wesley. It is the manner of men new-born in God (or, if the phrasing is preferred, of men who, being already in God, are lifted to some new level of life in Him) to speak of their experience in ways which seem to others extravagant—and even sometimes to themselves in the cooler atmosphere of later years. But let us submit the question to a plain pragmatic test. This will be far more fruitful than arguments as old and sterile as the vain discussion of whether the spark or the barrel of gunpowder had more to do with the explosion. A plain, pragmatic test is not inappropriate to one who applied the same test so often himself, and who has been recognised as, in some senses, the forerunner of Schleiermacher in theology and William James

---

[1] *Journal*, i, 418. [2] *ibid.*, ii, 262. [3] cf. Lee, 150. [4] *Journal*, i. 476.

G

in philosophy.[1] Is it in serious dispute that before this day John
Wesley was a man marvellously equipped but pitifully ineffective,
and that after this day he was an apostle? Let his *feelings* be left
aside for the moment, for he put only the slightest stress upon
them himself: neither the warmed heart of May 24th, 1738, nor
the doubts of June 27th, 1766, need confuse this question. *What
of the work?* What of the influence, religious and humanitarian, of
the formerly frustrated man before whom the mountains now
became as a plain? On those who depreciate the importance of
Wesley's visit to Aldersgate Street must rest the onus of explaining what, on their thesis, is surely inexplicable. To say that the
man had been found of God would seem to them to beg the
question, but not even they will deny that he had found himself.
The Revival had begun.

What was the effect of May 24th on Wesley's old and dominant
interest in Christian Perfection? It seems that at first he expected
not only to be justified in an instant by faith but, perhaps, to be
entirely sanctified as well. But in this—if, indeed, he really expected it—he was disappointed. It became part of his teaching,
as we have seen, that the Christian experience of salvation was in
two stages: the first consisting of justification and partial sanctification, and the second of *entire* sanctification. If, in his first
rapture, he had hoped for both together, experience quickly
changed his view.

Here is the big change of May 24th so far as it concerns his
quest for perfection: that while before he had toiled for it by
works, he was now convinced that it could only be attained by
faith. What Luther, through the Moravians, had taught him of
justification, he extended, in his own teaching, to sanctification
as well.[2] Believe and be saved!—and to be saved meant to be
sanctified as well as justified. God can do more with sin than
forgive it: He can destroy it. He can do more with righteousness
than impute it: He can impart it. He will not simply save us *in
sinning* but *from sinning*. The effort to make oneself holy is useless.
Wesley is convinced of that now. By faith God will work a
perfect cure.

Wesley owed an immense debt to Luther and Calvin. A careful
reading of his writings will prove his constant awareness of it.
Yet he was never an uncritical follower of either of them. He

---

[1] Piette, 478 f., cf. Cell, 49 f.   [2] *Sermons*, ii, 452 f.

believed that their interpretation of the gospel—Luther's particularly—did not deal seriously enough with the moral problem. The Calvinist doctrine of the Perseverance of the Saints as a contribution to the quest for holiness seemed to Wesley to be plainly contradicted by the facts of experience. The Catholic strain in him, which he owed most to his reverence for the Ante-Nicene Fathers, together with his passionate longing for holiness, led him to challenge some of the consequences of Luther's immense stress on faith only. It is not hard, therefore, to show in passage after passage from his works only a tempered appreciation of his great predecessor in the Evangelical Succession, and he included none of the works of Luther or Calvin in his *Christian Library*.[1]

He wrote in August, 1744:

"I love Calvin a little, Luther more; the Moravians, Mr. Law, and Mr. Whitefield far more than either. . . . But I love truth more than all."[2]

It was truth he really wanted. If, at times, he seems a mere eclectic, picking up something he fancied here and something he fancied there, and bundling incompatibles together, that impression evaporates on closer study. The precious things he took are not tossed together: they are truly synthesised. Indeed, they belonged together by the will of God and, what God hath joined together . . . Valuable things were lost at the Reformation. Wesley saw it with clear eyes. Himself, after the flesh, the product of generations of Church and Dissent, and, even after May 24th, 1738, deeply indebted in his own mind and soul to both, he had a breadth of view and balance of judgment not common in his century. The variety of those who opposed him at different times proves the point. He seemed "unsound" both to Anglicans and Calvinists. The humanistic Arminianism current in the Anglican Church at the period disapproved of his evangelism and his burning concern to get people converted. The Calvinists, on the other hand, were so troubled by his insistence on conduct that it seemed plain to them that he had reverted to the idea of salvation by works. Not a few of them plainly called him a "Papist."

Nor can it be denied that some of Wesley's expressions, when

---

[1] He included a short biography of each of them.
[2] *Letters*, ii, 25.

he was dealing with one aspect only of the matter, gave ground for misunderstanding.

But take his teaching as a whole: seek the heart of it: set aside a turn of expression here and there (which is clearly inviting a complementary truth even though Wesley has not paused to state it), and the doctrine he beat out is clear. Perhaps it becomes clearest of all in words like these. He writes:

> "Who has wrote more ably on Justification by Faith alone, than Martin Luther, and who was more ignorant of the doctrine of Sanctification or more confused in his conception of it? On the other hand, how many writers of the Roman Church (as Francis Sales and Juan de Castaniza in particular) have wrote strongly and scripturally on Sanctification, who, nevertheless, were entirely unacquainted with the doctrine of justification."[1]

To any modern defender of Luther in his wholeness, eager to contest Wesley's statement that Luther was ignorant of the doctrine of Sanctification, it may be enough, perhaps, to point out that so sympathetic an interpreter as Harnack has substantially admitted this defect in the great German reformer.[2]

Those who remember that it was Luther's Preface to Paul's Epistle to the Romans which led to Wesley's conversion, will find it more than a little surprising to discover Wesley's strictures on Luther's *Commentary on Galatians*:

> "I was utterly ashamed. How have I esteemed this book, only because I heard it so commended by others; or, at best, because I had read some excellent sentences occasionally quoted from it! But what shall I say, now I judge for myself, now I see with my own eyes? . . . How blasphemously does he speak of good works and of the law of God—constantly coupling the law with sin, death, hell, or the devil; and teaching that Christ delivers us from them all alike. Whereas it can no more be proved by Scripture that Christ delivers us from the law of God than that He delivers us from holiness or from heaven. Here (I apprehend) is the real spring of the grand error of the Moravians. They follow Luther, for better, for worse. Hence their 'No works; no law; no commandments.' "[3]

[1] *Works*, vii, 195.
[2] A. Harnack, *History of Dogma*, vii, 267 [E.T.]. But cf. Th. Harnack, *Luther's Theologie*, ii, pp. 460 f. [1886 Edn.] where the other side is set out. Dr. R. S. Franks kindly drew my attention to this second reference.   [3] *Journal*, ii, 467.

He openly warned his congregations against the *Commentary*.[1]

And the explanation of his recurrent criticisms is not chiefly that Luther was "deeply tinctured with mysticism" (though that was a ground in itself for severe condemnation from Wesley) but because "in the fury of his Solifidianism"[2] he disparaged works, "magnified faith to such an amazing size that it quite hid all the rest of the commandments,"[3] and had no obvious or deep concern with the master passion of Wesley's life—the longing for holiness.

There are times when Wesley himself seems almost to display a fury in his *anti*-solifidianism, and the explanation of this is almost certainly his horror of antinomianism. He had not forgotten what Zinzendorf said to him in Gray's Inn:

"We spit out all self-denial; we tread it underfoot. As believers, we do everything that we wish and nothing beyond. We laugh at all mortification. No purification precedes perfect love."[4]

If antinomianism is little more than a name now, it was a dreadful reality in the eighteenth century and a snare—the facts are indisputable—to which those who stressed *faith only* were peculiarly prone. Combining the doctrine of Stillness with an immense stress on faith, certain teachers all but wrecked the Methodist societies in the first months of their life in urging people to seek faith by neglecting all the means of grace (public worship, the sacraments, prayer, Bible study, etc.) and utterly confusing the uninstructed minds of those who listened to them.[5] Impossible as it may seem to us now, many there were who claimed to be in a living relationship with God and were yet committing the most gross and disgusting sins.

John Nelson, one of Wesley's early helpers, had many a clash with those who exulted in what they called their "happy-sinnership." Nelson says:

"I met with one of them, the other day, so drunk that he could not keep the cart-road. I asked him what he thought of himself now, if death were to seize him in that wretched condition. He said, that 'he was not afraid to die, for he was as his Saviour would have him to be; and if He would have him to be holy, He would make him so; but he was a poor sinner, and he hoped to be so to eternity.' He said, 'You and John

---

[1] *Journal*, ii, 468.　　[2] *ibid.*, ii, 174.　　[3] *ibid.*, i, 419.
[4] *ibid.*, ii, 490.　　[5] *ibid.*, ii, 328 *ff*.

Wesley are enemies of the Lamb; for you want people to be holy here. But the Lamb shall have the honour of saving me: I will not offer to save myself, like you Pharisees.' "[1]

Thomas Mitchell, another helper, met such men too. He says:

"They could hardly bear the word 'holiness.' Nothing was pleasing to them, but 'faith, faith'; without a word either of its inward or outward fruits."[2]

John Haime, declining to filch from the dead on the field of Fontenoy by explaining, "I have got Christ. I will have no plunder," is left to mourn the death in action of three of his fellow-labourers, but mourns much more two others who fell into antinomianism. He says:

"One of these Antinomian preachers professed to be always happy but was frequently drunk twice a day. . . . The two Antinomians set up for themselves, until lying, drunkenness, and many other sins, destroyed both preachers and people."[3]

Wesley was prepared to call predestination (which he strongly opposed) an "opinion," but antinomianism he was sure was of the very devil himself.

Because he saw—or thought he saw—the origin of this in Luther's burning but partial vision, he was never wholesouled in his admiration of the man who passed on to him the torch of evangelical truth. And because he saw—or thought he saw—a central concern for holiness even in the errors of Pelagius, Wesley was ready to say a defensive word for a heretic.[4]

This, then, is the claim we make for Wesley's doctrine of Christian Perfection: that it brought back to Protestantism something it had lost, a dominating concern for holiness and the restoration of moral aspiration to its central place in the life of the believer.

And this also: that it delivered the aspiring soul from the insupportable burden of seeking to achieve holiness by personal toil and opened the door to achievement by God's gift of perfect love through faith in Christ.

Dr. Cell, as we have seen, has called Wesley's doctrine "an original and unique synthesis of the Protestant ethic of grace with

[1] *Lives of E.M.P.* (1871 Edn.), i, 140.   [2] *ibid.*, i, 254.
[3] *ibid.*, i, 290.   [4] *Letters*, iv, 158.

the Catholic ethic of holiness," and we feel, with Dr. Umphrey Lee, that that is "a wise and just observation."

The weakness of the synthesis is here: when Wesley insisted that the grace of God which justified us by faith would entirely sanctify us by faith also, he seems not to have allowed enough for the difference between a changed relation with God and a completely changed life. Put bluntly, one is an assertion about God and the other is an assertion about ourselves. When the defenders of this teaching in its oldest form say, "If you have faith in God for your justification, why can't you have faith in God also for your sanctification?" they overlook the difference too. It is not enough to say, in further defence of the point, "But we give *God* the glory for what He has wrought in our souls: we are not parading ourselves or lapsing into spiritual pride"— the challenge has still *not* been met. One is an assertion about God and the other—in its effects—is an assertion about ourselves. To say, "I know I am forgiven" gives all the glory to God. To say, "I know I am holy" may carry with it a similar desire for God's glory but it intrudes the self and invites psychological and ethical proof of the uttermost kind. Entire sanctification is an ethical claim which cannot be surpassed on this earth and it must submit to ethical tests. Those tests will not, of course, be resented, and this difference will not rob the synthesis of all value, but clearly the discussion moves on from theology to moral philosophy and psychology, and to that transition we have now come.

(C) Psychological

CHAPTER XII

WESLEY'S CONCERN WITH PHILOSOPHY AND PSYCHOLOGY

As Dr. Flew brings to a close his masterly historical study of the Christian ideal for the present life, *The Idea of Perfection in Christian Theology*, he asks, "Is salvation possible for the sub-conscious?" And he adds this, "That is the real question for the seeker after holiness in our time."

We can be certain that no satisfying examination of the doctrine can now be conducted which ignores psychology. Its very character calls for this enquiry. If its solid basis is in biblical study, and its strong superstructure in theology, no sense of completeness can be reached without reference to the younger and more tentative science. The search for sanctity, with its maze of dubious motives, and, still more, the claim to have attained it, demand the closest psychological scrutiny.

It is not without interest to enquire, first, what the state of psychological knowledge was in the eighteenth century, and what familiarity Wesley displayed with it. The questions are not hard to answer.

Wesley was a prodigious reader, and had fairly catholic tastes, but he is content for the most part, both in his *Journal* and *Letters*, to mention the titles and authors of the books he reads and confine his comments to a phrase. None of the great philosophers of the age seems to have affected him deeply,[1] and he was more interested in their ethics and metaphysics than in what might be called their psychology. Of Leibnitz he entertained the poorest opinion, and is confident that the German thinker was completely worsted in his controversy with Dr. Samuel Clarke. "So poor a writer have I seldom read, either as to sentiments or temper."[2] Elsewhere, he warns one of his correspondents against Leibnitz's works. They "would only unhinge and perplex your mind."[3]

---

[1] Natural philosophy interested him more. He published two volumes on it in 1763 and enlarged them to five in 1777. In an appendix of fifty pages to vol. v he sets out his attitude to mental philosophy.

[2] *Journal*, vi, 63.   [3] *Letters*, v, 199.

To Locke he gave a tempered and hesitating approval. On the whole, he thinks that "the late Bishop of Cork's[1] excellent *Treatise on Human Understanding*" is "in most points far clearer and more judicious than Mr. Locke's"; but later he published selected passages from Locke's great Essay in the *Arminian Magazine*,[2] and the *Works* include his critical comments on it.[3] Many of his comments are caustic and based largely on Locke's dislike of logic, and his ill-concealed contempt for Aristotle and the Schoolmen. Wesley concludes that Locke's strictures derive in every case from ignorance. He argues—justifiably, as most scholars would now agree— that Locke had too slight an acquaintance with logic, Aristotle or the Schoolmen to put them in the pillory.[4] The second half of the Essay, Wesley thought, was "by no means equal to the first."

Nevertheless, he speaks of him elsewhere as "a good writer" and commends the book as being of "admirable use to young students, if read with a judicious tutor" and "calculated to improve young persons from twelve to twenty"(!)[5]

For Hume, as might be expected, he has nothing but denunciation. He is the author of that "insolent book against miracles,"[6] "the most insolent despiser of truth and virtue that ever appeared in the world . . . an avowed enemy to God and man, and to all that is sacred and valuable upon earth."[7]

Butler's *Analogy* he read twice at an interval of more than twenty years[8] and he heartily approved it both times, though noting, on each occasion, that it is a deep book—far too deep, as he thinks, for those for whom it was intended.

Only on Berkeley does he comment in his *Letters* at any length, and this in a letter written to his mother from Oxford some four months before he was elected a Fellow of Lincoln. He is commenting on *Three Dialogues between Hylas and Philonous*, and making particular reference to the early part of the Second Dialogue. His letter displays a fair degree of logical acuteness (he became Lecturer in Logic the same year that he was elected to his Fellowship, 1726) but it cannot be said that he does justice to Berkeley's subjective idealism. Wesley resolves it all into tautology:

[1] Dr. Peter Browne (Bishop of Cork, 1710–1735). See *Journal*, iv, 192.
[2] Vols. v, vi, vii.   [3] *Works*, xiii, 416–25.
[4] Brett, *A History of Psychology*, ii, 258–264.
[5] *Works*, xiii, 424. *Letters*, vii, 227 *f.*
[6] *Journal*, v, 303.   [7] *ibid.*, v, 458.   [8] *ibid.*, iii, 232, v, 264.

"How miserably does he play with the words 'idea' and 'sensation'! Everything immediately perceived is a sensation. Why? Because a sensation is what is immediately perceived by the senses—that is, in plain English, everything immediately perceived is immediately perceived; a most admirable discovery, the glory of which I dare say no one will envy him."[1]

Not so easily was the Bishop of Cloyne to be rebutted, either by the charge of tautology from Wesley or the literal charging of a stone by Dr. Johnson. The subsequent history of philosophy has made that abundantly clear.

Riding from Aberdeen to Dundee in May, 1774, Wesley read what he called "Dr. Reid's ingenious essay." This was Thomas Reid, the founder of the "Scottish School" of philosophy. The essay Wesley read was almost certainly *An Inquiry into the Human Mind on the Principles of Common Sense*.[2] Wesley says:

"With the former part of it I was greatly delighted; but afterwards I was much disappointed. I doubt whether the sentiments are just; but I am sure his language is so obscure that to most readers it must be mere Arabic. But I have a greater objection than this—namely, his exquisite want of judgment in so admiring that prodigy of self-conceit, Rousseau —a shallow but supercilious infidel, two degrees below Voltaire! Is it possible that a man who admires him can admire the Bible?"[3]

Of Hutcheson he had no higher opinion. He read the *Essay on the Passions* in 1772 as he travelled to Luton.[4] He commends his literary style, but is so far from being convinced that the case is made out for a special moral sense that he thinks the acceptance of Hutcheson's point of view is tantamount to rejecting the Bible. He argues in two of his sermons[5] that the theory boils down to practical atheism, though he does not deny to Hutcheson his favourite word for all philosophers—"ingenious."[6]

Wollaston fares even worse with Wesley. His effort in *The Religion of Nature Delineated* to reduce virtue to truth carries him "further from the Bible than Mr. Hutcheson himself."[7]

[1] *Letters*, i, 25.
[2] It may have been *An Essay on Quantity*. See *Proceedings of the Wesley Historical Society*, iv, 207.
[3] *Journal*, vi, 22.   [4] *ibid.*, v, 492 f.   [5] Nos. xc and cv.
[6] *Works*, vii, 37, 188 f., 201, 270, 338, 342.   [7] *ibid.*, vii, 38, 200, 270.

"For Mr. Hutcheson's scheme sets aside only one of the two great commandments, namely, 'Thou shalt love the Lord thy God,' whereas Mr. Wollaston sets aside both: for his hypothesis does not place the essence of virtue in either the love of God or of our neighbour."

Of Mandeville's *The Fable of the Bees* he cannot trust himself to write with any calmness. Machiavelli, in the judgment of Wesley, is milk and water beside him, and he doubts if Voltaire would "have said so much."[1]

He notices Rousseau chiefly in connection with the theory of education set out in *Emile*, a brief answer to which he made in 1783.[2] Of Rousseau as a writer and a man he speaks with unrestrained scorn. "A more consummate coxcomb never saw the sun! How amazingly full of himself! Whatever he speaks he pronounces as an oracle. . . ."[3] *Emile* he characterises as "the most empty, silly, injudicious thing that ever a self-conceited infidel wrote."

I can trace no concern in Wesley's voluminous writings with the chief psychological interests of the century. He seems not to have studied with any closeness the "associational psychology" of Hartley, though he was interested in the theory of vibration, on which it was founded. But he approached it as an opponent of determinism, and he struck a blow at it because it seemed to give a philosophic basis for predestination.[4] The psychological side of Hartley's theory—which, as Joseph Priestley sought to prove, could stand without the physiological[5]—did not invite his ready pen.

Nor can I trace any reference to the "faculty psychology" which developed during the century both in Scotland and in Germany.[6] It is another proof that Wesley's interests were practical and not speculative. In a discussion on the doctrine of Particular Redemption he refers to "what Mr. Locke calls 'the association of ideas,' "[7] but he does not pursue the phrase even to the extent of another sentence. He labours to prove that "we break with no man for his opinion. We think and let think." His concern at the moment was with antinomian practices and not with psychological doctrine.

[1] *Journal*, iv, 157; cf. *Letters*, v, 373.   [2] *Works*, xiii, 434–7.
[3] *Journal*, v, 352.   [4] *Works*, x, 474–80.
[5] Brett, *A History of Psychology*, ii, 286.
[6] Murphy, *An Historical Introduction to Modern Psychology*, 29.
[7] *Journal*, iii, 179.

Indeed, it never was. His genius, as we said at the beginning of our study, was practical. It should not surprise us, therefore, to discover so little interest in academic psychology. The psychological aspects and implications of what he taught remain the subject of our close enquiry, but we can now be clear about our starting point. We have to ask what psychology was implicit in his teaching, and what light can this re-born science cast on these pilgrims of perfection. Was Wesley right in supposing that it is possible to live a "moment-by-moment" life? Had they posed the question all wrong when they asked if sin could be eradicated? Does the Holy Spirit influence the unconscious? What really had happened to these simple, honest men in that rapturous high moment in which they claimed to be cleansed from all sin?

These are some, at least, of the questions to which, in the light of modern psychology, we must address ourselves, and, failing an answer, our enquiry will seem a poor and incomplete thing.

Nor will the absence of psychological phraseology in Wesley's writings trouble us as such. No reflective thinker will say that keen-minded men were unaware of the problems to be solved until the new psychology fashioned its own technical terms. The problems were felt in New Testament times and in every age since. Even the "unconscious" leaps to mind in "another law working within my members," "evil is present within me," and "the old man." The theology with which these phrases are bound up is not our concern now but the very phrases point to an awareness of the problems on which modern psychology endeavours to throw a revealing light.

They were not less acutely felt in Wesley's time, and in the multiplying spiritual societies which looked to him for leadership. With the immeasurably deepened understanding of these problems which two centuries of thought have evolved, we can now turn to these questions one by one and hope to give a clearer answer than was possible when Locke, Hume and Hartley were still the most potent influences on psychological thought.

CHAPTER XIII

IS IT POSSIBLE TO LIVE
A "MOMENT-BY-MOMENT" LIFE?

WE have seen that it is of the very essence of Wesley's doctrine that the sanctified soul live a "moment-by-moment" life.[1] We have recognised that his teaching is deeply misunderstood if it is supposed that the faith of one high moment secures entire sanctification for a life-time, and we see, therefore, his dislike for the phrase "a *state* of entire sanctification." It must be a "moment-by-moment" life because the perfect faith of each moment is crowned with the perfect love of each moment, and life proceeds by a chain of glorious "nows."

But strong objection has been made to the whole concept of a "moment-by-moment" life. It has been argued that it is philosophically unsound: that life cannot be chopped up into fragments: that we do not receive it as a succession of discrete bits, and that Wesley builds, therefore, on a foundation psychologically impossible.

But Wesley neither thought nor taught that life is a succession of discrete bits. Elementary as his psychology seems after the passing of two centuries, he was well aware that life was no series of fading and unrelated states of consciousness. His insistence on a "moment-by-moment" life is burlesqued if it is said that he "chopped" life up into dissociated fragments. He knew that at any moment we are not only being but becoming, and that *whatever will be, is*.

Nor, as a keen thinker, could he have been quite unaware of the problem to which modern psychology has directed close attention—our sense of time. William James has expressed the opinion that the problem of time is "probably never even conceived of by those unaccustomed to philosophic meditation."[2] But, though the interests of Wesley were more practical than speculative, it is hard to suppose that when he urged his followers to a "moment-by-moment" life, he urged them to something plainly impossible.

[1] See p. 85 *f.*
[2] James, *Textbook of Psychology*, 280; cf. Bergson, *Creative Evolution*, 355 *ff.*

He did not approach the problem academically. If he had even tried to conceive a *present* moment of time, he would have discovered, as all students have discovered, the baffling impossibility of doing it. This present "has melted in our grasp, fled ere we could touch it, gone in the instant of becoming."[1] "Now" has ceased to be "now" and become "then," ere the sound has died upon our lips, and all examination of "present" experience is a post-mortem.

But this does not wipe "now" from our practical life. "Now" is real. Whether we accept the findings of Wundt and agree that twelve seconds is the longest bit of duration which we can apprehend at once, or leave "now" to the clear, if unmeasured, apprehension of the plain man, it is still real. It is, indeed, the most real of all my apprehension of time. It is true that feeling of passing time takes no cognisance of the clock. "A time filled with varied and interesting experiences seems short in passing, but long as we look back. On the other hand, a tract of time empty of experiences seems long in passing, but in retrospect short."[2] None the less, "now" is supremely important. "Now" I can think, or speak, or act—and now I can have faith. Now! And, holding that faith can be perfect in this moment, Wesley taught that God can, and does, make a perfect response.

Nor is it open to serious question that both for sin and for sanctity "now" is "the accepted time." When Dr. Tennant considers the world's subtle wiles in seducing an aspiring soul, he finds its greatest power here. It can say "now."[3]

Conversely, those who would make the ways of virtue winsome, and pick out the path to perfection for themselves and for other honest pilgrims, will find with Wesley that the time to stress is *now*, and the mode of life is "moment by moment."

Is it not so set out in the New Testament? Is not all anxious worry for to-morrow forbidden? Are we not urged to consider the birds who live from moment to moment (God feeding them); and the flowers which neither toil nor spin (God clothing them); and the grass, destined in a day for the oven, but not before God has looked upon it and seen that it was good?[4]

Is it not so set out in the lives of the saints? Baron von Hügel, in an address delivered at Beaconsfield in October, 1921, said:

---

[1] James, *Textbook of Psychology*, 280.   [2] *ibid.*, 283.
[3] Tennant, *The Concept of Sin*, 188; cf. F. W. Robertson, *Sermons* (Third Series), 18.
[4] Matt. vi, 25–34.

"St. Catherine of Genoa's method of life has also helped me much. She would quietly concentrate, each moment, upon that moment's special content—upon God's gift and will of special suffering or joy, of determination, effort, decision and the like, conveyed within that moment. . . . Indeed, a genial, quiet death to self lies in every minute, when the minute is thus taken separately as the dear will and the direct vehicle of God."[1]

Not less emphatically did some write of Juan de Avila. The Apostle of Andalusia was expert in this "moment-by-moment" living, and it is said that his perfect serenity

"was most striking, however multifarious his occupations, however uncongenial the persons with whom his duties brought him in contact, he was ever serene.

"He seemed always as though he had just issued forth from a long and fervent prayer, and his very look was enough to edify men."[2]

And, in our own century, new stress has fallen on this approach to the devotional life in a little book which defends and extols this "moment-by-moment" living. It is called *The Cult of the Passing Moment*.[3] Its author, Arthur Chandler, offers it as a tentative "theory of the spiritual life," and would seem to have come to it in large part by a study of the lives of the saints.

". . . it is the saints who have pre-eminently practised this cult; in fact, we might go further and say, with some plausibility, that it is just the cult of the moment which has made them Saints. Sanctity has consisted in their taking each moment as it comes, with its call to prayer or suffering or action, and obeying each single call whole-heartedly as a call from God."[4]

The author's aim—as Wesley's and ours—is to find the path to perfection, and he sets it down that "man's perfection consists

---

[1] von Hügel, *Essays and Addresses on the Philosophy of Religion* (Second Series), 227 f.

[2] He lived in closest contact with the "world" and never joined a religious order. See Peers, *Studies of the Spanish Mystics*, ii, 125, 127. Wesley admired de Avila and included some of his *Spiritual Letters* in his *Christian Library*, with which he sought to make his people familiar with the world's best religious books.

[3] By Arthur Chandler, sometime Bishop of Bloemfontein. My attention was drawn to this book, as to many others in the literature of sanctity, by Dr. Flew.

[4] *The Cult of the Passing Moment*, 16.

in the relation of correspondence or union in which he stands to the Sovereign Spirit."[1] Distinguishing his teaching from its apparent similarity to hedonism, which also puts stress on squeezing the most from the passing moment, and defending it against the objection that it would take all system and continuity from our lives, Chandler sees "each pulse of time . . . transfigured with eternal light"[2] and holds that this "cult" is "a supremely important channel by which to approach God, and thereby to express and develop the spiritual life."[3]

We may leave it there. We do not find the objections to Wesley's plea for a "moment-by-moment" life sustained. We think it proceeds from a misunderstanding of what he taught, and a pedantically academic approach to the matter.

Conversely, we find such a life commended in the New Testament, and find also that it is the open secret of the saints. Weightier testimony we do not desire.

[1] *The Cult of the Passing Moment*, 51.   [2] *ibid.*, 211.   [3] *ibid.*, 214.

CHAPTER XIV

CAN SIN BE ERADICATED?

WE have already noticed that the question of the extinction of personal sin was hotly discussed in Wesley's time, and still remains a matter of sharp dispute between exponents of holiness teaching.[1] Has psychology any pertinent comment to make upon the point? Is the question sensibly posed when we borrow the phrasing of holiness sects and enquire, "Can sin be eradicated?"

Dr. Sugden is surely right in his contention that Wesley "never quite shook off the fallacious notion that sin is a *thing* which has to be taken out of a man, like a cancer or a rotten tooth."[2] Full of practical concern for the improvement of men's character, but without much technical interest in psychology (even as it was understood in his day), it is dubious if he ever scrutinised his own mind on the matter or proposed to himself the question, "What are the psychological elements involved in the concept of sin?" If he had been asked where sin came from in men, he would probably have been content to answer, in the words of the New Testament, "Out of the heart of men. . . ." and leave the word "heart" as undefined as his Lord did. But that he continued to think of sin as a "*thing*" far the larger part of his writing on holiness bears witness.

"But sin is not a thing; it is a condition of balance amongst our motives."[3] To label certain operations of the unconscious as separate "instincts," and select a few of them (e.g. sex) as being, in some way, polluted, is unsound in ethics and is unsound in psychology too.

"The whole question of instinct is very much in the melting pot at present."[4] There is a growing body of opinion that the old classification of instincts has been arbitrary and stilted. No one can compare the various lists of instincts which are commonly given without feeling, at times, that the classification has been "forced" and the tabulation almost capricious. If there is general

---

[1] See p. 81.   [2] *Sermons*, ii, 459 (footnote).   [3] *ibid.*, ii, 459 (footnote).
[4] Waterhouse, *Psychology and Pastoral Work*, 13.

agreement in the naming of half a dozen instincts, there is no general agreement about as many more. Some "instincts" wait on the doorstep to be admitted to the classifications, and others, which seemed quite firmly established, are being pushed out. The word is so blurred that it can hardly be said to have scientific value. McDougall, who has himself illustrated the loose use of the word very fully,[1] offers, in the interests of clarity, a rather cumbrous definition of his own[2] but is found at the last somewhat dubiously making "appeal" into "a primary instinctive disposition" which "seems to be accompanied by a true primary emotion which, perhaps, is best called 'distress.'"[3]

There is nothing very hazardous in suggesting that the whole subject is calling for fresh thought, and that the fresh thought will begin with the conviction that the unconscious works in directions too various to be classified in the old scheduled way. If some kind of classification is compelled by the necessities of thought, it will take enough heed of the modification of instincts (even in the lower animals), and the fact that "instincts" are seldom found in a really *pure* state but are entangled and interwoven whenever we meet them, as to avoid excessive sharpness in the classification and plainly to allow that the yeasty life of man does not yield itself to exact tabulation.

This difficulty being recognised (though not, of course, resolved) it is of interest to notice how the word "instinct" has been employed in connection with the pursuit of holiness.

A popular writer like Dr. Stanley Jones talks of the "unconverted instincts";[4] of "instincts polluted by the streams of racial tendencies which have poured into them for ages"[5] and of the "poison of the old instincts."[6] Are the instincts polluted? Can they, in any accurate sense, be poisoned? Is it devout—or even sensible—to pray that the grace of God will deliver us from the instinct of flight, repulsion, curiosity, pugnacity, self-abasement, self-assertion, sex, gregariousness . . . or any other innate psychophysical disposition which has been classified as an instinct? All these may be motives to sin, and that they may not be overpowering motives might well be the substance of an earnest prayer, but no-one would argue that these instincts could be "eradicated" from human nature and leave the personality unimpaired. To be human is to have life on these terms, and in these forms. Other

---

[1] McDougall, *An Introduction to Social Psychology*, 21 *f.*
[2] *ibid.*, 29. [3] *ibid.*, 443 *f.*
[4] Jones, *Victorious Living*, 87. [5] *ibid.*, 118. [6] *ibid.*, 142.

beings may have life without these instincts, but no straining of the connotation could call them "human."

Sin is in the erring will—not thought of just as the rational element in personality but the whole personality organised to seek what is conceived as "the good." Our examination of Wesley's idea of sin has shown us that, for him, sin lay essentially in volition. Had he known the epoch-making works of his younger contemporary, Immanuel Kant, he might have reversed the famous opening sentence of the *Metaphysic of Ethics* and said, "Nothing . . . can be called bad without qualification but a bad will." The instincts may provide, in their demandingness, many motives, and the strength of their pull may vary with different individuals, but sin enters only when the self is identified with a motive seen to be wrong. Again, it was one of the fine fruits of Wesley's conversion that, while he saw sin centred in the will, he saw also that there was no salvation by personal strain, or effort, or the whipping-up of the will. He saw also with clearness, what Dr. Niebuhr has seen again in recent years, "Men cannot, by taking thought, strengthen their will." . . . "Deeds of love are not the consequence of specific acts of will." . . . "What men are able to will depends not upon the strength of their willing, but upon the strength which enters their will. . . ."[1]

Wesley held that by a "moment-by-moment" life of faith with God, a new strength enters the will, a new sense of spiritual discrimination is given to the aspiring soul, and new power imparted to the pilgrims of perfection.

Consequently, we may now say with definiteness, that they posed the question all wrong when they enquired, "Can sin be eradicated?" It becomes clear why the sharp disputes between extinction or suspension, and eradication or suppression, were so sterile, and why the controversy could not, and cannot, be settled by quoting καταργηθῇ. Sin, not being a *thing*, cannot be "rooted-out," "extinguished" or "eradicated." Nor, for the same reason, can it be well described as "suspended" or "suppressed." If, in the light of our conclusions, these latter terms seem closer to the facts, they are still not good terms. The very character of the metaphor obscures the truth. A balance and choice of motive invites a simile less solid than any of these, and one which recognises not only that sin is not a "thing," but that men and women are not "things," and that, howsoever God, in

---

[1] Niebuhr, *An Interpretation of Christian Ethics*, 225, 228.

His mercy, deals with sin in us, He does not disregard our personalities.

Nor can we deny an extra confidence in this suggested solution of the old dispute in that it seems to be in harmony with Wesley's own best thought. His idea of sin may be limited and inadequate, but it is clear and sharp—as sharp as life, and our own uncertainty of motive, will allow. When he fell to disputing of sin's eradication, he was less clear in his own thinking than experience of his writings would lead us to expect, and half-disloyal to his own definition of sin. He should have refused the question in that form—or re-phrased it in such a fashion that it raised the really relevant question of how God respects our personalities and yet aids us in the selection of motive and the maintenance of a good will.

But it is plain that confusion of thought here was fruitful of other problems. These seekers after perfection were terribly troubled about their dreams. Naturally! Having convinced themselves that sin was *eradicated*, they woke up many a morning and blushed at their fragmentary recollections of the night. Finding sin, not in the will but in some cancerous growth of the spiritual life which they believed the Celestial Surgeon had already cut out, how could they quieten their tormented minds when they remembered at early devotions on what excursions their vagrant self had been in sleep? To say the least, the problem would have pressed less hardly on their sensitive souls if they were not tied to the words "eradicated" and "extinguished." If sin was eradicated and extinguished, where did those seductions come from in slumber which they had followed with such "willing" feet?

They had no modern psychological theory of dreams to help them. They could not discuss whether or not fear explained them, and they would have recoiled sharply from the suggestion that it was wish-fulfilment. They were just left, like poor Mrs. Hester Ann Rogers (one of their shining examples of sanctification), solemnly pondering the question put to her by a correspondent, "Does He make your very dreams devout?"[1] or like the saintly John Nelson who said:

"My soul was so harassed with my wicked dreams, that I often awaked and found my pillow wet with tears, after think-

[1] Rogers, 51.

ing that the enemy would reason with me about some sin I had committed in my dreams."[1]

Had they focussed the problem correctly they would have been spared those heart-searchings. However complete the illusion that in their dream-life it was really their willing and eager selves which had committed this misdemeanour with gusto and that misconduct with a light heart, they would have recognised that there was no true identification of the self with it: at the very moment of returning consciousness they would have repudiated it in their mind, and their conscience would have spoken clearly, "It was *not* sin."

[1] *Lives of E.M.P.*, i, 26.

CHAPTER XV

DOES THE HOLY SPIRIT INFLUENCE THE UNCONSCIOUS?

WE have already had need in our discussion of Wesley's idea of sin to use the word "unconscious," but it is necessary, before we can grapple with the question which now confronts us, to decide with more precision what we mean by the term.

Precision here is hard. Dr. Scott Frayn, pursuing the same exactness in definition, frankly confesses that we are "little farther on, at the moment, than to be in a position to know definitely that something indefinite is a factor in our thinking."[1] Yet the existence of the unconscious may now be said to be established beyond scholarly dispute, and only the question of the right way of thinking of it (and some general agreement as to its limits) hangs like a haze over this area of psychological thought.

Freud analyses the perceptual system into ego, super-ego and id, corresponding (roughly, perhaps) to the individual content and the social content of the otherwise unspecified unconscious, i.e. the id.[2] Most other thinkers have borrowed a spatial metaphor and, working downwards from above, have stratified the mind into conscious, sub-conscious and unconscious. Some, indeed, add a super-conscious[3] though any discussion of that would be a digression here.

It is probable that this latter thought-form will prove more serviceable to scholarship than Freud's phrasing, especially if its metaphorical character is remembered and the picture of sharply defined and unrelated levels of the mind is not permitted to obscure the unity of our mental life.

But this three-fold classification has not proved entirely adequate for the development of thought. There is growing agreement that the unconscious must be divided again into the primary unconscious and the secondary unconscious: the former being concerned with racial memory and a repository of primordial images, the latter being thought of as a "receptacle" and

---

[1] Frayn, *Revelation and the Unconscious*, 15.

[2] Freud, *Group Psychology and the Analysis of the Ego. The Ego and the Id.*

[3] Murray, *An Introduction to a Christian Psycho-Therapy*, 27, 47–55.

almost as a compound of individual repressions. The primary unconscious is sometimes called the "collective" or "absolute" unconscious.[1]

It is when the question of the relation of morality to the unconscious is raised—and that is our peculiar interest—that the sharp differences of the various schools of psychological thought become acute. To the Freudian School the unconscious, "which is the main factor in the psychic life of man, is a kind of devil's cauldron, exhaling evil vapours and pouring forth evil powers,"[2] and "the perfectibility of man, which is the hope of Christianity, is a chimera."[3] To such a view Jung replies, "It should, indeed, never be forgotten—and the Freudian School needs this reminder—that . . . morality is a function of the human soul, which is as old as humanity itself. Morality is not inculcated from without. Man has it primarily within himself. . . ."[4]

It is almost certain that the effort of some scholars, who work on the border-lands of psychology and theology, to posit and prove the existence of a super-consciousness derives from the too-ready acceptance of the Freudian idea of the unconscious as a morbid underworld. Convinced as they are that any cogent explanation of religious experience cannot live with a theory which makes the unconscious wholly evil, they are driven to suppose what is, in effect, another and non-Freudian unconscious, dignified by the term "super-conscious" because its contents are more respectable. Dr. Scott Frayn argues—cogently, as the writer thinks—that "to suppose an unconsciousness which is evil and a super-consciousness which is good is merely to label different moral results with correspondingly different departments of the mind, which is to beg one question, at least, if not two."[5]

The unconscious cannot sin. A discussion on original sin would be a digression in the quest we are pursuing, though we are aware at this point of the important side-road we are passing by. What many regard as the "taint" in human nature is not removed by being ignored. It is simply in the clear, if limited, sense in which we have already defined "unconscious" and "sin" that we affirm again—the unconscious cannot sin. Indeed, in

1 Jung, *Collected Papers on Analytical Psychology*, 410.
2 Hughes, *The New Psychology and Religious Experience*, 301.
3 *ibid.*, 304.
4 Jung, *Collected Papers on Analytical Psychology*, 379.
5 Frayn, *Revelation and the Unconscious*, 34.

this sense, the statement is tautologous. It amounts to saying that the non-volitional is not volitional. If we run back through time and dimly descry our truly primitive ancestors, before the emergence of self-consciousness and when his life was regulated only by reflexes, we may call that life "amoral" but never "immoral." The morality, as Jung has said, may be potentially "within himself" but only volition can make it explicit. Nor does it need to be stressed that volition emerges as a shy and limited thing. At this stage in development, man is still largely the creature of reflex: he does not acquire at once a wisely and widely legislating will, still less does he escape from his past into a world of whimsy and libertarianism. But within a narrow orbit he can choose—and because he can choose, he can sin.

Does the Holy Spirit influence the unconscious—or the subconscious? Hypnosis has made its own not unimportant contribution of proof to the fact that, in the deeper levels of the mind, moral considerations still have weight and the writer has himself observed patients in deep hypnosis reject suggestions which trespassed on their moral code. But in what way would the Holy Spirit influence these deeper levels of the mind and—harder question still—how could that influence still be personal?

Perhaps the directest approach to the answer would be to point out that faith in this influence already underlies a good deal of established Christian practice. This, of itself, will not prove the point but it will provide a starting place and show the things to which we are already committed by implication.

How could a conscious response be made to the appeal of God if the Holy Spirit had not already influenced the unconscious?

Are we to suppose that children profit by Divine contact only in the degree of their slow maturing, and to the extent that they understand the possibilities of fellowship between human beings and God? Is it plain that there is no grace given to an infant in baptism?

Could intercessory prayer, in all its range and passion, continue long without faith that the Holy Spirit does influence the unconscious? We may hazard the guess that more than half the intercessory prayer offered in the world is offered for people who have displayed no willingness to open themselves to the influence of God. Is the influence of God, then, quite powerless?

Are not sudden conversions preceded by a process in the subconscious and unconscious and can we suppose that in that process God had no share at all?

Now the answer which Christian orthodoxy would give to all, or most, of those questions, would certainly involve a faith in the power and willingness of the Holy Spirit to influence the unconscious but we can have no satisfaction with the answer, and we cannot call it spiritual and moral, until we enquire more deeply into the character of that influence. Spiritual forces might work upon a man as well as physical forces but—as Dr. Oman has argued—if that force were omnipotent it would rupture any personal relationship and rob the result, so far as the subject of its operation was concerned, of all moral worth.

"Being pure outside force, it might have so perfect an individual relation to us as to . . . straighten out all crookedness of disposition, yet have no more personal relation to us than a storm has to a ship which, without permitting a rag of sail to be shown or the rudder to be stirred, drove it like a log into harbour. The storm would still be the same kind of violence which dashes more hapless vessels on the rocks; and this form of grace would still be the same kind of force as lands the non-elect into perdition."[1]

Nor can it be denied that seekers after holiness have sometimes asked in their unreflecting eagerness for this very thing. Feeling the strength of sin in them, and knowing their own half-palsied wills, they have cried out, as we have noted in Scougal, for "some stroke of omnipotence,"[2] or have pleaded like Charles Wesley:

Confound, *o'erpower* me, by Thy grace. . . .
Take away the power of sinning. . . .

but if God granted such prayers He would rob His children of every scrap of moral worth. He could get a "perfect" world overnight but not with free-beings (only automata), not with persons (only puppets), not with men and women (merely marionettes).

Nor is the question without the most practical and day-to-day implications. Many men, converted from lives of wild debauchery, who were enchained in habits as evil as they are imprisoning, claim that some miracle of this character has been done in them. The writer has known men who were drunken sots commit their lives to God and get a swift release from a craving which had raged in them for years. One of them was fond of saying, "When

1 Oman, *Grace and Personality*, 72 (edit. 1925).
2 Scougal, *The Life of God in the Soul of Man*, 56; cf. also Rolle, *The Fire of Love*, 160.

God saved my soul He quenched my thirst," and a long subsequent life of even sobriety gave immense emphasis to his words.

It is only fair to say also that one has known others take a similar stand but not enjoy the same release and enter with their new faith a long, grim battle with temptation.

But why one and not the other? Is it a deep mystery hidden in the will of God? Are we to say that one attained a quality of faith and trust the other could not reach?

It may be so. To test the strength of any man's faith, even our own, borders on the impossible, but it is not hard to believe that "the expulsive power of a new affection" is mighty to move the most obdurate sins which stain our souls, and perhaps the most pertinent word to anyone who pants to be clean is still the word of Christ, "According to your faith be it done unto you."[1]

But we must insist that this is no impersonal operation, no mere stroke of omnipotence. To concede so much would be to make nonsense of all our moral thinking, to bring us face to face with a God whose will was not simply hard to understand but plainly capricious, and it would sponge the words "holiness" and "morality" from our vocabularies.

Whatever influence the Holy Spirit exercises on the subconscious and unconscious, no question becomes a question of religion or duty until it meets us in the conscious mind, and even the most sudden conversion does not leap like the genie of the lamp out of nothing, but has at its heart some dazzling conscious insight of the true relation of the soul and God.

It can come in a flash because it is insight and not laboured thinking, and being concerned with the deepest things of time and eternity it can be completely revolutionary in its effects. Nevertheless, neither the suddenness of the vision nor the completeness of the transformation makes it an impersonal operation of omnipotent force upon a passive subject. It is a relation of persons and has its tiny focus in human consciousness —even though the unequal tryst concerns Almighty God and the latest stained but penitent sinner.

One suspects that the metaphor we accepted as necessary for clear thinking about the different "levels" of the mind may trap us here, as it has trapped others. The "levels" are not separate strata but merge the one into the other, and the transition from conscious through pre-conscious (memory) to sub-conscious and unconscious no more permits a firm line of demarcation to be

[1] Matt. ix. 29.

drawn, than life allows us to say concerning any one day, "Before this I was a boy and after this a man."

Whatever lies in the sub-conscious capable of rising to consciousness and inciting the will to evil, can rise also to consciousness to be defeated by the willingly received grace of God. So—if a mechanical metaphor may not seem too absurd in this connection—one can imagine a rotary movement of the mind in which desires and impulses clamour to consciousness only to meet the cooling, cleansing Breath of God and sink away again to carry health and purity to whatever level of our mental life becomes their home.

In this sense, then, we are prepared to give a plain answer to the question which confronts us now. We believe that the Holy Spirit does influence the unconscious. It may be, as has been suggested,[1] that there is a clear promise in the fourth Gospel which does, at least, look in that direction. Was it not plainly said to the Apostles that the Holy Spirit would bring to their remembrance all that Christ had said to them,[2] and this supposes His aid in the pre-conscious if not in the sub-conscious as well. Nor is it hard to believe that those amazing moments of vision which come to us all and seem to synthesise the scattered fragments of our mental life, knitting our nature together and partaking of the character of revelation, owe their origin to the same Divine source.

No man can say to what depths of his being this holy influence may not extend but it only becomes a subject of full moral cognisance as it is willingly received into a mind which is aware and responsive. Response, it is true, can lie at times half-latent in intention and seem no more directly volitional than the flower which turns itself towards the sun. How hard it is, for instance, for any man to measure the various influences which have worked upon him during his three years at the university, but how clear it is that he is not the same man at the end.

Far more beneficently does the Holy Spirit of God work on us, never doing violence to our personality but constraining and wooing us to a higher life. Faith in His willingness to do even more for us would multiply the transformations He has already wrought and to part of the record of which—so far as it concerns the eighteenth century—we must now turn.

[1] Frayn, *Revelation and the Unconscious*, 139–43.

[2] John xiv. 26; cf. also Romans v, 12 *ff.* and viii. 2 *f.* where a similar work of the Holy Spirit is implicit.

CHAPTER XVI

THE WITNESS OF WESLEY'S FOLLOWERS

WE have now reached that stage in our quest when it would aid us to consider the artless words of those early followers of John Wesley who claimed that the gift of holiness had been given to them. There is no lack of testimony. Wesley encouraged his people to write down what God had done for them, and the best of these accounts he was glad to publish in the *Arminian Magazine*. In the files of that magazine, therefore, the curious may find a wealth of witness concerning the doctrine of Christian Perfection.

All the features of Wesley's doctrine which we have discovered in his *Plain Account*, in his sermons, journals and letters are illustrated here. The essence of the gift is love. All conscious sin is banished. It comes by faith and in an instant, carrying its own assurance with it. It is given here and now, in the busy press of our mundane life, and yet it is enjoyed in a certain spiritual detachment from the cares of this world.

The words are simple, unforced and make no effort to reach the literary style so much admired in the eighteenth century. Sincerity shines through them. That the narrators had enjoyed some impressive experience none can doubt. We have yet to decide whether or not their own explanation is the sound one, but, before any conclusion is reached, they should be heard.

Let us illustrate, then, the characteristics of Wesley's doctrine from the witness of his own disciples.

(i) Love is the key.

John Oliver was born at Stockport in Cheshire in 1732. He was converted and joined the Methodists in 1748. It was in the summer of 1762 that the longing for entire sanctification took hold of him. He says:

"I was convinced more deeply than ever of inbred sin, and of the promise of God to save me from it. And never did man at a bar plead harder for life, than I pleaded with God for this salvation."

His prayer was answered. He went to Lincoln's Inn at the

invitation of a friend and they joined in prayer with some others for this specific thing.

"The Lord was conquered by our instant prayer, and we had the petition we asked of Him. I was baptized with the Holy Ghost and with fire, and felt that perfect love casteth out fear. Great was our fellowship with the Father, the Son and the Holy Spirit. . . . If ever I had access to the throne of grace, it was on this memorable day. Our Lord was inexpressibly near: it seemed we might ask and have whatever we wanted. . . .

"From this time I went forth in the power and spirit of Love. I felt nothing but Love, and desired nothing but more Love. . . .

"From that day to this, [he wrote on June 1st, 1779] I have not lost my sight of, nor my affection for, Christian Perfection. . . ."[1]

Alexander M'Nab is not less emphatic that the heart of the gift is love. He writes of his state of mind after its glad reception in these terms:

"I could, therefore, now believe I was in the favour of God, and found the peace of God in my conscience; the love of God in my heart; and my spirit ardently breathing for the whole image of Jesus. I could daily call Jesus, Lord, by the Holy Ghost; and the frequent application of the promises to my mind greatly strengthened my faith. All the work of nature now bespoke the presence and goodness of God to me. The ordinances of His house were my delight; His Law, as well as His Gospel, I esteemed inestimably precious; and my heart was filled with pity towards my fellow-creatures, who knew not Jesus."[2]

Richard Whatcoat received the coveted gift on March 28th, 1761. He was twenty-five years of age at the time. When the blissful moment came, he said:

"Suddenly I was stript of all but love. I was all love and prayer and praise. And in this happy state, rejoicing evermore, and in everything giving thanks, I continued for some years; wanting nothing for soul or body, more than I received from day to day."[3]

---

[1] *Arminian Magazine*, 1779, 427 f.   [2] *ibid.*, 1779, 245.
[3] *ibid.*, 1781, 192 f.

(ii) All conscious sin has gone.

John Pawson was born at Thorner, near Leeds, in 1737, and met the Methodists first in 1755. At the time, he shared the common prejudice against them and had "a hatred against them above all others." The great change came in him on Sunday, March 16th, 1760, when he felt the power of sin broken in him. He says:

"I continually walked in the light of God's countenance: no creature shared my affections with God; but I served Him with an undivided heart. I had no distressing temptations, but had constant power over all sin; so that I lived as upon the borders of heaven."[1]

"M.G." writes in the same strain of conquered sin. She says, of the days and months succeeding her reception of this additional blessing:

"I was all faith and peace and love. I called upon all in heaven to praise God with me. Since then I have been established in the Lord. My heart is like a piece of solid gold. And I daily grow in the knowledge of God. And His ways are ways of pleasantness to me, and all His ordinances my delight: nothing stirs me now. Whatever comes is right. God is always with me. He lives in me and walks in me: He has cleansed my heart and sits as King there."[2]

The blessing came to William Green—a Londoner—on December 12th, 1774. He was thirty-five years of age and had been converted almost four years when this further experience came. Describing the glad hour, and his emancipation from sin, he says:

"The promises flowed into my heart without obstruction. I easily perceived the change was universal, and felt that I was cleansed from all my idols, and from all my filthiness. And I seemed to have light equal to my love; so that in one week I had a clearer insight into the life of faith, than I had for several years. Thus Jesus saves His people from their sins."[3]

(iii) It normally begins at a definite moment.

William Hunter—like many others—is positive on the point.

---

[1] *Arminian Magazine*, 1779, 34.   [2] *ibid.*, 1780, 274.   [3] *ibid.*, 1781, 305.

He came from a village called Placey in Northumberland and was born in 1728. Some years separated his conversion from his sense of complete cleansing. He hoped at first that they were simultaneous but discovered later, he says, that—

"my nature was not so much changed as I thought: I found many things in me which opposed the grace of God; so that without continual watching and prayer, I was capable of committing the very same sins which I had been guilty of before."

He came to believe in this further gift of God—and to seek it. Writing eighteen years after it came, he describes the experience thus:

"I found unbelief taken away out of my heart: my soul was filled with such faith as I never felt before: my love to Christ was like fire, and I had such views of Him, as my life, my portion, my all, as swallowed me up; and oh! how I longed to be with Him! A change passed upon all the powers of my soul, and I felt a great increase of holy and heavenly tempers, I may say, with humility, it was as though I was emptied of all evil, and filled with heaven and God."[1]

But what came in a moment had to be received from God moment by moment. William Hunter did not believe that he was lifted to an abiding *state* from which he could not fall.

"I feel I need his grace every moment: I stand by faith, I have as much need of Christ as ever: I may truly say, 'Every moment, Lord, I want the merit of Thy death.' . . . I am kept by His power: I enjoy salvation: my heart is fixed, my anchor is sure and steadfast."[2]

Alexander Mather was born at Brechin in 1733 and became one of Wesley's most trusted helpers. The experience which is our chief interest came to him at Rotherham in 1757. At the time he set the story down (1779) he frankly admits that the experience was less clear than it had been in those early days. But he is insistent that it came in a moment.

"What I had experienced in my own soul, was an instantaneous deliverance from all those wrong tempers and affections, which I had long and sensibly groaned under. An entire

[1] *Arminian Magazine*, 1779, 594-6.   [2] *ibid.*, 1779, 597.

disengagement from every creature, with an entire devotedness to God: and from that moment, I found an unspeakable pleasure, in doing the will of God in all things. I had also a power to do it, and the constant approbation both of my own conscience and of God."[1]

And to the same effect, so far as the instantaneous character of the gift is concerned, writes Thomas Rankin:

"I was meeting with a few Christian friends who were all athirst for entire holiness, and after several had prayed, I also called on the name of the Deliverer. . . . While these words were pronounced with my heart and lips, 'Are we not, O Lord, the purchase of Thy blood? Let us then be redeemed from all iniquity,' in a moment the power of God so descended upon my soul, that I could pray no more. . . . The language of my heart every moment was 'Oh what has Jesus done for me!' "[2]

(iv) The blessing carries its own assurance with it.

It came to John Manners as he mowed grass. Busy on his father's farm in the Yorkshire Wolds, and rejoicing in this new and wonderful change—he calls it "a greater change than ever"—a dark thought crossed his mind. Suppose he was self-deceived? What if it was all illusion? He says:

"I desired the Lord, not to let me deceive myself, but give me a witness if I was saved from sin? And in about a week he gave me my desire, the full, clear witness of His Spirit. It has not left me one moment since. I am now always happy in God. I always felt His love, and all my tempers, and desires, and words, and actions flow from it."[3]

Thomas Joyce was a sail-maker. Born in Portsmouth in 1712 he was given in his youth to "all manner of wickedness" but began to seek God earnestly in August, 1747, and found the forgiveness of sins in November, 1752. He went on the quest for entire sanctification in the early days of 1757. It came on Tuesday evening, February 22nd of that year, and the inward witness came with it. He says:

"I broke out into prayer, pleading the promises, till I was all over in a sweat. But I could not leave off, till I felt that word applied, 'Thou art sealed unto the day of redemption.' I immediately felt a far greater change, than I did when I was justified. I felt my soul was all renewed, and a witness that sin was all destroyed. And from that time I have found a continual increase of light, and love, and holiness.'[1]

(v) The element of ascetism is usually there.

Thomas Clark was born near Ripley in 1724 and was confirmed by the bishop when eighteen years of age. His confirmation meant a great deal to him. When he was twenty-five he married, and after that felt that "the cares and desires of the world" had "deadened" him. Meeting the Methodists, a longing was born in him for a deeper spiritual life and a sense of immense pardon came at Whitsuntide, 1759. The only shadow on his joy now was "a sense of inbred sin": a conviction that evil still lurked in his nature. It robbed him of his power to eat, or work, or sleep. Release from this came on the first Saturday in August, 1759.

"I was then at my work, when I was filled with such love and power, that I could work no longer. My soul was melted with love, the tears ran down my cheeks, and soon after, these words came, 'I have cleansed thee from all filthiness of flesh and spirit' which followed me for a fortnight wherever I went. I thought, however, I would tell nobody of it: but I could not refrain. I never found any doubt since, having the witness in myself continually. I feel no will but the Will of God. Even my body seemed renewed as well as my soul. I have a wife and five small children; but I have no care about them. I work every day among the wicked; but I am not hurt or hindered by them. I am always happy in God, full of love and peace, and feel no deadness or heaviness, but a continual increase of loving faith, springing up into everlasting life."[2]

He has a wife and five small children but he has "no care" about them. The word "anxiety" would be nearer to his mind, one imagines, in the meaning of to-day—but the sense of detachment from the world is plainly there.

John Furz was one of Wesley's whole-time helpers. He had suffered much for the faith. He was, indeed, so narrowly missed by a shot fired at him while preaching on Salisbury Plain that the bullet singed his hair. Entire sanctification, so he believed, came

---

[1] *Arminian Magazine*, 1781, 421.   [2] *ibid.*, 1781, 534.

to him in an instant and when he thought himself to be dying. It was at Hornby in Yorkshire. His illness was so grave that all hope of his recovery had been abandoned. Indeed, to "comfort" him another preacher sent him a letter "to inform me, he would come and preach my Funeral Sermon, and rejoice over me." He goes on:

> "The good women that sat round my bed said, 'We never had a Preacher die here before. We shall have a great company of people to hear the Funeral Sermon.' I heard one of them say, 'Now he is going.' Meantime, the cry of my heart was: 'Lord, sanctify me now or never.' In that instant I felt the mighty power of His sanctifying Spirit. It came down into my soul as a refining fire, purifying and cleansing from all unrighteousness. And from that instant I began to recover."[1]

One has a guilty feeling that the good women sitting round his bed would experience at least a little disappointment that he did not live up (or die down) to their expectations, but, unmistakably, a sense of "otherworldliness" suffuses the whole story. Earth is a desert drear and heaven is their home.

From the mouth of many witnesses we have now received accumulated proof that the doctrine as Wesley taught it was the doctrine his people held and experienced. It would be doing less than justice to the honesty and coherence of these accounts to suggest that their leader had simply imposed his ideas on their mind. The witnesses are so numerous: the accounts are so different in detail, yet so similar in substance, that it is impossible to dismiss them as personal vagaries or odd coincidences. Something had happened. But what? Were they self-deceived (at least, in part)? Having heard there was such a blessing to be had, did they imagine the rest? Was it simply a case of finding what they set out to find—and finding it because they so set out?

Or was it just peace that had come: the peace which comes to any soul which ceases to strive?

Or were they wholly right, and was it sanctification, deeper, completer, more penetrating than anything they had ever known before?

Those are the pressing questions which will no longer be denied.

[1] *Arminian Magazine*, 1782, 638.

CHAPTER XVII

IS IT SELF-DECEPTION, SANCTIFICATION, OR PEACE?

IT seems impossible to the writer that anyone could attend "the testimony meeting," which has preceded this chapter, and deny that some impressive experience had come to the various people who have spoken. The testimonies may seem to some readers to be as *unvaried* as most of the instances quoted (for one reason and another) by James in his *Varieties of Religious Experience*,[1] but it is not without interest to notice in passing just where the similarities and dissimilarities between them occur. If all the witnesses are to be regarded as of one type because they share an immense earnestness about religion, it is clear that they are of quite varied types in their mental equipment, early training, and (though not to the same extent) their social background. There are dour Scots and keen Cockneys: Northumbrians and Yorkshiremen: men of Cheshire and men of Hampshire. Some grew up in pious homes and never seriously strayed from the paths of virtue: others came to God and this great experience after years of prodigality. Some were simple souls to the end of their days: others had great natural gifts and gathered no small store of erudition with passing time. All write as honest men.

Deceivers they cannot be—but were they self-deceived? If we have seen good reason to doubt their claim that sin had been *eradicated*, can we doubt that these men of sensitive conscience had obtained release both from conscious sin and even from the *strain* of temptation? Temptation they knew—but not the long battle with it. They have insight swiftly to recognise its nature and power to repudiate it. It does not get past the divine guard which garrisons their heart. They live a victorious life. They are conscious only of love—and that the love is supernatural is proved by one fact alone: it does not confine itself to the channels of natural affinity but it overflows to all. In short, they deeply love people whom, by nature, they cannot like.

They do not claim to obtain in a moment a blessing that *must* abide for ever. They dislike the word *state* as a description of their experience if only because it is *static* and this life, they hold, is a

---

[1] cf. Barry, *The Relevance of Christianity*, 32.

"moment-by-moment" life. We have seen reasons to regard the "moment-by-moment" life as both possible and spiritually desirable, but I cannot find anywhere in the literature of the eighteenth century any explanation offered by one of these devout souls concerning the method he employed (if any) to hold doubt at bay, to keep the channel of faith unimpeded for the inflow of divine love, and to maintain this constant victory over sin. They stress, of course, the disciplined use of all the means of grace. Private prayer, public worship, Bible study, informal Christian fellowship and the observance of Holy Communion are constantly mentioned, and are, beyond all doubt, a large part of the answer to the question. But nowhere do I find any detailed explication of their own mental processes in the sublime hour itself, or in the days of dubiety which must have followed.

I am obliged, therefore, to quote a couple of instances written in the "thirties" of the present century by two earnest men who hold this teaching and which, I am convinced, will serve to show how the vigour of faith overcame—and overcomes—all the doubt which attends a man's belief that God can deal drastically with sin.

The first is by George S. Ingram. He claims the same blessing these eighteenth-century Methodists enjoyed and writes of it thus:

> "Never had the Devil so tempted me to doubt God, as when He gave me grace to trust Him to sanctify me wholly according to His promise in 1 Thessalonians, v. xxiii-xxiv. Before I had risen from my knees he attacked me, and day after day as I waited for God's inward assurance that He had cleansed my heart from all sin, the Devil again and again attacked me with doubts that nothing had happened because I felt nothing. And every time, God enabled me to hurl that promise that He had given me at the Devil; and every time, he left me, defeated by the Word. And then in God's own time came His deep inward assurance that He had cleansed my heart from *all* sin, and *filled* me with His Holy Spirit, and that inward assurance has remained with me through the years as a very precious possession."[1]

Later, he describes the experience this way:

[1] Ingram, *The Fulness of the Holy Spirit*, 23. He gives also an analogy borrowed from a camera.

"Then the real fight of faith began. The Devil turned the artillery of hell against my soul for about ten days, as I waited for God to give me the inward assurance that He had cleansed my heart from *all* sin. At last, while reading the second chapter of Acts, God gave me the inward assurance I was *desperately longing for* . . . and into my soul there stole a deep peace."[1]

The other instance I take from Dr. Stanley Jones. He enjoys the experience too.

"I was a Christian for a year or more when one day I looked at a library shelf and was struck with the title of a book, *The Christian's Secret of a Happy Life*.

"As I read it my heart was set on fire to find this life of freedom and fulness. I reached the forty-second page when the Inner Voice said very distinctly, 'Now is the time to find.' I pleaded that I did not know what I wanted, that when I finished it I would seek. But the Inner Voice was imperious, 'Now is the time to seek.' I tried to read on, but the words seemed blurred. I was up against a Divine insistence, so closed the book, dropped on my knees and asked, 'What shall I do?' The Voice replied, 'Will you give Me your all—your very all?' After a moment's hesitation, I replied, 'I will.' 'Then take My all, you are cleansed,' the Voice said with a strange inviting firmness. 'I believe it,' I said, and arose from my knees. I walked around the room affirming it over and over, and pushing my hands away from me as if to push away my doubt. This I did for ten minutes, when suddenly I was filled with a strange refining fire that seemed to course through every portion of my being in cleansing waves. It was all very quiet and I had hold of myself—and yet the Divine waves could be felt from the inmost centre of my being to my finger-tips. My whole being was being fused into one, and through the whole there was a sense of sacredness and awe—and the most exquisite joy. . . .

"My will was just as much involved as my emotion. The fact is the whole of life was on a permanently higher level."[2]

Both accounts are substantially the same and both are in harmony with our researches in the eighteenth century. It is impossible to resist the inference that we are dealing with the

[1] Ingram, *The Fulness of the Holy Spirit*, 26.
[2] Stanley Jones, *Victorious Living*, 120.

same spiritual phenomena, and it is unnecessary to deny ourselves the light which one sheds upon the other.

What are the facts?

The basis is set in the Scriptures. These devout souls believe that they have in the Bible a plain promise from God to cleanse them from all sin—and to cleanse them now. Faith in the suppliant is met by some mighty movement of the Holy Spirit which is as a refining fire in regard to their sin, and a mighty overflowing Love in their relationships with others. They *will* to believe. They *do* believe. Doubts arise. Conscience itself challenges this daring faith. They call their doubts "the devil" and sometimes, it is to be feared, apply the same term to their conscience too. They keep affirming that the miracle has been done. Faith, mounted and spurred, goes into action and hews the doubts to death and the contest is closed by a sense of immense elation and the inward conviction that this is a victory surpassing any they have ever known before.

Is it now possible, in the light of our previous study, and with these witnesses serving our need, to attempt a clearer explanation of what has occurred?

For people who do not believe that the promise of this cleansing is in the Bible, most of the super-structure which these men rear will fall to the ground. But not all! Even they may hold that there is a cleansing from sin which, without being complete, is more radical than anything most Christians enjoy, and will be more than curious concerning the evidence of it.

To those who have been constrained by the New Testament evidence to a belief that God *is* committed to the most drastic treatment of sin in the life of the believer, the claim to have experienced this complete cleansing, together with the manner of it, will seem among the most important subjects towards which their attention could possibly be turned.

When earnest seekers raised the question two centuries ago, "Can sin be eradicated?", there was no certain answer, not only because they had posed their problem in the wrong way and were confusing a balance of motive with some half-tangible "thing," but also because, in the exultation of an experience which, at the moment, expanded their heart, they sometimes spoke as if something had been done in that moment which must last for ever and ever. They forgot, in short, their own best thought, namely, that this life is lived only "moment by moment," and no witness can legitimately run past the glorious "now."

No man knows what is in him. He may be an utter stranger both to a certain sin and even the temptation to it, not because his nature is incapable of seduction at that point, but because his circumstances have never presented it to him. A change in his circumstances might make him bitterly acquainted, not only with the temptation, but also with the sin. Had he proclaimed himself utterly free of that sin, and phrased his proclamation with an orbit beyond the moment of its utterance, he would claim a knowledge of himself which no man can possibly possess. He would certainly be guilty of ignorant presumption and might, indeed, utter a lie.

The saintly Dr. F. B. Meyer, a convinced believer in the teaching that Christ can give by faith "instant and constant deliverance from sin,"[1] had, until the mid-years of his career, no awareness of the sin of professional jealousy. So strange was it to him that he found it very hard to believe that it existed at all in the heart of a man sharing his holy calling. The very idea bewildered him.

But the time came when he knew it. For years his Devotional Talks drew immense crowds to the Northfield Conventions, but the day arrived when a younger man began to claim "surpassing" notice. The crowds left Meyer. Religious crowds are as fickle as any others. He faced sparse audiences because the multitude had gone to hear the Bible Expositions of the youthful Dr. Campbell Morgan. And jealousy stirred in the heart of the saint. He confessed so much to many friends. "The only way I can conquer my feeling," he said, "is to pray for him daily, which I do."[2]

No man knows what is in him. Hence the immense and matted difficulties and dangers (to which we must revert when we come to restate this doctrine) of proclaiming that one is cleansed from all sin. It invites misunderstanding. The most sympathetic hearer reads more into it than the speaker may intend. The element of time intrudes. He may mean no more than this: "At this moment I am conscious of nothing but love." But more has been implied if, indeed, more has not been said. People hearing the astonishing claim do not hear it only for the moment, but in terms of to-morrow . . , and the day after. And they remember it, moreover, when the life of the witness has become its plain contradiction. Hence the wide distrust of this

[1] Fullerton, *F. B. Meyer*, 194.

[2] *ibid.*, 37.

teaching and its neglect even in those churches in which it is "officially" believed.

In patient and sympathetic questioning through a number of years of people who claim to have enjoyed this deep cleansing, I have met none who never experiences a stab of jealousy, or a mood of irritation, or a sense of pride, or a lustful thought. I have met many in whom they were rare, and many in whom their immediate consciousness led to their immediate repudiation. But who that wears this flesh will deny that when a stab of jealousy comes, or a mood of irritation, or a flush of pride, or a carnal thought, it is already "me" in the moment of my first awareness? Sin does not always beset me from without and grant so much as a fleeting minute to say "Yes" or "No." It stabs *in* me. *I*, for that moment, am vain. In the first split second of awareness, it is in possession. Repudiation is eviction, for it is already in. How then can I talk of eradication, or frame a testimony which will cover a moment beyond "now"?

Yet a great claim may be made. In the light of the heaped-up testimony of these honest witnesses, we can see plainly what the mercy of God has been able to do in response to such resolute faith. That faith moves mountains, we have been divinely taught, and that the impediment of sin in our souls is not more obstructive than mountains we may—with more faith—dare to believe. The faithful soul affixes itself to the confident expectation that God will give him the victory in every conflict with sin. He knows he is "in" the will of God in desiring victory, for sin is the one thing that God will not tolerate. He *holds* the faith and battles for it against the demon of doubt. He stands up, as did Mr. Ingram, to "the artillery of hell" or—like Dr. Stanley Jones—he walks around the room "affirming it over and over" and pushing his hands away from him as if to push away his doubts. All his mind is fixed on God and on purity, and his heart is all compounded of confident belief that God can do something in him which he can never do for himself.

And God does it! He does not "eradicate" sin. A false psychology lies behind the very hope of that, even (so the writer believes) when it is phrased as a hope that a man may "consent" to eradication. But He moves out to the believing soul with inexpressible power and, in ways as varied as men are varied, He gives victory in the fight with temptation by drawing the heart towards Himself and all Wholeness, and fills that heart with positive and objective love. The prolonged study of testimonies covering more than two centuries, and conversations with many living witnesses, lead me to this affirmation. It will not be resented if I say that some personal experience also beckons me on. Not all the wild vagaries of eccentrics, nor the unlovely lives of some who have claimed to be holy and contradicted their claim by their conduct, can divert our minds from the core of truth which lies at the heart of this teaching. It seems to the writer that the substance of Wesley's teaching is sound. God is able, not only to save us *in* sinning but *from* sinning. He can do more with sin than forgive it: He can break its power as well. It may cease to "have dominion over" a man.

But how comes it that this teaching should be exposed to the sad absurdities of eccentrics and that many who have claimed this blessing should have so patently contradicted it by their unlovely lives? No-one who has studied the teaching in its historical unfolding will deny that this is the case.[1] One does not dwell chiefly on the unbalanced women who were called "Bundling Perfectionists" and who "attempted to increase their spiritual virtue by killing the sense of shame which had been put as a curse upon Adam," flinging themselves into all sorts of compromising situations and even running naked through the countryside.[2] Nor yet on John Humphrey Noyes, the founder of the Oneida Perfectionists with their "complex" marriage system and opposition to all monogamy out of respect to communistic ideals. Many, alas! in our own day have made this bold profession in a hectoring and aggressive way, showing few of the graces of gentleness and barely a trace of humility, while there have been others who have publicly affirmed it of themselves at the very time when they were guilty of the grossest sins.

It was bitter experience which led an American bishop to exclaim: "We shudder at the very mention of this holiness teaching." Well within living memory a prominent exponent of it had to hurry out of the country after the revelation of his own immorality. On the Sunday evening before the ghastly *dénouement*, he had publicly announced from a pulpit that he was free of all sin!

Less heinous by far, but not without its psychological interest, is the explanation of the sudden withdrawal from public life of Mr. Robert Pearsall Smith who, in the seventies of the last century, achieved such wide fame as an apostle of the "Higher

---

[1] cf. Hampson's *Life of Wesley*, iii, 61.
[2] H. W. Smith (Mrs. R. Pearsall Smith), *Religious Fanaticism*, 55 f.

Life." It is difficult to believe now what immense, if transient, interest the visit of this American teacher exercised on evangelical opinion in Europe, but Dr. Warfield has not hesitated to say that it was "nothing less than amazing." [1] Put in a phrase, his message was not markedly different from the teaching we have been examining here; he taught that by an act of faith it was possible to become "dead to sin": he differed from Wesley, he believed, in insisting that the recipient of this grace is saved from all sinning, though not from all sin. "Eradication" of sin was an idea abhorrent to him. "We remain in ourselves sinful and liable to sin" he would say, though whether he fully understood Wesley's teaching—at least, at its clearest and best—may be doubted. [2] A great meeting at Oxford in the autumn of 1874 stirred the Protestant world and many heard Wesley's doctrine—with this apparently new accent—as though it was being proclaimed for the first time.

Mr. Pearsall Smith became famous. His photograph could be bought in the London shops: thousands hung on his words: queens consulted him in Belgium and Holland: in Germany the Emperor lent him a church and the Empress Augusta received him in audience. Back in England, Mr. Smith announced in the Dome at Brighton, "All Europe is at my feet." Dr. Warfield exaggerates only a little in saying, "There is nothing more dramatic in the history of modern Christianity than the record of this 'Higher Life Movement.' " [3]

Suddenly, the apostle withdrew from public life. A newspaper announcement said that he had been compelled to cancel his public engagements and return to America. The story went round that some old physical trouble caused by a fall from a horse years before had re-asserted itself, and when this story was disbelieved his friends issued a statement that he had "inculcated doctrines that were most dangerous and unscriptural, and that there had been conduct on his part which, though it was free, they were convinced, from all evil intention, had rendered it necessary for him to abstain from public work." [4]

His son, with even more relish than Edmund Gosse displayed in *Father and Son*, has enjoyed telling the world where his father went wrong.

Mr. Pearsall Smith, it seems, ignoring the desperate warnings of his saintly and wise wife, and ignoring also the fact "that

[1] Warfield, ii, 504.   [2] *ibid.*, ii, 521.   [3] Logan Pearsall Smith, *Unforgotten Years*, 51.
[4] *ibid.*, 52. Warfield, ii, 506 *f.*

nature, in one of her grossest economies, has placed the seats of spiritual and amorous rapture so close to each other that one of them is very likely to arouse the other," [1] had expounded to select gatherings of spinsters of a certain age how the "Higher Life" could be imparted by the salutation of "a holy kiss." When jealousy intervened between the recipients of "the holy kiss," scandal ensued, the plain, honest seekers for a higher quality of life were utterly discomfited, and great occasion was given for the Philistines to rejoice.

Are the exponents of holiness teaching more prone than ordinary men to follies and eccentricities, to spiritual pride and spiritual blindness, or is this merely another illustration of unhappy events claiming notice on the ground of their rarity, and impressive simply because they are almost incredible?

The answer appears to be this. Doubtless, special attention *is* directed towards the failings of anyone claiming to be free of conscious sin—as it should be—and proving again the unwisdom of such public affirmations, but it cannot be doubted either that, in one particular at least, all who assert this faith in the manner of Mr. Ingram and Dr. Stanley Jones expose themselves to special danger. We have already glanced at the peril in passing. It belongs to the militancy of faith when seeking this experience to rise from one's knees asserting that the miracle has been wrought. All doubt is of the devil. It must be beaten down by the affirmations of faith. To believe and to have are synonymous. Any dubiety is guilty unbelief.

And it is just at *that* point that the greatest danger lurks. When uncertainty concerning the health of my soul troubles my mind, it does not normally come from the devil but from my conscience. I recall the stab of jealousy—I may be conscious of it at that very moment—or I feel the flush of petty pride. To call the regret and repentance which this sinful awareness quickens in me "the devil," is to slander one of my best friends. To silence that admonitory voice by bawling louder that I am holy will damage me in the most sensitive part of my soul-life, and wound the most trusty mentor I have on the path of spiritual progress.

And this, surely, is what some of these unbalanced teachers and false guides have done. They have blunted their own conscience, believing that what they were doing was to the glory of God. When that inner monitor of the soul stirred in disapproval,

[1] Logan Pearsall Smith, *Unforgotten Years*, 54.

they flung "a promise" at it, and called the warning "unbelief."
With passing time the conscience ceased to function with any
accuracy or power and they are found proclaiming themselves
free of sin while guilty of conduct which a worldling would know
to be wrong.

The number of these sad casualties has probably never been
proportionately large but their lapse is a recurring phenomenon
in the history of this teaching and to understand it is part of our
task. We may answer the question, therefore, with which this
chapter began, by saying, of this high experience, that it is a true
tryst with God and the impartation of Divine power in the battle
against sin, but we have recognised also where self-deception
sometimes creeps in. To preserve the vigour and demandingness
of faith, the focussed concentration on God and purity, the hunger
and thirst after righteousness which is so manifestly blessed, and,
at the same time, never to tamper with conscience and dope it
with a lie . . . there is the task, as there is the triumph, of the quest
for holiness on which we have embarked. Holiness is a gift of
God. Faith is the means. To direct the energy of faith to its great
Object and, while appropriating the gift, to heighten the sensitivity of conscience . . . this is the upward mountain path
which runs right on to the top. There is an abyss on either side
of this path. It can be followed only on one's knees. But we have
found the path which we were seeking. When Wesley discerned
that path, he was sure that he had found the path to perfection.

One question still remains on this aspect of the subject. It
need not detain us long.

Certain scholars, convinced that the claimants of this experience have unquestionably made some contact with God, but
unconvinced that it is fittingly described as "sanctification,"
have said that what they really receive is peace. Dr. Warfield
takes that view. He says, "What the Christian receives . . . is
not sanctification but peace."[1]

I cannot feel that this comment takes sufficient heed of the
fact that we are examining a religious experience which, by
common testimony, is subsequent to conversion. Whether or not
the experience is well described as "a second blessing" some will
doubt, but the witnesses, howsoever they express themselves,
are clearly able to distinguish the first committal of their lives
to God from this later quest for complete cleansing.

[1] Warfield, ii, 491.

Peace came with forgiveness at their conversion. Heartease and guilt-free rapture belonged to their first tryst with God. It is true that many of them talk of inner unrest at the discovery that sin still finds place in them, but it would distort the great mass of their testimonies if we concluded that they had to wait for this further experience before they found peace. Peace, they would say, they have had already, and no close study of conversion data leaves the student in doubt that interior rest, even though it may subsequently be intermittent, is one of its commonest concomitants. It belongs to the borderland of theology and psychology to discuss whether the peace is a gift from God or simply the inner harmony which registers the end of mental strife (or both).[1] Some men who have rejected not only the Christian faith but all theism have spoken of a "peace" which came to them when the struggle about the existence of God was over and they had taken up their permanent abode in unbelief. Joseph McCabe says:

> "I have had thirty years' intercourse, by letter or conversation, with men and women over the whole English-speaking world who have given up the belief in God and, though in some cases the critical period was painful, I never met one who wanted to get back the belief or deplored the loss of it."[2]

He rejects Professor Montague's remark that "atheism does not lead to badness but sadness" as "preposterous." My own experience reverses that of Mr. McCabe. I have met many people who found faith impossible but very few who did not frankly admit that they would like to believe.

But for us the question is a diversion. Peace of a kind no doubt comes to any man at the end of toilsome mental effort, but whether that peace is comparable to what the Christian calls "the peace of God" we may take leave to doubt. Logan Pearsall Smith, who has lost faith himself, and can enjoy lampooning it in others, looks back to the religion of his childhood and his own belief in sanctification with something more meaningful than a jest upon his lips. He says—and seems to mean—"I have felt nothing in my life which I can compare with that holy joy."[3]

[1] Hughes, *The New Psychology and Religious Experience*, 243 f.
[2] McCabe, *The Existence of God*, 154.
[3] *Unforgotten Years*, 65.

CHAPTER XVIII

THE NAME OF THE DOCTRINE

A CONSTRUCTIVE task invites us now. We have examined Wesley's doctrine of Christian Perfection in the light of the biblical, theological and psychological scholarship of our day and we have now to enquire what changes the passing of two centuries has wrought. Can this doctrine still be preached? If it cannot be preached precisely as Wesley preached it, with what differences may it, and must it, be offered to the people? Is it an integral part of the Christian gospel, and does every man who omits it offer only a maimed message? Are the deep objections felt against it by some theologians in the eighteenth century—the Calvinists for instance—the same objections which are pressed against it to-day, or have the arguments changed in character as well as multiplied in number? Is there something inevitably individualistic about this teaching, or is it social at its very heart, so that to talk of its social "implications" is to misconceive its nature and to treat as an excisible appendix what is vital to its life? Put in the plainest terms possible, " Can we, as related persons in this world, be free from sin, can we know it, and should we say so?" These are the large questions to which we must address ourselves now.

But before we attempt to answer these questions and endeavour to restate Wesley's doctrine in the thought-forms of our age, one particular part of our aim should be made clear. Dr. Curtis, in his brief but sympathetic account of Wesley's teaching, talks of "all his inconsistencies" in expounding it,[1] and other scholars have noted this judgment with approval.[2] None of them, however, not even Dr. Curtis himself, has paused to draw out the inconsistencies, and it is important for our purpose to set some of them down.

It will be felt by many that Wesley was inconsistent in making this doctrine central in his teaching, urging his people to "press

---

[1] Curtis, *The Christian Faith*, 382.
[2] e.g. Rattenbury, *The Evangelical Doctrines of Charles Wesley's Hymns*, 300.

on to perfection" and to testify concerning it, yet never testifying himself. The point is not answered by saying that Wesley was sure the blessing could be obtained but had never received it himself, because it is germane to his exposition that God will never deny a bold, importunate faith. Had he then lacked faith—or had God forgotten to be gracious?

These are the facts. He was sure that there was a special gift of God concerning holiness but, whatever testifying he urged upon his people, he never said himself, "I am freed from all sin." We may anticipate our own conclusions by saying that it is Wesley's example which we shall find impressive and not Wesley's advice.

It has been felt also that there is inconsistency in Wesley's oscillations between perfection given in an instant and perfection as a growth. But Wesley faced this objection in his own day and believed that he had answered it. His analogy of human birth carries the substance of his reply: there is growth in the womb before birth and a long, long growth after, but the birth itself is a matter of moments and can be timed upon a clock. He would have said, concerning the life of holiness, that you do not grow into it: you are born *into* it, and grow *in* it. It is true that, if one takes isolated phrases from his writings, first about the instantaneous character of the birth and then the slow maturing of the growth, it is not hard to sharpen the contrast into a series of antithetic phrases and produce the appearance of plain inconsistency. But that is to do despite to his meaning. Written in the margin of his own copy of one of Charles' hymn-books (still preserved at Richmond College, Surrey) is a comment on a verse which deals with the impartation of holiness to the soul. It is not a human achievement. Both John and Charles are agreed upon that. It is a gift of God. But when Charles writes as though the gift always came as a gradual growth, John comments, "Both sudden and gradual." Nor would he have admitted any inconsistency in this. His rejoinder to the remark of Dr. Vincent Taylor that "there is no support in New Testament teaching for the view that sanctification is a sudden and miraculous gift of the Spirit in response to importunate prayer"[1] would have depended on the connotation of the word "sanctification" as used here. Freedom from conscious sin, he believed, could be given in an instant, but for the impartation of the rich wholeness of holiness, eternity, he would have argued, is too short.

[1] Taylor, *Forgiveness and Reconciliation*, 184.

Finally, Wesley appears inconsistent in speaking of sanctification sometimes as a state and sometimes as a moment-by-moment life. When he addressed his mind to the question he repudiated the idea of a "state"; but ever and anon he slipped back into phraseology which belongs to the realm of the static. He was almost compelled to do so by the dual thread of thought in his mind. The idea of an instantaneous birth, as we have seen, was the substance of at least half his thinking, and to be born one moment and unborn the next is a strain which no metaphor will bear. Indeed, he was impeded by his own analogies the further he went, and what had helped his thought at one stage hindered him at the next.

If we add to these inconsistencies his difficulty about a name for the doctrine, his preference for one term but his more frequent use of another, we shall begin to get not only the measure of our task but also a clue to its accomplishment.

This is our hope: that our restatement of the doctrine will not only respect the findings of modern scholarship but remove the inconsistencies (real or apparent) from Wesley's own exposition. We begin with the belief that Wesley made his own task harder by contending for things which do not belong to the marrow of the New Testament truth, and thereby imperilled the acceptance of what he was most concerned to give. It will seem to us a confirmation of any position which we take if, though it run counter at some points to Wesley's own exposition, it can be shown to be more consistent with its heart.

As to the name. Many names have been given to this teaching in the various forms which it has taken, each carrying its own peculiar flavour of meaning. Most of them are biblical in origin, and those which have been coined in recent years have been fashioned for the sake of freshness and because other old and honoured terms had worn thin. In Wesley's time it was called Christian Perfection, Sanctification, Holiness, or Perfect Love. More recently, it has been called the Higher Life, Victorious Living, Fulness of Life, and Constant Victory. Among those for whom the pursuit of holiness has taken a more mystical turn than it did with Wesley, we meet other names: *unio mystica*, *via unitiva*; Beatitude, or the Vision of God.

It is not suggested for a moment that all these names mean, or were intended to mean, precisely the same thing. A chapter could be written on the *nuance* which each carries, and the shade of distinction delicately drawn. But such a degree of *finesse* is not called for in our study, though some appraisal of the terms is compelled. The teaching has been suspect in part because of the name. Juliet must have known herself, even when she soliloquised on her famous question, "What's in a name?", that there was more in a word than her love-sick heart was disposed to allow. All life confirms this. Not for nought does a fishmonger call dog-fish "rock salmon," or a house-agent describe an unfurnished floor as a "flat," or a textile merchant call artificial silk "rayon," or a bookmaker describe himself as a "turf accountant." There is much in a name. It could be said, without any fear of contradiction from those who have studied the evidence, that no small part of Wesley's difficulty in pressing this doctrine on his preachers turned upon his ill-advised use of a name.

Reviewing the terms, then, which we have set down as descriptive of the *summum bonum* of the individual life, and seeking the one which best describes the teaching Wesley's name is associated with, we may begin by setting aside the mystical terms, if only because of Wesley's abhorrence of most things mystical. Attempts have been made to prove that Wesley's criticisms of the mystical writers have been exaggerated[1] and it may freely be allowed that the word "mysticism" is so blurred that it can be given a connotation wide enough to cover Wesley himself. But these attempts do not really succeed in vaulting over the difficulties, and they can never be made plausible enough to foist a mystical term on a Wesley doctrine.

Just as resolutely should we set aside the terms Victorious Living, Beatitude, Fulness of Life, and all others whose stress falls on the peace, joy, happiness and triumph of the believer. From them the inference is falsely, but quite naturally, drawn that we should be holy for the dividend it pays and not because God is holy. A subtle subjectivism shifts the emphasis from God and His work, to man and his enjoyments, and that is reason enough for passing over terms which carry such an implication even in an undertone.

Between the terms Perfection, Sanctification, and Holiness, there is a difference more solid than a *nuance*. Dr. Platt says that the term perfection is "distinguished in Christian thought from holiness and from sanctification as a question of degree, or as a

---

[1] Bett, *The Spirit of Methodism*, 57–63. Rattenbury, *The Conversion of the Wesleys*, 231–9.

K

specific from the generic. Many Christians who urge the possibility of holiness plead the impossibility of perfection."[1]

The word "perfection" is an extraordinarily difficult term.
Wesley and Fletcher found it so. That was why, in their day, they
made such laboured distinctions between Paradisaical, Medi-
atorial, and Christian Perfection,[2] and that is why subsequent
writers, sympathetic to their teaching, have distinguished the
terms relative and absolute perfection, the perfection of the
stage and the perfection of the end. Oddly and sadly enough, the
adjectival use of the word Christian with the word perfection has
not burnished the noun but tarnished it. This was inevitable. An
illimitable term must shine in lone splendour. The misguided
effort to furbish it is worse than gilding the lily and has the
precisely opposite effect from the one desired. When Wesley
linked the sublime name "Christian" with the sublime term
"perfection," he produced a title which was not sublime. In the
critical minds of those who followed him keenly, and in his own
frank exposition too, Christian Perfection was set out as something less than perfection, and he was exposed to the sneer which
we have noted already: it was possible to be a perfect Christian
without being a perfect man.

The term "perfection," for what Wesley had in mind, must be
dropped. Indeed, it appears plain that he wanted to drop it
himself.[3] It is a mystery that he made such free use of a name he
did not like and which was so fruitful of trouble and misunderstanding. He used it, no doubt, for the same reason that he used
the name "Methodist": because others used it and because it
was the swiftest way to recognition.

The names "Christian," "Quaker," and "Methodist," all
began as nicknames and all have been redeemed. The brick-bat
has become a badge of honour. But the word "perfection" cannot
be wrested in that way. It has its own lustre and a long, long
history. It has also a fatal defect. It was, and is, ambiguous. This
ambiguity, as Archbishop Trench once pointed out, "it shares
with τέλειος itself; . . . both are employed now in a relative, now
in an absolute sense. . . . The Christian shall be 'perfect,' yet not
in the sense in which some of the sects preach the doctrine of
perfection, who, as soon as their words are looked into, are found
either to mean nothing which they could not have expressed by
a word less liable to misunderstanding; or to mean something

---

[1] E.R.E., ix, 728.   [2] Fletcher's *Works*, vi, 270.   [3] *Letters*, iii, 167.

which no man in this life shall attain, and which he who affirms he has attained is deceiving himself, or others, or both."[1]

Wesley comes under this condemnation. The pity is that though he had a better term at hand and did not hesitate, on occasion, publicly to profess his preference for it, he let it lie, and made more frequent use of the other. Herein is no small part of the explanation of the neglect of this teaching even among his own followers. Before he slipped into the grave,[2] the "perfect" had become a joke behind his own back and the precious thing for which he had contended was lost while the wits were poking fun.

His better term was "perfect love." It will seem, at first, no better than the term it supplants, in that the word "perfect" still finds place in it, and that must, perhaps, be admitted as a danger still. But it is strangely less aggressive as an adjective than a noun. And here the English word "love" cannot stand alone.

It is a calamity that the word "love" is so wide, so blurred, so amorphous. We must use the same term to cover the flutterings of adolescent emotion in spring, and the mighty passion which moves in the heart of God. Into this one word we pour in sad and profane confusion, ἀγάπη, ἔρως, φιλία, στοργὴ and even ἐπιθυμία. Difficulty besets us whatever we do. If we keep "perfect" as an adjective we have still its lurking ambiguity to face. If we let "love" stand in its own unbuttressed strength, the pull of the gutter will be upon it all the time. *Roués* speak of their conquests as "love."

But few will doubt that Wesley had a better term in "perfect love" than in "Christian Perfection." To begin with, it is positive. The common idea of perfection as sinlessness gave a picture of the ideal in terms of negation. It never grappled with the tremendous sins of omission. Even the words "sanctified" and "holy" are no better in this regard. They certainly carry the idea of being purged from impurity but no hint of being robust in active goodness. "Perfect love" reverses that: it is a spirited principle no more to be confined within the narrow limits of the individual heart than a perfume can be gathered up and returned to the bottle once it has escaped.

Consequently, it is social too. Holiness, conceived as perfect love, can never be a selfish cult the devotees of which are greedily bent on their own joy, peace, power, poise, or conquest over sin.

[1] Trench, *Synonyms of the New Testament*, 76.
[2] Hampson's *Life of Wesley*, iii, 197.

Into such unsocial conduct many who have set out on this path have been trapped. The terms they used to describe their quest gave us a hint of the danger. Because it was the peace of God they sought, or victory over sin, or fullness of life, it seemed to them completely unimpeachable; but the gratification of some self-desire does not become unselfish because the end of it is respectable: it is still selfish, though one pursue the uttermost refinement of personal holiness, if the quickening motive is still *for oneself*.

And therein lies a clue which we must follow later when we come to consider the social character of perfect love in more detail. For some reason not fully explicated, the early Methodists never worked out the communal implications of this teaching.[1] It remained the passionate but private pursuit of individuals. It inclined to be a cult rather than a crusade. Scriptural exhortations to be "separate" from the world, and the mirth and mis-understanding which the teaching engendered, all fostered its individual character and made its exposition little more than the occupation of "conventions" and the special interest of a coterie.

It goes without saying that, even in this narrowed orbit, it had social *implications*. Men and women bent on the conquest of sin in their own souls, and seeking to enjoy the peace and blessedness of God, become, whether they want to or not, distinctive in the community and exercise a wholesome influence upon their fellows. But this teaching as commonly given had no overt and resolute social *concern*. Individual holiness was the aim and social benefits were a pleasing by-product. Even when they appeared to have a social mission it was largely salvage work: the re-clamation of drunkards and harlots. Such work, when they did it, was beautiful and Christlike, but it was not normally related to any big communal thinking and included no robust hope for the redemption of society. It was an individual snatching an individual from the burning building, but the bigger question, of whether the blaze could be got under control, seemed not to arise. Social redemption with personal holiness as a blessed by-product would have seemed utter folly to them. They would certainly have rejected the suggestion that it is impossible to live a perfect life in an imperfect world.

It is no part of our immediate purpose to suggest that we have the whole answer to the complicated relationship of the self and its world. Our concern at the moment is with terms, and this much, we feel, is quite clear. Both from its positive character

[1] Dale, *The Evangelical Revival and Other Sermons*, 33–9.

and its essentially social nature, the term "perfect love" is preferable to the term "Christian Perfection." For the reasons we have indicated, it seems preferable also to the other terms which have been employed. That Wesley himself preferred it seems to confirm our choice; and to the examination of perfect love as the best description of the Christian ideal we can now turn.[1]

[1] For another consideration of these varied terms—and a different conclusion—see K. E. Kirk, *The Vision of God*, 466 *ff.*; cf. also Taylor, *Forgiveness and Reconciliation*, 198–214.

CHAPTER XIX

LOVE—IN LOVE'S DIVINEST FEATURE

I<small>T</small> would be well to approach our appraisal of the term "perfect love" by a frank facing of those features of it which cannot but be regarded as defects. We have glanced at some of them already in passing. The ambiguity of the word "perfect" has constantly to be borne in mind, though we have suggested that the adjective is a less serious hindrance to clear thinking than the corresponding noun, but it is the English word "love" which invites us, and yet obstructs us, more.

Not only is its current meaning far too wide for our purpose—as any student of the Greek New Testament is sadly aware—but it is far too shallow too. It is too shallow because it is too wide.

The word "love" as commonly employed denotes a mere emotion. The speech of the streets and the thought of the streets confine it to feeling. In vain the thinker and philologist protest against this debasing of a great word: the plain man persists in using the word as though love were only an emotion. If a doubt is cast upon his love for a cause or a person, he knows no other test than the test of feeling. Confronted with the question which perplexed John Newton years ago:

> 'Tis a point I long to know,
>> Oft it causes anxious thought;
> Do I love the Lord or no?
> Am I His, or am I not?

he can make no better answer than to place his finger on the pulse of feeling and seek to settle the gnawing doubt that way.

Yet it is not hard to show even a man who reads as he runs that this test is altogether inadequate. Feeling fluctuates. It may not be capricious but it is certainly fluctuating. Even in our human relationships, we do not always *feel* our love. If love were only present when the feeling-tone is strong enough to be self-conscious, every form of human affection would be a poor and intermittent thing. The most loving husband does not always feel his love. The most devoted mother is not always aware of her affection. Days, weeks, months even, may slip by without any floodtide of emotion expanding her heart, but if it were suggested that at such periods she had ceased to love her child, she would toss the suggestion scornfully aside.

Moreover, feeling is affected by health, circumstances and physical comfort. Neuralgia or sea-sickness can rob people of all *sense* of love, even on a honeymoon. A man may be on the way to sainthood, but on the day his business is sold up to placate his creditors, he feels nothing but a sense of defeat. A woman may be of virtue all compounded, but the day she weeps beside her husband's grave she knows no feeling but one of unutterable loss. Feeling is tidal. There are deep psychological reasons why that should be so. The restless tides of feeling can never be a true index to a deep and constant love.

The reason surely is this. If feeling were at white heat all the time—a plain impossibility—it would still only be a third of this complex thing we call "personality." What of thought? What of will? Love cannot be love—most certainly it cannot be perfect love—until it interpenetrates the whole personality and knits our nature into a wholeness which, by nature alone, it does not possess. Clearly, it is not enough to have love only in the emotions. At the very beginning of our understanding of this strong term we must see it deep also in the thought and the will.

Moreover, if love is only in the emotions, it cannot be stern and it cannot punish. Sentimental musings on love would leave one believing that love has no method with sinners but to let them off, and that God's whole policy is to forgive on easy terms.

All honest observation of life contradicts this. Consequences run through all nature and through all God's dealings with men. When God forgives sin, He does not necessarily remit its penalties. The prodigal came home to an estate every bit of which belonged to his elder brother. He had wasted his substance in riotous living and the inheritance was not divided again simply because he had come home. In being magnanimous with his penitent prodigal, the father was not unjust to his first-born.

But he welcomed him home as a *son*, not as a servant, took him in with the filth of the swine-trough still on him, and said in effect, "Son, we will live the shame of it down together."

God's love can be stern because it is love as an attitude and not merely as an emotion. His love can punish, but His punishments are always remedial and never vindictive.

It is because the idea of love is limited in common use to the realm of emotion that so much cynicism is uttered about it and people can laugh and say, "Love is chemistry." But the witticism dies as a blasphemy upon the lips of anyone who follows Love Incarnate through the thronged villages of Galilee, sees the bloody sweat of Gethsemane, and witnesses the noise, and thirst, and agony of the bitter Cross. Here is love ingenious, strategic, resourceful, indestructible. Here is love seeking, serving, praying, bleeding. Here is love in feeling, thought and will.

Howsoever we fashion our thought of perfect love, we must shape it in the light of that Life in which alone it found its fullest expression in this world.

And now we are in a position to weigh the merits of the term. The defects of common usage are there, and recognised, though not, of course, removed. Removing mountains is easier than re-minting a word. But we have seen graver objections to the other terms we considered, and no term can claim a higher warrant in the Scriptures than love.

"And one of the scribes came, and heard them questioning together, and knowing that He had answered them well, asked Him, What commandment is the first of all? Jesus answered, The first is, Hear, O Israel; the Lord our God, the Lord is one: and thou shalt love the Lord thy God with all thy heart, and with all thy soul, and with all thy mind, and with all thy strength. The second is this, Thou shalt love thy neighbour as thyself. There is none other commandment greater than these."[1]

On unimpeachable authority the two supreme commandments are keyed to love. Even the "new" one which the Fourth Gospel gives us is a glad repetition.

"A new commandment I give unto you, that ye love one another; even as I have loved you, that ye also love one another."[2]

Into the question of whether our ideal is love for God or love for man, we will not enter because we see no necessary antithesis there. We do not believe in a love for God which does not express itself as love for man, and love for man divorced from love for

---

[1] Mark xii. 28-31.   [2] John xiii. 34.

God is, much observation has forced us to conclude, a poor, anæmic thing.

But to return. In the last chapter we saw reason for stressing the *positive* character of the term and the inwardness of that we must now draw out in greater detail.

It is one of the demerits of the term "Christian Perfection" that its ideal is static, and that however positive the phrase may sound it is really a summation of negatives. It brings to mind some triumph of exorcism. "Sinlessness" is its keynote. Evil is cast out.

Duty is the path which leads thither—a precise and awe-ful observance of rules, whether it be the code of the Stoic or the Pharisee, the monk, or the Puritan. And "duty" as the keystone of ethics leaves much to be desired. It is sombre, straining and straitened. It freezes "the genial current of the soul." It catechizes every simple pleasure to make sure that it is truly re-creational and brings everything to the severe test of its effect on soul-health. It rations laughter and on leisure it looks askance.

Strict duty takes no heed of circumstances—which is only another way of saying that it takes no heed of common life. A lie is a lie—even when it can prevent a massacre. It dreads an exception like the plague and hides behind the rule, fearing to face the scrutiny of actual fact.

Right at its heart there is a holy egoism. Because its own rectitude or sanctity is the undeviating aim and not the adoration of God or the love of one's neighbour, self sits enthroned. Not a crude self, but a self in sack-cloth and ashes, an immolating and macerating self—but still self! Just as egoism may express itself in the secretive but unresting scheming to be a dictator, a bishop, or a party-boss, so it can essay this flinty road of duty to be a saint. Whole areas of life will be willingly sacrificed to it, and (half-unconsciously) the happiness of relatives as well, and the selfishness is so hard to unmask because it wears a halo. God alone knows the truth about our souls but, in the degree that we can stand it, He is not unwilling to tell. Charles Wesley prayed:

> Teach me, *as my soul can bear*,
> The depth of inbred sin.

And one of the hardest things to bear is the discovery that our passionate devotion to "duty" as the means to holiness may be a disguise of exhibitionism and that the concept of duty, in any case, is not free, or vital, or wide enough, for the full purposes of God.

Jacobi's protest against Kant's moral rigorism is well known:

"I am the Atheist, the Godless one, who, in spite of the will that wills nothing, am ready to lie as the dying Desdemona lied; to lie and deceive like Pylades, when he pretended to be Orestes; to murder like Timoleon; to break law and oath like Epaminondas, like John de Witt; to commit suicide with Otho and sacrilege with David—yea, to rub the ears of corn on the Sabbath day, merely because I am hungry, and because *the law is made for the sake of man and not man for the sake of the law....*"[1]

It is not an accident that the men who have most given themselves to the slavish observance of duty—Stoics, Pharisees, ascetic monks and Puritans—are, for the most part, hard and cheerless souls. They seem to have been quarried, not born. Noble and austerely splendid as their best types unquestionably are, they fail in one of the chief tests of true sanctity; and prove that this is a false path for us. They are not *happy*, and the flaw is fatal. They could not pray with George MacDonald, "Lord, make my spirit good and *gay*." They do not recognise joy as a necessary mark of the saint, and they would make all life not merely serious (which, of course, it is) but solemn (which it need not be).[2]

Into how different a world we come when we come into the world of supernatural love. This is no sum of negatives. Sin, it is true, is expelled by "the expulsive power of a new affection" but one is not left with a holy void. Christian morality is not a list of things to be left undone. It is an active, vital principle, positive, rich, pulsating with eager life. It touches other life on all sides. It enters into a hundred relationships and glows with the gladness of fraternity.

How sharp the change is from the chill world of duty may be judged by imagining a home in which everybody is busy trying to do his duty and contrasting it with a normal Christian family thrilling with impulsive love. What a nightmarish place the home would become with children and parents constantly reflecting on the call of moral obligation in this situation and in that, and never abandoning themselves to the simple impulses of unreflecting affection!

[1] Quoted by Mackenzie, *A Manual of Ethics* (5th Edn.), 200 *f.*
[2] For the survival of Puritanism and the lack of joy in J. H. Newman, see von Hügel, *Essays and Addresses on the Philosophy of Religion* (Second Series), 242.

Now Wesley never tired of insisting that love was the main-spring of the holy life and, having made the world his parish, he saw that no human being could be excluded from God's family life. What, perhaps, Wesley did not see but what we may notice with more than ordinary interest was that, had he held to his better title of perfect love and permitted nothing to deflect his stress from it, certain serious defects in his doctrine would never have developed.

For instance, it has been widely felt, as we have noticed in Chapter IX, that his definition of sin is defective. He held that it was a voluntary transgression of a known law. But this ill-assorts with the idea of perfect love as the mainspring of holiness. Sin is more adequately and extensively defined as a failure in perfect love and, if it is so defined, the definition will pass the most rigorous scrutiny. If, indeed, it seems to fail as a definition, it fails (if that were possible) by excess and not by defect, but, whatever be the truth about this, Wesley would not have been led off into sterile discussions about whether sin could be eradicated or not. The weight of the doctrine would have rested elsewhere and "sinlessness" would have been thrust from the forefront of thought simply as a happy consequence, if God so gave it, of something positive and more important still.

Nor will it be forgotten that Wesley's defective doctrine of sin is nowhere more defective than in its failure to deal with the sins of omission. How could it? If sin is a voluntary transgression of a known law, the sin is the positive thing and the holiness (reversing Browning) "is null, is nought, is silence implying sound." Those subtle, sometimes chronic and always deeply serious sins of omission have slipped through the net. No known law has been transgressed. Yet they remain a deadly leprosy of the soul and fruitful of the most terrible penalty which can overtake humankind.[1]

But holiness conceived as perfect love is utterly free of this defect. Love has a keener vision than duty. It notices things. It could not tolerate the year-in-and-year-out neglect of dear ones which the most dutiful men in some moment of self-revelation have discovered in themselves, and recognised in the very second of awareness as the fruit of deep self-centredness. If someone had drawn Tennyson's notice to the fact that, in the poem of dedication he had written to the gracious lady who was his wife, four lines were about her and the other nine about

[1] Heb. ii. 3.

himself, he would probably have been astonished. A sense of self-importance is myopic: it blinds as it grows. No reflections on duty can clear the vision. The sin is too subtle and the test is too coarse.

But supernatural love can reveal it. It has vision. It does not lumber forward by ratiocination: love *divines*.

Not only would Wesley, had he both held to the name and put the stress on perfect love, have avoided these defects in his doctrine, but the weakness of his great synthesis would not have developed so obviously. If we found it impossible—and we did—to accept the reasoning that, because we have faith in God for our justification, we must have faith in God for our sanctification also (when that second phrase is taken as meaning entire sanctification imparted in a moment) we did so only because the static idea of sinlessness was set up as the goal, and attention was directed to a sum of negations. The synthesis would not have been unchallengeable had the thought been all directed towards perfect love, but the integration swifter and the cohesion closer, and a dynamic love would have knit together "the ethic of grace and the ethic of holiness."

The positivity of love is the answer to each of these weaknesses, for the fruit of goodness is not found by lopping off healthy branches of the tree of life, or exalting asceticism to the skies. Hating oneself can become as obsessional as hating others. Not purgation and more purgation, but love and more love. The way forward is to let purgation be the by-product and let love crowd sin out. "We are not saved by what we know, but by what we love." [1]

And, in addition to these considerable gains from centring all in perfect love, the *given-ness* of holiness so conceived would have been far more intelligible than Wesley's exposition sometimes left it. To be made holy in a moment, when holiness is thought of as eradicated sin, seems to savour more of magic than of religion, and leaves the plain man sadly perplexed and asking, "How can holiness be *given*: surely holiness can only be *achieved*?"

But, if the stress is kept on love, while its given-ness may still outrun experience, it will carry no hint of contradiction on its face. For even the plain man knows that there is a given-ness about love—even human love. He cannot explain its rise in his own heart and yet he will not deny that it is there and that it is an ultimate in the realm of motive. If, enquiring the reason of the

[1] Cell, 349.

most sacrificial deed, he receives the simple answer, "She loved," he asks no more. The enquiry is over for him and all other questions die on his lips.

Nor is it a big step in thought from the given-ness of human love to the given-ness of divine love. Faith can take it. It may seem like a step in the dark but there are not only human analogies: there is a wealth of Christian testimony. Of nothing do the witnesses of this experience speak more than of the love of God which expanded their hearts, seeped through their whole beings, and overflowed in love to all. That it was supernatural love may be proven by the simple test we have offered before: it is not confined to the channels of natural affinity. Like their Lord, the recipients of His love love where they do not like. It is impossible to think that Christ *liked* rotting lepers, bloated publicans, loose women or wild demoniacs; yet it is undeniable that He *loved* them.

Those to whom, in response to faith, He gives this supernatural love, love in that way. It is not more of the love they had before: it is love with a new quality. Like Saul Kane in Masefield's *The Everlasting Mercy*, they feel—

that Christ has given them birth, to brother all the souls on earth,

for, while this love begins with conversion, it has come to multitudes in still richer measure through the spiritual experience which it is the purpose of this monograph to examine. Commissioner Brengle's witness will serve as example. He begins his little book on this theme with the startling sentence, "On January 9th, 1885, at about nine o'clock in the morning, God sanctified my soul," and then goes on:

"It was a Heaven of love that came into my heart. I walked out over Boston Common before breakfast, weeping for joy and praising God. Oh, how I loved! In that hour I knew Jesus, and I loved Him till it seemed my heart would break in love. I loved the sparrows, I loved the dogs, I loved the horses, I loved the little urchins on the streets, I loved the strangers who hurried past me, I loved the heathen—I loved the whole world."[1]

The heart of the experience is love—and love is a gift. When the moralist, in keen defence of ethical principle, asserts that holiness

[1] Brengle, *Helps to Holiness*, iii *f.*

cannot be given, this is the reply. The heart of holiness so conceived is supernatural love—and love is a gift. With J. B. Mozley we may say:

"Love in the Gospel sense is that general virtue which covers the motives; like some essence which we can hardly get at, it is not itself so much as it is the goodness of everything *else* in us; not a virtue so much as a substratum of all virtues; the virtue *of* virtue, the goodness *of* goodness."[1]

Love is the key to holiness.

One serious challenge to this view must be noted before we leave this phase of the problem. Dr. P. T. Forsyth, in his little book, *Christian Perfection*, restates with trenchancy and great aphoristic skill what might be called the Zinzendorf tradition concerning holiness.[2] He defends a sinful perfection as against a sinless perfection. He insists that *perfection is not sanctity but faith.*[3] Visitations of sin have a ministry in the redeemed life: they are a barrier against spiritual pride and a motive for faith. "To cease to feel defect is to cease to trust."[4]

It is not hard to imagine the kind of reply which Wesley would have made to this. He would, no doubt, have answered certain of the points separately and insisted that he argued for no absolute and infallible perfection from which all sense of immaturity was excluded, and certainly that he robbed none of his followers of a sense or need of trust. He would have replied also to Forsyth's unexceptionable remark that "it is better to trust in God in humiliated repentance than to revel in a sense of sinlessness"[5] by saying that his people were not encouraged to revel in a sense of sinlessness, and none who has read his *Advices*, or Fletcher's *Address to Perfect Christians*, could doubt his word. To the suggestion that a little sin keeps one humble, he would have replied with Fletcher that this opened the door to antinomianism,[6] and perhaps he would have endorsed the retort of a much simpler expositor of his teaching who replied to the same defence of a little harboured sin by saying, "Why not have a great deal, and be perfectly humble?"[7] His deep objection, however, to the case set out by Dr. Forsyth would be the same which he held against

---

[1] J. B. Mozley, *University Sermons*, 32 (edit. 1876).   [2] See p. 125.
[3] Forsyth, *Christian Perfection*, 84.   [4] *ibid.*, 12.   [5] *ibid.*, 134.
[6] Fletcher's *Works*, vi, 280 *ff*.   [7] Cook, *New Testament Holiness*, 49.

similar teaching in the eighteenth century and which we have
noticed as explaining his hesitating approval of Luther at certain
points. The contention does not deal seriously enough with sin.
God utterly abhors evil, and wills to deliver us from it. Between
God and sin there can be no compromise, and all talk about
"visitations" of evil which have a half-beneficent ministry is a
dreadful ignoring both of its deadly nature and also of the fact
that it never just "visits": it stains and stays.

But it is Dr. Forsyth's attitude to love which concerns us most
now. Perfect love, as Wesley conceived it, carried sinlessness as
a consequence. Love, as Forsyth thought of it, is "faith in its
supreme and perfect form . . . the impassioned expression on the
face of faith,"[1] but *not* sinlessness. And this is only to express
again, and from another angle, the major difference which we
have noticed above. Yet it is not only a *difference*. The similarity
is almost more impressive. Wesley, passionately pursuing his
ideal of sinlessness, can find no better title or richer conception
for the ideal than perfect love. Forsyth, insisting that salvation is
by faith, and regarding sinlessness as half a delusion and half a
snare, is convinced that the maturity of faith is love. Both roads
converge in love.

It would be folly to ignore the depth or importance of the
difference, but it is surely no extravagance of hope to see in
this confluence of thought the promise of a new synthesis, and
to anticipate not only the union of "the Protestant ethic of grace
with the Catholic ethic of holiness" but also the reconciliation of
the two chief schools of thought on sanctification in Protestantism
itself.

Clement of Rome, writing to the Corinthians, says, "By love
all the elect of God were perfected,"[2] and by love, also, we shall
see more aspects of that many-faceted thing called Truth.

---

[1] Forsyth, *Christian Perfection*, 5.

[2] *The First Epistle of Clement to the Corinthians*, XLIX (Lowther Clarke translation,
p. 76).

CHAPTER XX

NO MAN KNOWS WHAT IS IN HIM

WE come now to the hardest and least defensible part of Wesley's doctrine: the part which concerns assurance.

Assurance was a dominant note in his effective preaching from the beginning. He held that a man could not only be saved but *know* that he was saved. He said, "When God pardons a mourning, broken-hearted sinner, His mercy obliges Him to another act—to witness to his spirit that He has pardoned him."[1] His mercy obliges Him! . . . God is committed to it. So Wesley believed and so he taught.

It was on this point that Wesley parted with Jeremy Taylor as his trusted mentor. Taylor held, "A true penitent must all the days of his life pray for pardon and never think the work completed till he dies. Whether God has forgiven us or no we know not, therefore still be sorrowful for ever having sinned."[2] Wesley repudiated that as he would have repudiated John Henry Newman's similar criticism of assurance and his firmly expressed conviction that all we may have is a sober trust.[3] "God's mercy obliged Him to do more than pardon" said Wesley: it obliged Him to put a glad confidence in the penitent's heart that all was forgiven.

This assurance is not well described as "feeling" if feeling is thought of as some swelling tide of emotion. Wesley was not an emotional man himself and references to his feelings are not common in his *Journal* and *Letters*, once the Revival had begun. In fact, the desire to feel *more* is a more recurrent note than the actual expression of feelings,[4] yet of feeling for feeling's sake he was justly suspicious. It is probable that what Mrs. Rogers had in mind when she wrote, "I must feel, or I cannot be happy,"[5] would not have won the approval of John Wesley. He once remarked of his saintly mother that her feelings for others were by no means as strong as those of his poetic father— but she *did* ten times more.[6] This must be borne in mind by any

---

[1] *Letters*, iii, 138. [2] *ibid.*, i, 19.
[3] *Apologia*, 6 (1890 Edn.). [4] *Letters*, vii, 319. [5] Rogers, 72.
[6] *Letters*, vi, 18.

who would banish Wesley's teaching on assurance as simply
"feeling" and particularly in assessing the worth, say, of Dr. J. B.
Mozley's criticism of Wesley's doctrine of Christian Perfection,
where feeling would appear to be the whole subjective test.[1]

A psychological examination of the spiritual intuition which
Wesley called "The Witness of the Spirit" is not in the line of
our main purpose now. It is important only to remark that he
carried over, without any apparent sense of crossing a gulf, the
conviction that we could be assured that our sins were forgiven,
and affirmed that we could be assured of our sanctification as well.
It is impossible to believe that a man of Wesley's mental acuteness
was unaware of the different character of these assurances, or
counted it as unimportant that one could be submitted to tests
which were impossible for the other.

But I can find no discussion in his writings of the difference.
He believed that one could be free of all conscious sin and could
enjoy God's assurance of the fact. Of that happy state he advised
his people (not without warnings against pride and the possibility
of self-deception) to speak aloud and tell the world what God had
done for them. To keep silent concerning so wonderful a blessing
was dishonouring to God and impoverishing to one's neighbour.

How many people took his advice?

He did not take it himself. It may be, though Wesley's conviction that this was the privilege of all believers casts more than a
little doubt on the idea, that the blessing he urged on others had
passed him by. But this is certain. The most convinced adherents
of his teaching have been unable to discover him making this
bold claim for himself. The man who sedulously sought this
testimony in others and exulted over it when he found it, is
himself dumb on the point. Samuel Bradburn is reported to have
asked him on one occasion to give his own experience, and he
answered:

> Jesus, confirm my heart's desire
>   To work, and speak, and think for Thee;
> Still let me guard the holy fire,
>   And still stir up Thy gift in me;
>
> Ready for all Thy perfect will,
>   My acts of faith and love repeat,
> Till death Thy endless mercies seal,
>   And make the sacrifice complete.

[1] J. B. Mozley, *Lectures and Other Theological Papers*, 178.

L

It was no answer. That was only aspiration, and aspiration creates no problems: it is the claim to have achieved (or received) which startles thought.

Nor did his brother Charles make the claim. Indeed, Charles became so fearful of the unbalanced irresponsibles who were proclaiming themselves as holy as the angels[1] that, as we have seen, he wrote solemn admonitions in verse against the dangers of this public avowal of holiness.

> The purest saint that lives below
>   Doth his own sanctity disclaim,
> The wisest owns I nothing know,
>   The holiest cries, I nothing am.

and—

> Whene'er Thou dost Thy grace bestow,
> Lest *proudly* I the blessing *shew*,
>   A second grace impart,
> "Tell it to none"—with vain delight,
> "Tell it to none"—in mercy write
>   Upon my broken heart.[2]

And, strangely enough in some ways, it is as hard almost to find in the literature of early Methodism as it is in the New Testament, the plain statement, "I am freed from all sin." Thomas Walsh, who seemed to his contemporaries to be clearly enjoying the experience, declined to make the public affirmation and solemnly adjured the friend who received his private witness to give it no more publicity.[3] Indeed, it is astonishing how comparatively little there is in all *The Lives of Early Methodist Preachers* about *this* assurance. Some of them make no reference to it at all. Some of them only added their testimony to it as a postscript and when Wesley reminded them.[4] None of them enjoys it in the hour he is writing.

The one clear, unequivocal witness of the phrase, "I am freed from sin," is the saintly and widely honoured John William Fletcher, Vicar of Madeley. He made the claim, as we have noted,

---

[1] *Letters*, iv, 192.

[2] *Short Hymns on Select Passages of Holy Scripture*, ii, 151; cf. Rattenbury, *The Evangelical Doctrines of Charles Wesley's Hymns*, 304.

[3] *Lives of E.M.P.*, iii, 225.

[4] *Arminian Magazine*, 1779, 594. 1780, 202.

in Leeds on August 24th, 1781,[1] four years before he died, and said that he had received the blessing four or five times previously but had lost it through not confessing it. We owe the story to Mrs. Hester Ann Rogers, who was present and whose evidence there is no reasonable ground to doubt, but I can trace the statement in that form nowhere in Fletcher's own considerable writings.

Certainly, he always writes from that angle, and it is hard to imagine that any man could set down the *Address to Perfect Christians*[2] and still hesitate at the statement attributed to him by Mrs. Rogers. Yet Wesley hesitated. His *Advices* are not less from the "inside" than Fletcher's *Address*, but, if Wesley ever trembled on the edge of saying, "I am freed from sin"—

> . . . something seal'd
> The lips of that Evangelist.

Here, surely, is the significant point. When the normal devout souls testified to this "second blessing," they testified in terms of love. The stress fell there. They are "filled with love," or "conscious of nothing but love," or "loving everybody they know." They did not normally talk of being "freed from all sin." If the teaching of their spiritual father permitted and even encouraged such language (with the definitions and reservations he had laid down) it was still not the natural language of their adoring hearts.

They talked of supernatural love. Something, they felt, had been given to them that was not of this earth and it burned with love in them even for those at whose hands they had suffered persecution. They dwelt on the positive and active side of this new experience: not on its negations and exclusions, wonderful though some of them might be.

And here we find ourselves in harmony with conclusions we have already reached by other paths. Wesley's spiritual instinct, and that of the mass of his people, was sounder than Wesley's logic. The stress belongs to supernatural love, not eradicated sin. There are deep, deep reasons why no man can say, with all respect to the saintly Fletcher, "I am freed from all sin." It is, indeed, a thing *not* to say. It is gravely dangerous to utter such sentiments. If it costs any students of this teaching a pang to part with Wesley

---

[1] Rogers, 224-9.   [2] Fletcher's *Works*, vi, 400 *ff*.

at this point, it must console them to remember that, if they have
rejected his counsel, they have followed his example.

Why is it dangerous for anyone, even a devout soul conscious
of nothing but supernatural love, to say, "I am freed from all
sin"?

First, because they are using the words with a limited meaning,
the limitations of which may not be clear to the people who hear
the witness. They mean, "I am not *conscious* of committing sin,"
and the worth of a testimony of that character necessarily turns
on the sensitivity of the conscience of the person giving it. It
may mean a great deal: it may mean very little.

Secondly, a claim of this tremendous character is hard to
harmonise with a moment-by-moment life. The witness may be
intended to refer only to the moment of its utterance but no-one
used to the normal commerce of conversation would hear it that
way. Indeed, it is questionable whether, with the definition of
sin here used, the statement is in any way remarkable and whether,
if it refers only to the moment of its utterance, it is worth making
at all.

Thirdly—and more deeply—if the words are understood to
have any reference beyond the immediate moment (and normally
they are) it is a witness shaped in ignorance because no man knows
what is in him. We have noticed already that a man may be an
utter stranger both to a certain sin and even to temptation at that
point, not because his nature is invulnerable there but only
because his circumstances have never presented it.[1] The tendency
to it may be in him all the time.

Did David, composing one of his sublime psalms, ever suppose
that he could be the seducer of Bathsheba and the virtual murderer
of her husband? Or Peter, protesting undying loyalty to his Lord,
so much as imagine that he would thrice deny Him before the
cock crew? Did Bishop Andrewes, weeping over the manuscript
of his *Private Prayers*, and beseeching God for holiness, dream
that he could be guilty of the paltry partisanship and sad infamy
which have stained his name? Or Samuel Rutherford, making the
shadow of the Almighty his permanent abode, guess at the
fierceness of passion which would shake his soul when engaged
in a quarrel?

We cannot think it. Surely, in the depth of their penitence, we
may read the measure of their horror. They did not know what

[1] See p. 135.

was in them. No man knows. Happy in the memory of past mercies and multiplying spiritual victories, a man may travel with increasing confidence and quiet peace, and he will exult particularly in this glorious gift of supernatural love, but he will not say, "I am freed from all sin." God *may* free a soul from sin while still in the body. Who dare put a limit to the grace of God? The glorious possibility beckons every aspiring soul. But He will not tell him that it is done. The angels may whisper it to one another. Other men may feel sure that a saint is in their midst. But he himself will not say, "I am freed from all sin." Rather will he say with Paul, "I judge not mine own self . . . He that judgeth me is the Lord."[1]

Fourthly, the awful danger of presumption and pride, and the self-induced spiritual blindness which is a recurring phenomenon of this claim, should check every public utterance that all sin has gone.

That it is a recurring phenomenon of this teaching (particularly in its extreme forms) is indisputable. If the critics of this doctrine have exaggerated the danger, and fastened their attention on the sad and rare calamities rather than on the blameless and lovely lives of those who have adorned the doctrine, it still remains true that the danger is there, that sin is peculiarly horrible in those who claim perfection, and that it is not to be set down simply to the common frailty of men. There is a particular *reason* for this particular phenomenon.

If a man is convinced that he is free from all sin: if, moreover, by some freak of faith he is convinced also that to doubt his freedom from sin is dishonouring to God and tantamount to disbelieving the Bible, he will necessarily be less likely to recognise the presence of sin when it rises in his soul. With his own hands he has built a wall between himself and self-knowledge. He puts a bandage around his own eyes whenever he looks inwards, though when he looks outwards on others it often appears that his eyes are not only unbandaged but sharp with censoriousness. Normally, he has two standards, or, if he has but one, it is only for other people: the perfect outsoar every gauge. I have known a devotee of "holiness" speak with scorn of folk who would make *any* use of a train on the Sabbath day, yet use the same train on a week-day himself and only buy a half-ticket for his child over fourteen. "She is quite small," he said.

It is remotely far from my mind to suggest that this double

[1] 1 Cor. iv. 3 *f.*

morality is common among the claimants to perfection, but no one can become a close student either of the literature or the lives of these believers without meeting it. The best of their leaders know the danger.

How swiftly censoriousness sometimes follows in the wake of this assurance may be judged from the unhappy instance of the drunkard whom God used Father Stanton to convert. "Go and get drunk again," was Stanton's terrible interruption of his bitter criticisms of other people. "I liked you better then."

Nor does the danger of this moral blindness belong only to odd individuals. It has often been remarked that the last defence of slavery was made from a pulpit, and it is not hard to imagine the cogent case which could be made out for its continuance from the slave-holding habits of the Hebrew patriarchs and the fact that Paul sent a runaway slave back to his master.

There is a bill of sale still extant belonging to the slave-owning days in America in which the effects of a church deacon recently dead are offered to the highest bidder. Successive items are:

> A library, chiefly theological.
> Nine slaves, very prime.

The question has been asked: Could the library (chiefly theological) redeem the nine slaves (very prime)?

The Society for the Propagation of the Gospel not only owned slaves but did not deny using the driving-whip years after Parliament had condemned it.[1]

But our concern is not chiefly with these instances, nor yet with the slow exposure of a double morality in the corporate thinking of the Church. We are concerned with the moral blindness of good people which Christ so heartily denounced when He said:

> "Woe unto you, scribes and Pharisees, hypocrites! for ye tithe mint and anise and cummin, and have left undone the weightier matters of the law, judgment, and mercy, and faith. . . ."[2]

How does it happen that these moral experts go wrong? Doubtless in the way we have suggested. Instead of keeping the stress on love they have thought of sinlessness and made it a

---

[1] Mathieson, *British Slavery and its Abolition: 1823–1838*, 216 (footnote).
[2] Matt. xxiii. 23.

cardinal article of faith to believe that it has already been wrought in their hearts. The idea that one has already achieved becomes, therefore, an impediment to spiritual progress. The yearning soul, conscious of nothing but God-given affection, yet panting for more, is displaced by a soul which is subtly content, and the heart from which active sin would have been crowded out by that high and expanding love now has room to admit the masked envoys of evil. So "sanctity" and sin live together in the heart. In some senses they so live in the heart of most men but with a difference. God can still work in the heart of a man conscious of need; but those unconscious of it make themselves incapable of progress even in the hands of the Almighty.

There is, perhaps, but little value in pointing out also how impermanent is the assurance of complete cleansing seeing that most people who believe in it follow Wesley in believing also that sin can enter again the fully sanctified heart (even in their sense of the word "sin") and rob the most assured of their assurance. It would, perhaps, savour too much of a mere debating point to raise the question, "If the heart is completely cleansed, where did the sin come from which made them need complete cleansing again, and will not this sad memory cast doubt on the new assurance when it comes?" From the primary misconception of sin as a "thing" all these confusions flow.

There is but one way for earnest and adoring souls to witness to the mighty love which God gives to those who ask Him. They must so live that other people will be forced to find the explanation of their lovely lives in Christ. When the inevitable questions arise, they can attempt to whisper the open if unspeakable secret of it and say that this is God's free gift of supernatural love through faith in Christ. They will be careful to speak seven words about Him for every single word about themselves, and when, having done their utmost, they feel with poor Cordelia—

> I cannot heave my heart into my mouth;
> I am sure my love's more ponderous than my tongue,

it will comfort them to remember that the convincing witness is not their word but their life. One thing they will never say; "I am freed from all sin."

CHAPTER XXI

A PERFECT LIFE IN AN IMPERFECT WORLD?

ON the evening of July 27th, 1879, in Carrs Lane Chapel, Birmingham, Dr. R. W. Dale, the distinguished divine and educational reformer, delivered an address on the Evangelical Revival. The address became famous in Free Church circles—and beyond. Speaking with appreciation, and yet with real detachment, Dr. Dale attempted a dispassionate appraisal of the work of Wesley and his helpers, and, in the course of it, he said:

> "There was one doctrine of John Wesley's—the doctrine of perfect sanctification—which ought to have led to a great and original ethical development; but the doctrine has not grown; it seems to remain just where John Wesley left it. There has been a want of the genius or the courage to attempt the solution of the immense practical questions which the doctrine suggests. The questions have not been raised—much less solved. To have raised them effectively, indeed, would have been to originate an ethical revolution which would have had a far deeper effect on the thought and life—first of England, and then of the rest of Christendom—than was produced by the Reformation of the sixteenth century."[1]

Dr. Dale did not further develop his point. It is not possible to say, with complete conviction, precisely in what directions he looked for the "great and original ethical development" and exactly where, in his opinion, "genius and courage" were lacking; but enough is known of his own approach to Christian truth and sufficient is plain concerning the deficiencies of Wesley's doctrine to leave no reasonable doubt of the area of Dr. Dale's disappointment. The doctrine received no adequate *social* development, though it had social *consequences*. The most narrowly individualistic teaching, as we have seen, has social consequences. It *must* have, because no life in this world is possible with complete segregation; the tendrils of personality, even in the most hermit-like soul, intertwine with those of others, and strongly

[1] *The Evangelical Revival and Other Sermons*, 39.

held convictions, or richly received grace, will reach a man's neighbour whether the man wills it or not.

But Dr. Dale held that the gospel is social in its nature and not merely in its implications, and he believed that sanctification, being part of the gospel, is social by nature too. It seemed to him a major misfortune that the burning passion for perfection which he had noticed in Wesley, and in the early Methodists, did not issue in a doctrine of social perfection or, at least, of social regeneration. So complete, indeed, were their individual pre-occupations that, so far as Dr. Dale could judge, they were not even aware of the deficiency and failed to raise the questions at all. The urgent, inescapable question, "Is it possible to live a perfect life in an imperfect world?" which presses so hardly on every keen, modern pilgrim of perfection, seems never to have seriously bothered them. God, they felt, dealt with them as individuals. In the secret recesses of the soul every man is a solitary. We come to all the high moments of life alone. So we are born and so we die. So also we are born again. What John Henry Newman said of himself is true, in its degree, of all men. In that awesome moment, when a self-conscious sinner holds tryst with the Almighty, he is aware of nothing but "two and two only absolute and luminously self-evident beings, myself and my Creator."[1]

If some precursor of Dr. Dale had challenged the simple souls, whose testimony meeting we attended, concerning the individual emphasis of all their thought on holiness, hesitatingly, perhaps, and with their sweet and unaffected simplicity, they would have answered in that way. The only social holiness they could conceive was a combination of individual instances of holiness. To the men of their time personality was wholly individual, and such expressions as "the group mind" (had the phrase then been coined) would have seemed to them little more than a strained metaphor. For them, holiness was intrinsically individual and they would have regarded any subtle distinctions between *individuals* and *persons* as pedantry. Man in his separateness, and man in his relations, was a stratification of thought but never of life, and into the consequences of their limited thinking they felt no need to go.

But there is a price to pay for all neglect—especially in thinking. If holiness has become the occupation of coteries and the serious concern only of conventions; if the people who pursue it most

[1] J. H. Newman, *Apologia*, 4 (1890 Edn.).

assiduously seem to their neighbours to be almost detached from the world (and to rejoice in their detachment); if more and more of the richness of life (poetry, art, music, fun, sport, the drama) are thrown away, and a distinction is not always made between the sensuous and the sensual; if it is counted as a virtue to live in a spiritual world within this material world, and not to struggle with all the difficult compromises involved in translating the one into the other . . . if this be true of the people who have made holiness a "hobby," it is partly because this distinction between individuals and persons has not been made, or been made only to be despised as "academic."

Nowhere is this clearer than in William Law, who, as we have noted, was among the first to inspire Wesley with an interest in Christian Perfection. Law says, drawing to the close of his moving book, *A Practical Treatise upon Christian Perfection*:

"It now only remains, that I exhort the Reader to labour after this Christian Perfection. Were I to exhort anyone to the Study of *Poetry* or *Eloquence*, to labour to be *Rich* and *Great*, or to spend his Time in *Mathematics* or other Learning, I could only produce such Reasons as are fit to delude the Vanity of Men, who are ready to be taken with any Appearance of Excellence. For if the same Person were to ask me, what it signifies to be a *Poet* or *Eloquent*, what Advantage it would be to him, to be a great *Mathematician*, or a great *Statesman*, I must be forced to answer, that these Things would signify just as much to him, as they now signify to those Poets, Orators, Mathematicians, and Statesmen, whose Bodies have been a long while lost amongst common Dust. . . . For when we are at the *Top* of all human Attainments, we are still at the *Bottom* of all human Misery, and have made no further Advancement towards true Happiness, than those, whom we see in the Want of all these Excellences. Whether a Man die before he has written *Poems*, compiled *Histories*, or raised an *Estate*, signifies no more than whether he died an hundred, or a thousand Years ago." [1]

Nothing could be plainer. Verse, eloquence, statesmanship, scholarship, mathematics, business: nothing matters. Only holiness! But it is a holiness lean, ascetic, solemn and pitifully

[1] Law's *Works*, iii, 232 *f*.

unattractive. Put at its crudest it comes to this. God is interested in us only when we are saying our prayers.

The influence of Methodism on social conditions has been much discussed. J. L. and B. Hammond take the view that, while communal good came from the Evangelical Revival, it was a limited and narrowed benefit, and, on the balance, they incline to the idea that it was an obstruction rather than a help to social progress. "The teaching of Methodism was unfavourable to working-class movements." They are led to contrast, for instance, the spirit of Methodism and the spirit of the trade unions. Methodism taught patience: the trade unions impatience. Methodism taught resignation in evil conditions: the trade unions mobilised opposition. Methodism stressed spiritual individualism: the trade unions made class loyalty a virtue. Even the Methodist's neighbourly love, it is argued, was only a method to get one's neighbour converted.[1]

Shrewd and just as many of these comments are, they are not balanced. They take no deeply serious account (though they mention it) of the incontestable fact that many early leaders of the trade-union movement were Methodists, and that their passion for social progress was not at variance with their religion but related to it. The Tolpuddle Martyrs would be inexplicable if the Hammonds were entirely right. Dr. Rattenbury suggests that the authors of *The Town Labourer* erred in judgment by assuming that the then entirely clerical Conference of the Wesleyan Church was a clear mouthpiece of the mind of all Methodism.[2]

That was far from the truth. There were other branches of Methodism and, even within the Wesleyan Church, there were strong opponents of those who usually shaped the Conference resolutions. Nor must it be assumed too easily that the conservative school which did produce and carry the resolutions was composed entirely of smug reactionaries. If Methodism saved England from the kind of terror which tore France from end to end—and eminent historians incline to the view that it did—the explanation is to be sought in the unwillingness of its leaders to identify their movement with the aims of the passionate (and largely free-thinking) radicals of the day, who would have hurried the country into bloody revolution as swiftly as their counterparts across the Channel.

Élie Halévy gives a fairer picture of the times. Soberly he

[1] J. L. and B. Hammond, *The Town Labourer: 1760–1832*, 277–87.
[2] Rattenbury, *Wesley's Legacy to the World*, 226.

surveys the facts. Perhaps his concern is more to explain how in England social changes have "been accomplished with such a marked and gradual continuity"[1] rather than to study in some isolation the conditions of the working man; but his tribute to Methodism, while far from being uncritical, is full and ungrudging.[2] It will always be a mystery to those who are strangers to the experience of evangelical conversion why evangelists are not "sensible" social reformers. No doubt John Wesley was as confusing to William Cobbett as Jesus Christ was to Simon the Zealot. But Simon the Zealot came to understand. If tradition may be trusted, he had the chance after the Crucifixion of joining in a revolution or going as a missionary. He went as a missionary.

But let us step still closer to the facts. It is not enough to talk about the "concern" of these perfectionists even with social *conditions*. We need some analysis of their "concern."

If we think in terms of social *salvage* they were and are in the very van of the host of God. The poor sufferers from the sad conditions of life were the constant objects of their pity and help. They suckled a hundred philanthropies. The sick, the widows, the orphans, the unemployed: the drunkards, harlots, smugglers, slaves: all were the recipients of their care. If they did not give sufficient thought to the economic reasons why multitudes then got drunk, or women took to the streets, or coast-dwellers prayed for a wreck, that lack of reflection did not prevent their naming these poor, abandoned souls as their brothers and sisters and doing their utmost for them. Charles Wesley was more than half a snob before he was converted, but two days after the experience came he wrote:

> Outcasts of men, to you I call,
>   Harlots and publicans and thieves!
> He spreads His arms to embrace you all;
>   Sinners alone His grace receives. . . .
> He calls you now, invites you home:
> Come, O my guilty *brethren*, come!

Nor was this salvage work confined to picking up the broken pieces of an ill-adjusted economic system. There was constructive social service involved in it as well. It is true that there is a noble monotony about Wesley's *Journal*. Taken as a whole, it would

---

[1] Halévy, *A History of the English People in 1815*, i, 335.
[2] *ibid.*, 371 *f.*, 389 *f.*, 393, 399 *f.*

seem that its author had no interest in anything but *souls*. Read more carefully, however, and taken in conjunction with his other writings, it is clear that a keen mind and a shrewd judgment were busy not only with the bodily needs of men but with the deeper, harder questions concerning the origin of those needs and were considering how the social maladjustments might be overcome. The acquisition and use of wealth,[1] the economic consequences of luxury,[2] the shifting population from the country to the towns,[3] the problem of unemployment[4] and the limits of legitimate speculation,[5] all receive some comment from him. In the thinking of to-day, many of the comments may seem naïve, but any sound judgment upon them is compelled to make allowances for the limited ideas of an earlier age. Even to expect such an approach to the problem as, for instance, Dr. Garvie's, in *The Christian Ideal for Human Society*, is unreasonable. Convinced as Wesley was that "Christianity is essentially a social religion; and that to turn it into a solitary one is to destroy it,"[6] it is not to be expected that he had seen all that was involved in this under the principle that T. H. Green made explicit:

> "It is equally true that the human spirit can only realise itself, or fulfil its idea, in persons, and that it can only do so through society, since society is the condition of the development of a personality."[7]

As Green also points out, there is always a standard of ultimate good beckoning a man above conventional morality but it cannot be individualistic.

> "That standard is an ideal of a perfect life for himself and other men, as attainable for him only through them, for them only through him; a life that shall be perfect in the sense of being the fulfilment of all that the human spirit in him and them has the real capacity or vocation of becoming, and which (as is implied in its being such fulfilment) shall rest on the will to be perfect."[8]

Dr. Cell comments on "the naïveté of Wesley's economic

[1] *Sermons*, ii,309. [2] *Works*, iii, 271, vii, 250, viii, 162 f, xi, 56, 157.
[3] *ibid.*, iv, 73, xi, 142 f. [4] *ibid.*, xi, 54 f.
[5] *ibid.*, viii, 164. [6] *Sermons*, i, 381 f.
[7] Green, *Prolegomena to Ethics*, 201. [8] *ibid.*, 419.

ideas and the remedies proposed" and shows that, whatever merit they had in the eighteenth century, they hardly possess it now.[1] The matted problems associated with the acquisition and use of money are not solved with the simple sermon divisions, "Gain all you can: save all you can: give all you can." Indeed, it is hard to believe, however much he preached his simple remedy for economic ills, that a man of Wesley's mental stature really believed that he was commending a complete cure.

It has never been seriously claimed as a fruit of evangelical conversion, or the gift of perfect love, that it made a man a brilliant political economist or a Christian sociologist of the first order. It *is* claimed—and weighty evidence substantiates the claim—that the entry of the Holy Spirit into a man's life will deal radically with his own sins and begin at once to shape his thinking in the context of the universal family which God intends mankind to be.

It cannot be denied that Christians have been slow to realise the outworking of those family obligations. Cynics (and some who were not cynics) have been at pains to point out how honestly pious a man could be in his private life and yet be socially pestilential. Not a few instances could be given even from the nineteenth century of men who lived a long life "in compartments," asserting with one breath that they were "saved" and with the next that "business is business." The latter phrase often covered some dubious device of their crafty trade. Plain hypocrites most of them were not. They lived in two worlds. Yet they were guilty in keeping these worlds apart.

Of the many instances which could be given, perhaps the case of Lord Overtoun will suffice. "He filled the varied rôle of merchant prince, county magnate, Churchman, evangelist and philanthropist, and later took his place among the legislators of the Upper House of Parliament."[2] He was particularly devoted to Sabbath Observance, Sunday-school teaching, Bible-class work, Temperance instruction, and Evangelical missions both at home and abroad. His money derived from certain chemical works at Shawfield and it was Mr. Keir Hardie who, at the height of his lordship's career, drew public attention to the following facts:

---

[1] Cell, 373 *ff*; cf. 392, 394. See also Lee, 275, 289.
[2] D. Carswell, *Brother Scots*, 192.

1. That Lord Overtoun's employees were paid at the rate of 3d. to 4d. per hour.

2. That they worked twelve hours a day, with no time off for meals.

3. That many of them also worked seven days a week.

4. That the manufacture of chrome was exceedingly deleterious to health, workers contracting abscesses which were familiarly known as "chrome holes."

5. That the sanitary conditions at the works were well-nigh as bad as they could be, and that it was even doubtful if the Factory Acts were being complied with.[1]

His lordship was silent in the face of these charges, defending himself only by saying that he was so busy with public and philanthropic labours that he left the actual management of his works to others. His defence will seem to some only to aggravate the crime and certainly to illustrate our point. If he was as ignorant of the conditions of the people who made his wealth as he claimed to be, it was a guilty and shameful ignorance. But that is how these perplexing contradictions occur.

Such men were born into an economic system which they did not make but in which, keeping the same rules as their competitors, they won their wealth; loving the game, and not seeing how they could possibly alter it themselves even if they wished, they lived their life compartmentally, moving from one area of life to the other at different hours of the day, and on different days of the week, but never attempting a real fusion of life. The business part of their life paid homage to the spiritual part by princely benefactions to good causes, but no synthesis was ever achieved.

As time went by and the light broadened, mitigations of the economic system were introduced: profit-sharing was tried: the welfare of workers became a deep concern of Christian industrialists; but the framework of the system remained. It was the *same* system—underpinned. The hope that the system could be altered challenged the conscience and troubled the mind of the Christian socialist sons of Christian conservative fathers. And

[1] Carswell, *Brother Scots*, 207 f.

when the preacher intruded into industry with a couple of questions, asking employers why they paid wages and their employees why they went to work at all, the questions, which appeared to be silly at first, began to torment by their pertinence, and new vistas opened before the eyes of men who saw work no longer as a curse, but as a divine vocation and a way of glorifying God.

A constant tension seems to be the burden of our generation. It does not know the new answer but it will not be fobbed off with the old. The discontent which precedes fresh thinking is its portion and, in so far as that affects the pursuit of holiness, it affects it this way. Men are concerned about holiness in all the relationships of life and not merely as a private occupation. The hundred situations in which the conscience of an earnest disciple can be strained by the shabby deceits of competitive business life, but against which it is so perilous to protest if he is to live at all, are known to all to whom plain men open their hearts. To say that it is impossible to live the Christian life in commerce is an exaggeration, and sometimes it is just a "defence mechanism" against the accusation of an outraged and restive conscience. But no one can listen patiently to the stories of tasks laid on underlings by unscrupulous employers without feeling how desperately impeded is the path to perfection. The story ends so often with the words, "I had to do it. I must live." One can answer the latter phrase, of course, by saying with General Booth, "You needn't"; and doubtless that *would* be the answer to the assistant brothel-keeper or the prentice procuress or the professional abortionist, but the issue is not usually as morally clear as that, and it often seems to the mass of men merely a raising of scruples which only a person concerned about perfection would pause to consider. Yet, in the nature of things, it is just there that the strain comes and some kind of compromise seems inevitable, and if a man cuts the discussion short by affirming his conviction that it is impossible to live a perfect life in an imperfect world, he must not resent it if he is reminded that Christ did.

Yet, even here, we must be careful to make clear what we mean. Christ only lived a perfect life in the sense that He always acted with a perfect motive. He did not always do what a perfect man would do in a perfect world. In the latter, for instance, there would have been no whip for the Temple traders, no "woes" for the Pharisees, no tribute money for the foreign conqueror. Nor would He have gone to the Cross.

But let us focus the problem still more sharply and face its flinty character unflinchingly, not by an illustration taken from commerce, but by one borrowed from international relationships. Let us consider *war*.

The hour in which his country goes to war is one peculiarly terrible for any pilgrim of perfection in which personal danger, or even the loss of his own unimportant life, are the very least of his concerns. Let us assume that he is convinced, after the most careful collation of evidence, that his country is in the right and has honestly striven for peace, but is withstood by an opponent so resolute that peace is possible only by capitulation. One of three or four courses proffer themselves to his perplexed mind.

(i) He can take the full pacifist position, or, at least, one of the positions so described, because what is "full" pacifism is a matter of dispute and one group is tempted at times to excommunicate the others. But one thing he will *not* do: he will not kill. With his eyes fixed on the Cross, he will assert that the Christian way is to suffer (meekly not weakly) but never to slay. At any personal cost, therefore, he will abstain from slaughter.

But his "perplexed" conscience is not completely at peace even after that decision. How much can he do "as one who would be perfect" and not sin? Can he join the Army Medical Corps, and so help others to fight again, though under a vow never to use a weapon himself but only to succour and save? If he cannot make munitions, can he make medicines for the military authorities? Should he work on the land or fight the fires? Is the risky service of bomb-disposal a work so obviously remedial and yet so obviously brave that he could almost regard it as specially "made for him"? Or should he be adamant to all appeals to do anything even remotely connected with the war until, at last, the State puts him into prison?

And, even in prison, he will still have his perplexed moments. He strives against the vanity of thinking himself a martyr. He prays, and it is part of his iron conviction that those who pray are rendering the richest service to the community—but he must *eat* also. And if his country depends for her food supplies on overseas trade, he knows that his every meal is likely to include something which a brave man has ferried across the mine-infested seas. Even in prison, therefore, he is living on another man's pluck. It sounds almost parasitic! He is not entirely without an answer, but . . . but . . . is it perfection?

M

(ii) Another line of action would be this. Tormented by conflicting duties which seem irreconcilable; feeling, on the one hand, the horror of evil men having the world in thrall and able systematically to poison through education the minds of succeeding generations of children, but feeling no less sharply the horror of offending that strange Man upon the Cross, whom pious writers have been able to turn (according to their bias) into an Imperial Cæsar, or an Eschatological Preacher, or a Liberal Reformer, but into whose hands they have never been able to place a rifle and bayonet, some disciples have felt reluctantly compelled to turn their backs deliberately on Christ while they were engaged in slaughter, and endure the thought that there can be no fellowship with Him while the bloody task is in hand.

Only those who have walked this dark way can imagine the inky blackness of the starless night, though the last spate of post-war reminiscence will quicken the imagination of those who really want to understand.[1] But for those on this path there is not even the pretence of perfection.

(iii) A third possibility (open to those who can pitch a tent in a wilderness) is to stress the pilgrim nature of our mortal life and to insist on the necessity of tension, not merely because life forces it on us, but because, being related to two worlds and engaged in translating a heavenly ideal into an earthly actuality, we are denied all hope of present fulfilment or present completion. It is freely allowed that pilgrims may rest awhile—but they cannot *settle*.

Hence, it is argued, the tension must continue. The disciple caught up in bitter war fights, and fights hard, but loathes it all the time he labours at it, and disciplines himself to look daily to his Lord and His perfect will, lest, in the heat of battle, and by the slow strain of slaughter still prolonged, he forgets he is a pilgrim, and his real and waiting task is to build the New Jerusalem.

But this is conscious compromise. It is not to be despised too readily because of that. It is the very theory of compromise: the clear-eyed conviction that the life we live, and the world God has set us in, compel such temporising. It does not even disguise itself in pseudo-philosophical language as "the principle of accommodation." It is overt and plain compromise. But who will call it perfection?

(iv) There remains the position of the disciple who definitely

[1] e.g. Montague, *Disenchantment*, 71.

equates the best that one can do in any circumstances with the perfect. Sometimes he says the "relatively perfect," or "the perfect for all practical reasons." These limiting phrases will seem to many to take the heart out of the word and so despoil it as to make it an offence to use it in this way at all. That question must be deferred for a moment. It has hung over us since we set out on this path. It is a question of terms—and more. Does not a deep and dangerous absurdity lie at the very heart of the phrase *relative perfection*? But, if so, how shall we describe that ethical height which is demonstrably above man's normal moral achievement and is really the highest of which a man is capable?

Imagine a disciple convinced of the justice of his country's cause, and convinced also that the cause is so great that his country's particular interests are almost trifling in comparison. Assume him to be convinced that precious things are at stake affecting the true well-being of all mankind. He sees as a clear duty the need to fight, and he looks upon the men who have made themselves his enemies as misguided by poisoned education and the denial of news. He recognises that what they do they do believing it to be the best, but he is sure that they have half-consciously become the terrible agents of evil.

Against them he fights with might and main. He cannot hate them because he believes that they are deceived, and because he is a follower of One who said, "Love your enemies." But he resists their evil will and he resists it to blood. He may be the bomb-aimer of an aircraft and take the most scrupulous care to hit only the military objective which is his target for the night, but none knows better than he that a bomb is not a precision weapon and, with all the care of which he is capable, he may hit a home for crippled children or a maternity hospital instead. With this dilemma he lives night and day. If he has peace of heart it is partly because he resolutely thrusts the warring arguments from his mind, but also because, terrible as his task is, he deeply believes that it is the best possible in the circumstances. Can he call it perfection? His life is a little thing, he feels, beside an unquiet conscience. Can those who sent him on the errand scorn his perplexities, and deny their scrap of communal responsibility? If he were to say that he does not hate the enemy and can even feel love for them (as persons) while hating the things they do, shall we laugh at him and talk of the tears of Torquemada? Or shall we set the whole problem aside and simply say again, "It is not possible to live a perfect life in an imperfect world"?

The early Hebrew patriarchs lived at peace by isolation but, with the passing years, isolation was found impossible for their multiplying descendants, and peace had to be sought by other and harder means.[1] The quest for perfection meets with similar difficulties. Once it seemed possible by isolation. In the hermitage or the monastic cell, in the rural life of eighteenth-century England, many of the hard problems of human relationships could be ignored but, as the shrinking world forced international contact on the most unwilling, new problems for perfection had to be faced. Living a life without sin by "escaping" the world grew increasingly impossible in practice and theoretically dubious too. The difficulties had to be solved, not fled from. But it is a necessary consequence of facing them that perfection seems to recede farther and farther away, and the doubt intrudes as to whether or not the dissolving oasis is not a mirage.

It is not without interest to note, in passing, what attitude these eighteenth-century saints took to war. They all denounced it—some of them with the most terrible invective. Wesley himself says:

"Hark! the cannon's roar! A pitchy cloud covers the sky. Noise, confusion, terror reign over all! Dying groans are on every side. The bodies of men are pierced, torn, hewed in pieces; their blood is poured on the earth like water. Their souls take their flight into the eternal world; perhaps into everlasting misery. The ministers of grace turn away from the horrid scene; the ministers of vengeance triumph. . . .

"And what is it which drags on these poor victims into the field of blood? It is a great phantom, which stalks before them, which they are taught to call *liberty*! It is this

Which breathes into their hearts stern love of war,
And thirst of vengeance, and contempt of death.

Real liberty, meantime, is trampled under foot, and is lost in anarchy and confusion."[2]

"All our declamations on the strength of human reason, and the eminence of our virtues, are no more than the cant and jargon of pride and ignorance, so long as there is such a thing as war in the world. Men in general can never be allowed to

---

[1] C. Ryder Smith, *The Bible Doctrine of Society*, 2 f., 88 f.   [2] *Works*, vii, 404 f.

be reasonable creatures, till they know not war any more. So long as this monster stalks uncontrolled, where is reason, virtue, humanity? They are utterly excluded; they have no place; they are a name, and nothing more."[1]

Much else said Wesley just as heatedly on the same point. But the full pacifist position he never took.

Some of his followers did take it—notably John Nelson, the stone-mason, who became so dependable and valiant a Methodist preacher. Pressed for a soldier at the instigation of the clergy and the ale-house keepers, he declared himself a pacifist and refused even to carry his musket. Touched by his sincerity and the quality of his character, his comrades carried it for him.[2] Imprisoned and then court-martialled, he held unshaken to his convictions. He said to the court-martial:

"I shall not fight; for I cannot bow my knee before the Lord to pray for a man and get up and kill him when I have done. I know God both hears me speak and sees me act; and I should expect the lot of a hypocrite if my actions contradict my prayers."[3]

Finally, he was discharged from the Army.

It is clear, therefore, that two centuries ago some yearning souls, panting after perfection, were perplexed concerning their duty to the nation at war. John Nelson and John Haime set the contrast at its sharpest. Doubtless, they met many times at the annual Methodist Conference: Nelson, who had been imprisoned for his conscientious scruples against war, and Haime who had fought so valiantly at Dettingen and Fontenoy and even described himself in the heat of the former battle as having a heart "filled with love, joy and peace."[4] Did they never discuss the point? Is it possible that these fellow pilgrims, who desired nothing so much as the perfect will of God, never sought to aid each other at this stubborn place of difference?

But if they ever reached agreement on what the sanctified should do in an hour like that, neither of them placed it on record. They went down at the last into the Valley of the Shadow, both pilgrims of perfection but differing deeply on this. And there —in substance—the problem remains until this hour.

[1] *Works*, ix, 223. [2] *Lives of E.M.P.*, i, 127.
[3] *ibid.*, i, 109; cf. 132, 136. [4] *ibid.*, i, 280.

But new vistas rise on our view. The old individualistic interpretation of holiness grows less and less satisfying. It has been recognised as a limitation all through this quest. The suggestion that religion is a purely individual concern, having no relation to the economic and political framework of society, is offensive to our judgment and to our deepening religious thought. The contention that the work of the Church should be confined to developing the spiritual life of people in their separateness, merely as a preparation for the life to come, can be set out persuasively and devotionally, but it is, nevertheless, false.

To begin with, it ignores etymology. Whatever else it is, it should not be called "holiness" (or "wholeness")[1] because it deliberately ignores wide areas of life. It forgets that the heavenly end should shape our life *now*. It falsely assumes that our Lord came of set purpose to snatch us from the natural order, and denies, therefore, by implication, the sweep of redemption, and even the hope of restoring the whole organic scheme of things to God. It assumes also that the present world order (organised into a system of sin, softened a little here and there by kindly mitigations, but planned and developed in neglect of God) is not a constant affront of His majesty and Lordship, but has been supinely abandoned by Him to the forces of evil. It fails to satisfy the deep longings of the consecrated heart by narrowing the spiritual life to personal devotion and tacitly assumes that, even if God did send His Son into the world to redeem the world, the *world*, through Him, will not be saved.

It must not be supposed that this social concern in the heart of a modern pilgrim of perfection is the same thing as a man-made plan for "a better state of things." Followers of Christ have no confidence that men can make "a better state of things" alone, nor do they find sufficient motive in the prevalent discontent to set out on the toilsome task of social redemption. They are passionate for this thing because they believe *God* wills it. It is His world and will only work His way. God has had His saints in the present order (and under conditions worse even than these) and there are senses in which it is an overstatement to say that it is impossible to be a Christian in the world as it is, but none of these legitimate comments settles the point. *This* world is not the end of our striving, or the whole purpose of our existence, but a Christian social order could be used by God to shape men to

---

[1] This etymological point has no reference, of course, to either the Greek or Hebrew words.

spirituality as clearly as Christian men are being used by God to challenge and shape the social order to His will. Because man is both individual and social in his nature, God's redemption compasses both, and there is no satisfying view of holiness which will ignore either.

Consequently, for the modern pilgrim of perfection, the word "sin" takes on a wider connotation. It is seen in social guises too: the selfishness which clings to dubious theories of economics, and which refuses to examine criticism directed against them, because these theories serve as a protective cushion to the conscience: the jealousy which guards existing privileges and will not meet a challenge concerning their legitimacy: the wilful ignorance of the circumstances of other people's lives though it is acknowledged that they share an equal place in God's regard.

Moreover, these aspiring souls find their consciences assailed by shafts which had not troubled them before: the absence of a really fair chance of rich Christian life for those of their fellows who are haunted by continual unemployment: the impossibility of finding a sense of divine vocation in work which is plainly inimical to the best interest of the race, or in tasks utterly mechanical and the tedium of which no effort is made to reduce: the subordination of industry to finance which has created centres of economic power exercising something analogous to tyranny over multitudes of men: the vast inequalities of opportunity which still exist in regard to health, education and leisure.

Those who would be perfect can no longer find their definition of sin exhausted by lewd thoughts, drunkenness and the use of a cinema on a Sunday. They see sin also in an evil social system, some of the buttresses of which may be set in their own class and in their own soul. And when they confess sin, they have need now to ask forgiveness, not only for the sins which they have long recognised as such, but also for their failure to follow their Master in the redemption of social life.

Not only is "sin" widened in meaning; "perfection" is widened in meaning too. It gets richer and does not concern itself only with "private" virtues. Salvation is by a Saviour not by a system. The Saviour's plan will only be worked effectively by those who have His Spirit and who have known His personal salvation within themselves. That is not to say that Christians can never work with non-Christians, nor is it to suggest that everyone must be individually converted before the Christian order can take shape on the earth. But it *is* to say that the high rôle of leader belongs to those who are consciously committed to Christ and who receive His daily guidance for daily life.

There is no system devisable by man which will work with automatism to perfection, and which an evil will cannot subvert. The deepest personal religion is called for from all who would fulfil the enlarging opportunities of God's new order on earth, and the demand is made to Christians in every stratum of our present social life. From some it will require the surrender of exclusive privilege and extreme wealth: from others it will call for victory over sloth and self-indulgence: from all it demands honest labour of brain and hand. But to what dazzling possibilities are we beckoned?—creative work of a quality never before achieved by whole communities, and to toil which shall be noble, ungrudging, and truly a maximum because it is offered as a sacrifice to God through one's fellows.

There will be much for the pilgrims of perfection to learn: patience with the slow development of those who have been unprivileged in time past and may be loath to learn: patience with those in whom it seems so hard to create any desire for nobler things: courage to face the subtle evasions of sin in their own souls and to overcome the temptation to return to the narrower concept of holiness because it was less costly and more comfortable.

The highest quality of life will be needed in those who essay these tasks. Both to shape this God-inspired order, and effectively to work it, will demand more than the average in moral achievement. But those in whom God's perfecting process is at work will not be unequal to it. Self and society are not at war in them. Because supernatural love fills their consecrated hearts, and directs their keen minds, they are the true pioneers of the new order and they march in the van of the victorious host of God.

Nor have they parted with the text they loved so dearly in their most individualistic days—but they see more in it: "For God so loved the *world*, that He gave His only begotten Son."

CHAPTER XXII

THE VISION OF A GOAL

OUR task draws to a close. We set out to discover what Wesley taught on Christian Perfection and, recognising in him the father of all modern "holiness movements," as we kept close to his own writings, his doctrine took shape before our eyes. It was not hard to distinguish what Wesley taught himself and what others *said* he taught.

It was not difficult either to recognise in the subsequent developments of this teaching those who could claim with justice to be his spiritual successors and those who taught things which Wesley himself would never have sanctioned. Its biblical basis, theological presuppositions, and psychological implications, we passed in critical review.

The evidence led to certain clear conclusions. Not all the texts on which Wesley built can sustain, in the light of modern scholarship, the interpretation he placed upon them, but his more general claim that the whole tenor of the New Testament points to the necessity of ethical and spiritual perfection seemed to us to be beyond dispute. The contention of others that this perfection is always, in the New Testament, set in the distant future after death does not seem to be upheld.

The difficulty over terms became most acute when we scrutinised Wesley's theological presuppositions. His definition of sin as "a voluntary transgression of a known law" was clearly defensible but just as clearly limited, and one which has failed to satisfy many of Wesley's most sympathetic interpreters. His definition of the word "perfection" has proven still more unsatisfying to a yet larger number.

Indeed, there are those who would solve the central uncertainty concerning this doctrine by confining all enquiry to the effort at reaching a clear connotation of this one term. Most people who take the view that this simple solution is possible would reject any and every adjective applied to "perfection." "It neither needs nor admits them," they would say, "the word is an ultimate. It *must* stand alone. A thing is perfect or not perfect, just as a thing is unique or not unique." To talk, therefore, of "relative" perfection, or "sinless" perfection, or "Christian" perfection, is to blur one's own thought and confuse the issue.

The pros and cons of that controversy have risen on our view more than once as we have travelled this road. We have seen solid reason for not making the word "perfection" the keystone of our thought, not chiefly because the word cannot go into company with a partner but because, unhappily, the idea of perfection in common thought is a sum of negations, the lean result of triumphant prohibitions.

Perfect love was the term which appealed to us more, both because it avoids to some extent the inherent philosophic utterness of that high and austere word "perfection"; and because it is positive in all its implications and social in its very nature, and avoids the difficulties which beset Wesley in his limited definition of sin. That the term was highly favoured by Wesley himself, and is the commonest and most natural word on the lips of those who claimed this gift from God, only serves to deepen our satisfaction in it.

Nor did we find that the new psychology had robbed the old quest for holiness of all hope of success. G. A. Studdert Kennedy in a "rough rhyme" sets out the analysis of sanctity which some modern psychologists have made.

> He takes the saints to pieces,
>   And labels all the parts,
> He tabulates the secrets
>   Of loyal loving hearts.
> He probes their selfless passion,
>   And shows exactly why
> The martyr goes out singing,
>   To suffer and to die.
> The beatific vision
>   That brings them to their knees
> He smilingly reduces
>   To infant phantasies.
> The Freudian unconscious
>   Quite easily explains
> The splendour of their sorrows,
>   The pageant of their pains.
> The manifold temptations,
>   Wherewith the flesh can vex
> The saintly soul, are samples
>   Of Œdipus complex.

The subtle sex perversion,
  His eagle glance can tell,
That makes their joyous heaven
  The horror of their hell.
His reasoning is perfect,
  His proofs as plain as paint,
He has but one small weakness,
  He cannot make a saint.[1]

But it was not the inability of psychologists to make saints
(even supposing that it was legitimate to expect that they might)
which caused us to pause. We were concerned to discover where,
if anywhere, the psychological implications of this eighteenth-
century search for holiness might be judged by the standards of
to-day to be in error. Our enquiry was not without fruit. It
became clear that their quest for the *eradication* of sin was misconceived and proceeded from premises demonstrably false. Sin
is not a *thing* to be cut out. Clearly their psychology was wrong
here, as was also their hope that Omnipotence might, in some
mysterious way, overwhelm their wills, "take away the power of
sinning," and yet still leave their personalities unimpaired.

But nothing emerged from the enquiry to prove that the quest
itself was misconceived; that holiness is a mirage seen only by
those who, fearing or failing to recognise that their only home
is on this sordid earth, turn to the vain phantasies of nature "all
made new." Nor did any fact come to light convincing us that
this multitude of raptured souls who hold that they have received
from God the gift of supernatural love *must* be mistaken.

The claim to have reached perfection's height on this earth we
were unwilling to hear from any man, not because we set any
limit to what the mighty God can do with a soul in this mortal
life, but because no man can have so intimate a knowledge of
himself as to make it. And from all the difficulties which confront
us when we consider the question of living a perfect life in an
imperfect world we take refuge again in the gift of God's love.
We live our mortal life in the midst of a process and some things
will not be clear till the end. But it can never be wrong to open
one's life to the fullness of God's grace. Divided loyalties and
inescapable compromises may beset the pilgrim of perfection on
every side, but they cannot dam his heart against the inflow of
the love of God, and its inevitable outflow in love for God and
man.

[1] Studdert Kennedy, *The Unutterable Beauty*, 120 f. (1940 Edn.).

Here, then, we stand. Is Wesley's doctrine whole? Can the marrow of it still be preached? Have we really jettisoned his distinctive teaching in dropping the word "perfection" and denying the possibility of "eradication"? Is what survives no more than Warfield said of all this holiness teaching: just "living up to the light that is in us"?[1] Does it "boil down" (for the great commandments, alas! have lost their awesomeness by familiarity) to "loving God and one's neighbour," which every Christian acknowledges as his standard, though he may be without any interest in perfectionism at all?

It is quite plain that whatever freshness this examination of Wesley's doctrine may have, no plea for the substance of the doctrine itself has the slightest hope of succeeding with those who hold, in the words of the Westminster Catechism, that "no man is able, either of himself, or by any grace received in this life, perfectly to keep the commandments of God; but doth daily break them in thought, word and deed."[2]

If that be true, if our nature is so ineradicably polluted and beyond the resources of grace to cleanse, then Wesley's doctrine is false in its traditional form and, perhaps, only of tepid interest with the changes which we have been bold enough to suggest.

"What emphasis," it will be asked, "in putting stress upon the gift of supernatural love, do you place on the expulsive power of this new affection? Does it exclude all sin? *Can* it exclude all sin?"

The answer we have been led to give to this question will not seem as direct as some would desire. We hold that it *can* exclude all conscious sin—and "conscious" sin is not to be waved aside lightly as a grovelling term in a man of sensitive conscience. It is an immense thing to say of any man who lives intimately with God that he is not *aware* of sin, and to infer at once that he cannot possibly live close to God and be unaware of sin savours more of a retort than a reply.

We must insist again that no man can put a limit to what grace can do with a soul on this terrestrial plane, and, while our self-ignorance should prevent any mortal from claiming that the work has been done, it would do despite to the whole spirit of the New Testament (as we read it) to affirm categorically that it *cannot* be done. "Can God do nothing with sin but forgive it?" John Wesley asks; and his brother exultantly answers:

---

[1] Warfield, ii, 526.
[2] *Westminster Confession: The Larger Catechism*, Q. 149.

> He breaks the power of cancelled sin,
> He sets the prisoner free.

God has called us to holiness, "Be ye holy for I am holy" saith the Lord. Does God command the impossible?

Augustine admitted the possibility of perfection on this earth by divine power and grace but hedged it about with so many impediments that it remains—as Dr. Mozley remarks[1]—more of a name than a reality. Indeed, Augustine finds a reason why this should be so: he dwells on the humility created by a sense of sin.

Many have followed Augustine in this. That they should plead for humility is altogether fitting, for it is the fairest of the graces and all our progress can be measured by our growth in it. But to put in a covert plea for sin, or, at least, to make a defence of this deadly leprosy of the soul as a means to humility, is surely strange. How much sin keeps us humble? Is it not in the nature of sin to make us proud and less likely to repent? In not the cleansed soul's awareness of utter dependence on grace in every moment of life not enough to beget the coveted bloom of humility upon the spirit?

Another objection to Wesley's teaching on holiness comes from those who assert that antinomianism is its inevitable consequence. Dr. Warfield speaks of "that Antinomian tendency which is the nemesis that follows on the heels of all forms of perfectionism."[2] Dr. Piette inclines to the same view.[3]

Neither of these writers, however, allows enough for the fact that precisely the same charge was brought against the Calvinist opponents of this teaching, and with, at least, as much pith. John Nelson fought many a wordy contest with men who asserted that they were predestined to swearing and other vices,[4] and who claimed to be in a state of "happy sinnership." He convicts them of "seeking happiness without holiness."[5]

Nor are the Antinomian Calvinists to be classified as men who merely *said* these things to quieten a restive conscience and withstand an eager evangelist. They meant what they said. They had a theory and a theology behind it. Because Christ had become righteousness for them, there was not only no need to seek it for

---

[1] J. B. Mozley, *Lectures and Other Theological Papers*, 168.
[2] Warfield, ii, 528.   [3] Piette, 462.
[4] *Lives of E.M.P.*, i, 25; cf. 34.   [5] *ibid.*, 33.

themselves but something approaching blasphemy in attempting to do so. Some of them wallowed in sin.

If extravagances were committed on both sides in this eighteenth-century wrangle (and who will say that they were not?) it is folly to assert that antinomianism is the inevitable outcome of holiness teaching without recognising that it has been a recurring phenomenon among the militant opponents of this doctrine. And not unnaturally! Underline the worthlessness of all our own righteousness, emphasise the utter pollution of human nature, put it beyond hope that even by grace one may live a day without sin in thought, word and deed, and then stress faith, and faith only, and it is not a little unlikely that vagaries will creep in. They may also creep in, it is true, among "perfectionists." It has been no small part of our effort in this book to face up to the dangers which beset holiness teaching, and understand them. But those who bundle all "perfectionism" together as heresy ignore at least half the evidence if they charge the exponents of holiness with seducing people into antinomianism, and do not recognise the awful danger which their own emphasis involves. Paul saw the danger with his steady eyes. To Luther it was not so clear.[1]

To believe that the human heart can be cleansed from sin is a bold, big thing to believe, and we have protested against any easy assumption that it has been done because this is fraught with dreadful dangers, not the least of which is a subtle discouragement against being honest with oneself. But the opposite conviction, so it seems to the writer, is not less terrible. To hold the fixed conviction that it simply *cannot* be done and that one must always mentally provide for sin in one's life suggests all kinds of rationalisation to our sinful minds. How easy to ignore Paul's injunction, "Make not provision for the flesh, to fulfil the lusts thereof." How eagerly this desiring heart fixes on "inevitability" as an ever-ready excuse. Can any man confidently and unswervingly press on to the utterly unattainable?

Imagine a Christian minister who regards this teaching as a dangerous error mounting the pulpit to conduct divine worship. He begins by reciting certain passages of Scripture:

"As He which called you is holy, be ye yourselves also holy in all manner of living."

[1] But cf. Lindsay, *History of the Reformation*, i, 429 *ff*., Moffatt, *Love in the New Testament*, 95, 110, Whale, *Christian Doctrine*, 146, Otto, *The Idea of the Holy*, 107 *f*., H. R. Mackintosh, *The Christian Experience of Forgiveness*, 148 *ff*., 243.

"He hath granted unto us His precious and exceeding great promises; that through these ye may become partakers of the divine nature, having escaped from the corruption that is in the world by lust."

"Put on love, which is the bond of perfectness."

"I beseech you therefore, brethren, by the mercies of God, to present your bodies a living sacrifice, holy, acceptable to God, which is your reasonable service."

"If we confess our sins, He is faithful and just to forgive us our sins, and to cleanse us from all unrighteousness."

The first hymn is:

> O for a heart to praise my God,
> A heart from sin set *free*.

For the Invocation he uses the collect in the Anglican service of Holy Communion and the people pray with him as he says:

"Cleanse the thoughts of our hearts by the inspiration of Thy Holy Spirit, that we may *perfectly* love Thee. . . ."

And the second hymn is "Love divine, all loves excelling," in which minister and people sing with fervour:

> Finish then Thy new creation,
> *Pure* and *spotless* let us be.

For the First Lesson he reads the 51st Psalm with its haunting plea for cleansing:

"Blot out my transgressions. Wash me throughly from mine iniquity, and cleanse me from my sin. . . . Wash me, and I shall be whiter than snow. . . . Create in me a clean heart, O God; and renew a right spirit within me. . . ."

Whatever the psalmist meant by all that, the people know what they mean. Then they sing the Te Deum, mounting up to the great appeal:

Vouchsafe, O Lord, to keep us this day without sin.

And for the Second Lesson Romans vi is read:

"We who died to sin, how shall we any longer live therein? . . . Our old man was crucified with Him, that the body of sin might be done away, that so we should no longer be in bondage to sin. . . . Even so reckon ye also yourselves to be dead unto

sin, but alive unto God in Christ Jesus. . . . For sin shall not
have dominion over you: for ye are not under law, but under
grace. . . . But now being made free from sin, and become
servants to God, ye have your fruit unto sanctification. . . ."

When the worshippers turn again to petition, the minister uses,
among other prayers, the collect for grace:

"Grant that this day we fall into no sin, neither run into any
kind of danger."

The sermon is preceded by the hymn, "God of all power, and
truth, and grace," which includes the lines:

> Purge me from *every* sinful blot;
> My idols all be cast aside

and the service concludes with a hymn of consecration:

> Take my life, and let it be
> Consecrated, Lord, to Thee. . . .
>
> Take myself, and I will be
> *Ever*, *only*, *all* for Thee!

The act of worship is completed by the Benediction, with its
three-fold promise that the grace of the Lord Jesus Christ, and
the love of God, and the fellowship of the Holy Spirit will be
with minister and people for evermore.

Yet—after that—the minister returns to his home with the
unshaken conviction that not even by any grace received in this
life can he avoid daily sinning and that, despite all the promises
and prayers, he cannot live for twenty-four hours without stain
in thought and word and deed.

But let us approach the problem from another angle, practical
rather than theoretical, and by the observation of life rather than
books. There are three things which strike a discerning critic of
the Church to-day.

(i) First, many Christians live on a sub-Christian level. That is
not a judgment made in spiritual pride, nor yet a judgment which
necessarily omits the critic himself. Its truth is keenly felt by
sensitive souls in the Church, even more, perhaps, than by those
outside.

The Church is living far below the New Testament offer and
promise. There is not enough difference between the people
inside the Church and those outside to be impressive. Men
cheerfully ignore the Christian faith, repudiate public worship,
private prayer, and all the means of grace, and live, so they believe,
as good a life as their church-attending neighbours. And in
thousands and thousands of instances the professing Christian
lacks that quality of life which would inevitably, though uncon-
sciously, rebuke such inverted Pharisaism, and make it self-
conscious and ashamed.

Not even her most earnest devotees would claim that the
Church is a mighty and effective instrument for God in this world.
Without belittling her thousand secret philanthropies or abating
one jot of the claim that, with all her faults, she is the nearest
expression of God's will in this world, it remains true that, in the
western world, she is disunited, enfeebled, and in retreat. The
gates of hell prevail against her.

In her multitude of needs, what need, if any, out-tops all the
rest?

The need for holiness. Holiness is potent and mighty. Like the
word of God it "is living, and active, and sharper than any two-
edged sword, and piercing even to the dividing of soul and spirit."
It rebukes sin. It creates the appetite for itself. It blasts doubt
and fosters faith. No man is quite the same after contact with a
saint. He may fly from him, and even, in the obduracy of his
sinning, hug his sin the tighter, but always, uneasily, he remembers.

And if, moreover, we think of holiness, as we have been
learning to do, in terms of the strong positive gift of perfect love,
it strains the imagination, and floods the heart with new hope,
even to conceive the impact on the world of a Church made new
in perfect love. If God would but re-visit His people thus, then
would we see:

> The gates of brass before Him burst,
> The iron fetters yield.

(ii) In the second place, it has struck many discerning observers
of the modern Church that very many of her members lack any
sense of goal. Even to the thoughtful, membership of the body of
Christ is just . . . membership. Their eyes are not held by a vision
of glory and they are not dumb before the wonder of God's

N

uttermost purpose in their lives. They do not say with bated breath:

> He wills that I should holy be.

There is little about them to suggest resolute pilgrims knowing their goal and holding on their course with unswerving zeal, displaying that "toil unsevered from tranquillity" but yearly maturing and refining for heaven in everyone's gaze but their own. They do not seem that kind of pilgrim. Indeed, the general scene is so frosty, and the gait so waddling, and the journey so undirected that, as has been remarked, they seem more like penguins than pilgrims.

A clear conviction received into the mind that God is able, and willing, and eager, to deal drastically with sin in us, the sins of the mind as well as the sins of the flesh, the jealousies, pettinesses, irritabilities, resentments, egotisms: the earnest attending to God that one may receive this *present* salvation, and know in experience the deep difference between a straining effort to do the thing oneself, and the bewilderingly wonderful awareness that God has done something Himself; such a conviction and such an experience beckon the pilgrim on and make it obvious to all that he is a man on a journey with a pre-view of his goal. Indeed, he sings as he travels: the note is set to aspiration rather than complete and present achievement, but he puts no limits to the power of his God.

> O that I now, from sin released,
>   Thy word may to the utmost prove,
> Enter into the promised rest,
>   The Canaan of Thy perfect love!

(iii) Thirdly, there are not a few acute observers of modern Church life and thought who remark upon the wide neglect of the doctrine of the Holy Spirit and would explain the lack of spiritual power chiefly by this.

That the doctrine is neglected few will deny. Some scholars reject the "personality" of the Spirit and would prefer to be called "binitarians" than "trinitarians." The mass of Church people receive the doctrines of the Spirit's "personality" and His power "as taught," but their powerless lives remind one of none so much as the men at Ephesus whom Paul challenged with the words, "Did ye receive the Holy Ghost when ye believed?"[1]

---

[1] Acts xix. 2.

Now, we have seen that Wesley did not care to describe the gift of perfect love as "the reception of the Holy Spirit," as some later teachers have done,[1] because he held that the Holy Spirit was given when a man first believed, and entire sanctification he regarded as a subsequent blessing. But that the life and literature of early Methodism are full of the doctrine of the Holy Spirit none who is acquainted with them will hesitate to affirm, and that God the Spirit was peculiarly associated with sanctification is abundantly clear. Wesley says that it is the Holy Spirit which is responsible for—

"the conversion and entire sanctification of our hearts and lives. . . . The title 'holy,' applied to the Spirit of God, does not only denote that He is holy in His own nature, but that He makes us so; that He is the great fountain of holiness to His church; the Spirit from whence flows all the grace and virtue. . . ."[2]

Wesley's precursors in this teaching are not less emphatic that sanctification is a special work of the Holy Spirit. Scougal affirms it.[3] Marshall makes it clear.[4] All claim that the New Testament is behind them.

Paul's doctrine of the believer's mystic indwelling in Christ, and Christ's in the believer, they link up with the Holy Spirit too. They seem to draw a contrast between having life *alongside* God, and having life *in* God. The promise of the Johannine discourses that the Spirit "abideth *with* you and shall be *in* you" is precious to them.[5] They find a rich meaning in the change of preposition.

Is it only a coincidence that, in an age when the doctrine of the Holy Spirit is neglected, the Church is feeble and ineffective, and does not seem to be rich in lovely lives of compelling Christlikeness? Or have we a hint here that the wise will be swift to heed?

Power was promised with the Holy Spirit[6] and the first fruit of the Spirit is love.[7] Christians to-day need power and perfect love. On the plain promise of Christ, God is pledged to give the Holy Spirit to them that ask Him.[8] He *gives*. The Spirit is not to be strained after. Only those who have strained after holiness by

---

[1] See p. 83.   [2] *Works*, vii, 485 *f*.
[3] Scougal, *Life of God in the Soul of Man*, 9.
[4] Marshall, *The Gospel-Mystery of Sanctification*, 127.
[5] John xiv. 17.   [6] Acts i. 8.
[7] Gal. v. 22.   [8] Luke xi. 13.

N*

their own taut effort and set wills know the weariness and disappointment of it. One is always on guard: "edgy," over-braced, vigilant to the point of being fearful, living on one's nerves and getting on other people's. The more one struggles and fails, the more irritated one becomes by conscious defeat. There is no peace, no poise, no inward rest. Slowly the conviction seeps into the mind: "I was better when I did not try."

And then to "let go and let God"! Just to *receive* the Holy Spirit! To believe and find it true! To practise the moment-by-moment life! Surely, none but those who have had both these experiences can really know the bliss unutterable which belongs to those who "enter into the promised rest." While they can barely look back to the days of strained self-effort without a shudder, they turn with thrilling eagerness to the present enjoyment of the rest which remaineth to the people of God. [1] Busy but not harassed! On the stretch for the Kingdom but not way-worn! Buying up the moments in this royal service but all quiet within!

Two other points call for notice here.

(*a*) The Holy Spirit, with the great endowment of power against sin, is a gift, but a *supernatural* gift. The point is important. So many ministers of God to-day defend their ineffectiveness on the ground that they do not possess certain gifts. They are not eloquent, or they lack popular appeal: they do not possess organising power, or they have no skill as church financiers. All these are gifts, it is true, and gifts not to be despised, but—in the sense in which we are now using the words—they are natural gifts, and none of them alone, nor all of them together, can outweigh the supernatural gift of the Holy Spirit. Here is the secret of power because here is the secret of holiness. Eloquence dies on the ear and popular appeal is evanescent—in the pulpit as in vaudeville. The gift of organisation is only valuable in the Church as it is a servant of God's Spirit. Unhappily, the machinery has often become so cumbrous that the waning spiritual life cannot work it and, as for the overstressing of financial genius in the Church, it is largely the folly of failures who will not face the root cause of their defeat. Men who make debts and men who clear them largely cancel each other out.

If all this talk of special natural gifts could be redirected to understanding and seeking the supernatural gift of the Holy Spirit, how vast would be the gain! If God's cause can only succeed in a church furnished with a minister possessed of

Yes !

[1] Heb. iv. 9.

outstanding natural gifts, what a hopeless outlook for the cause of God!

It is not so. The apostles were ordinary men—but they had been to Pentecost! And the apostles turned the world upside down.[1]

(b) It will not be inferred by any unhurried reader that our stress on the active principle of holiness as a gift cancels out all discipline from the devotional life. It belongs to the vanity of our human nature usually to exaggerate our own small part in our dealings with God, and sometimes to exaggerate it so much that the stress falls entirely upon it, and God is all but elbowed out of the scene. There is a big price to pay for that folly. The central fact of the gospel, namely, that it is a gift, an offer, something which God does, is virtually forgotten, and we are back again at the humanistic self-effort from which it pleased God to deliver us.

Yet we have our part to play—small, but not unimportant. Should a millionaire give a fortune to a pauper, the pauper must take it. If the King grants a pardon to a felon, the felon must accept it. When a mortal goes to God for forgiveness and the Holy Spirit, he must receive the gift and, if he is wise, receive it daily for each new day as it comes.

That is where discipline comes into the holy life: not the toilsome, straining, failing effort to be good; but the faithful attending on God to receive. Those who have the gift and lose it, normally lose it by neglect of this. Nothing has become clearer to us in our quest than the fact that the faith of one high moment cannot secure holiness for ever: it is a life of intimate relationship (which issues in mystic indwelling) and faithfulness shows itself in our consistency in attending.

Wesley was a man of iron discipline from his youth up. During the years which he spent in what he afterwards came to regard as "legal night," he was unshaken in discipline, and when illumination came he carried the discipline over to be the servant of his enlightened mind. It stood him in good stead. Early and late and often in the day, he waited on God and his waiting had its rich reward.

Most Christians reverse Wesley's order. Enlightenment comes first and they need to forge the discipline afterwards. Some fail to do it, and the precious thing they found slips from them. They may even come to doubt if they discovered any secret at all, and in

[1] Acts xvii. 6.

chill cynicism write it off as the ebullience of adolescence. They
have ceased to wait upon God and this is the heavy price.

There can be no real continuance of the holy life in the soul of
any man who does not continually wait on God. Only those who
"attend the whispers" of His grace can hear Him "inly speak."

We have said that nothing incites to holiness (or perfect love)
like the contemplation of it—but it must be contemplation, not
in the abstract, but in Christ and in the saints. We have not shrunk
in this book from studying people who, consciously or unconsci-
ously, have caricatured it. Let us complete our survey by glancing
at some who adorned it; students and exponents of Wesley's
doctrine who, in their own writings and by the testimony of
credible witnesses, appear clearly before our eyes, and the
cumulative effect of whose evidence makes it impossible for any
unprejudiced student to brush the whole thing impatiently aside.

It is fitting that Fletcher of Madeley be the first. We have
already noted Voltaire's reputed tribute to him. The celebrated
mocker seems to have had an unfeigned admiration for Fletcher,
whose life he regarded as the nearest to Jesus Christ's of any he
had the opportunity to observe.[1]

Wesley said of Fletcher:

"I was intimately acquainted with him for thirty years. I
conversed with him morning, noon, and night, without the least
reserve . . . and, in all that time, I never heard him speak an
improper word, or saw him do an improper action. To conclude: Within fourscore years I have known many excellent
men, holy in heart and life: But one equal to him, I have not
known; one so uniformly and deeply devoted to God. So
unblamable a man, in every respect, I have not found either in
Europe or America. Nor do I expect to find another such on
this side eternity."[2]

Overton, the historian of the eighteenth century, made a close
study of Fletcher's life, and said, "He was more than Christian,
he was Christlike."[3]

Fletcher's wife, who naturally had the closest opportunity of
observing and sharing his toilsome, sacrificial life, and saw him
when he was over-tired and ill, knew how often he was called

---

[1] See p. 32.   [2] *Works*, xi. 365.
[3] Abbey and Overton, *The English Church in the Eighteenth Century*, ii, 113.

from his bed at night during an epidemic of spotted fever (from which eventually he died), and helped him to pare down their expenditure to a dangerous minimum in order to have more to give away; she said that his life was "the most angelic I have ever known."[1]

Fletcher, as we have had more than one occasion to notice, held and defended Wesley's doctrine of perfect love. With some parts of his exposition we have felt compelled to differ, but his life leaves us lost in wonder, love and praise.

John Brash, also, was a defender and expositor of Wesley's doctrine. He was a living example of it too. Born in 1830, and living on until 1912, there still survive many people who knew him well and who think of God and heaven at the merest mention of his name. One who knew him intimately for more than half his life said:

"In him, holiness was a transparency. Yet 'he wist not that his face shone.' If I mention that for forty-three years it was my happiness to enjoy a close and uninterrupted friendship with him, it is that I may testify that, through all those years of intimacy, I never saw in him either in spirit, word, or deed, anything out of harmony with the spirit of Jesus."[2]

The reviewer of one of his little books, commenting long afterwards on its effect upon his mind, said:

"The first reading of it will never be forgotten by me. Again and again on a devotional morning, I have reached down that little book, never without the same powerful stimulus. And even now the touch of the good man's memory seems to renew one's life. If all who have spoken of holiness among us had been such as he, how different would the position of the doctrine have been; and if this doctrine had been in its right place, how many other things would have been different, too!"[3]

The Rev. Walter Hawkins also offers his witness. He had long known by repute the quality of John Brash's life but had a singular opportunity to observe it closely during two trying

[1] Tyerman, *Wesley's Designated Successor*, 559.
[2] Page, *John Brash*, 6.   [3] *ibid.*, 145.

months in which they travelled together around the Mediterranean Sea. Day and night, aboard and ashore, they were together. He says:

"The scenes in those eventful weeks recur often, and one startling reflection came to me in retrospect one day which I have never had any reason to correct, namely, that I could not recall one act, or word, or look which I could not naturally expect from our Lord Himself, were He upon earth again. It is a tribute one may well hesitate to trust in black-and-white, but it is deliberate, and I dare not withhold it. Truly 'such honour have *not* all His saints.' But I imagine there are many others who knew this saint, and could quite thoughtfully endorse my testimony. Whenever I am tempted to doubt the doctrine of Christian perfection I think of John Brash, my old fellow traveller, and—I press toward the mark."[1]

Let the last instance be Benjamin Hellier, yet another exponent of Wesley's teaching and one who "adorned the doctrine." Classical Tutor in the mid-years of the last century at Richmond College, Surrey, then Governor of Headingley College, Leeds, he made the paths of holiness winsome by a piety which was irrepressibly gay. The Rev. Dr. W. F. Moulton bore witness to it,[2] and the Rev. Dr. E. H. Sugden,[3] and the Rev. Dr. G. G. Findlay. Dr. Findlay said that he never knew "a saint more blameless and unworldly, yet more pleasant and conversable."[4] Benjamin Hellier's children said:

"He did not within our knowledge ever profess to have attained entire sanctification, and yet no one would have more readily accepted such a statement than the members of his own family. And he himself records that he enjoyed 'constant victory over inward and outward sin, perfect freedom from anxious care, and implicit trust in God.'

But he considered this experience to be negative rather than positive. 'In one sense I think I am perfect in the love of God, inasmuch as I do not willingly allow myself in what is contrary thereto: but in another sense I am not perfect in love —it does not produce in me all its legitimate fruits.' "[5]

[1] Page, *John Brash*, 269.   [2] *Benjamin Hellier by His Children* (Introduction).
[3] *Sermons*, ii, 150.   [4] *Benjamin Hellier*, 170.   [5] *ibid.*, 57.

It was characteristic of the man, and a proof of his deep insight into true holiness, that he felt he should have had an "intenser joy."

This high quality of life seems almost to have been left as a "legacy" in this family. It was of his brother, J. B. Hellier, that Edgar Wallace, the writer of detective fiction, said:

"J. B. Hellier was a perfect man. . . . I believe that much of the good which is within me came because I knew him. He is an everlasting barrier between me and atheism."[1]

We may leave it there. Sanctity is not the monopoly of any one communion, but its origin and growth are of vital interest where-ever it is found. Many of the world's "great" men were very little men. It is the saint who stands by the throne in the Court of the King of Kings. Some we can name, but far more "there be which have no memorial," the fragrance of whose lives God has used to sweeten His world.

Many of these have I seen among the spiritual heirs of John Wesley, since, in the providence of God, I first made contact as a stranger with this people. Few held important office even in their own communion. Most of them lived comparatively obscure lives. But it was plain to see almost on their faces that here was a stream of sanctity, deep, distinctive (in some ways), and as arresting and appealing as true sanctity ever is. The stream seems not so full as once it was, but I have tried to trace it to its source through two centuries of changeful mortal life, back to John Wesley himself, and through him to the main tide of the Holy Catholic Church, and to the Great Shepherd of the sheep who is pledged to make us "perfect in every good thing to do His will, working in us that which is well-pleasing in His sight, through Jesus Christ; to whom be the glory for ever and ever."

[1] Margaret Lane, *Edgar Wallace*, 84. The authoress has confused the two brothers, Benjamin Hellier and J. B. Hellier. Benjamin Hellier died in 1888.

BIBLIOGRAPHY

WESLEY AND HIS TIMES

C. J. ABBEY and J. H. OVERTON. *The English Church in the Eighteenth Century*. 2 vols.

The Arminian Magazine. 1779–1800.

HENRY BETT. *The Spirit of Methodism*.

J. WESLEY BREADY. *Lord Shaftesbury and Social-Industrial Progress. England: Before and After Wesley.*

G. C. CELL. *The Rediscovery of John Wesley.*

GEORGE EAYRS. *John Wesley: Christian Philosopher and Church Founder.*

MALDWYN EDWARDS. *John Wesley and the Eighteenth Century.*

JOHN FLETCHER. *Works.* 9 vols. (1806–1808 Edn.)

J. R. GREEN. *A Short History of the English People.*

ÉLIE HALÉVY. *A History of the English People in 1815.* (Pub. T. Fisher Unwin.)

J. L. and B. HAMMOND. *The Town Labourer: 1760–1832.*

JOHN HAMPSON. *Memoirs of the late Rev. John Wesley, with a Review of his Life and Writings, and a History of Methodism.* 3 vols.

THOMAS JACKSON. *The Lives of Early Methodist Preachers.* 6 vols. (1871 Edn.) *The Life of the Rev. Charles Wesley.* 2 vols.

BISHOP LAVINGTON. *The Enthusiasm of Methodists and Papists Compared.*

WILLIAM LAW. *A Practical Treatise upon Christian Perfection.* (Vol. III of *Works.*)

W. E. H. LECKY. *A History of England in the Eighteenth Century.* 7 vols. (1892 Edn.)

UMPHREY LEE. *John Wesley and Modern Religion.*

MAXIMIN PIETTE. *John Wesley in the Evolution of Protestantism.*

J. E. RATTENBURY. *The Conversion of the Wesleys. Wesley's Legacy to the World.*

HESTER ANN ROGERS. *The Experience and Spiritual Letters of Mrs. Hester Ann Rogers.*

JOHN S. SIMON. *John Wesley the Master-Builder. John Wesley and the Religious Societies. John Wesley and the Methodist Societies. The Revival of Religion in England in the Eighteenth Century.*

ROBERT SOUTHEY. *The Life of John Wesley.*

JEREMY TAYLOR. *Rules and Exercises of Holy Living and of Holy Dying.*

AUGUSTUS M. TOPLADY. *Works.* 6 vols.

L. TYERMAN. *The Life and Times of the Rev. John Wesley.* 3 vols. *Wesley's Designated Successor.*

C. E. VULLIAMY. *John Wesley.*

HORACE WALPOLE. *The Letters of Horace Walpole.* 9 vols. (Cunningham Edn.)

W. J. WARNER. *The Wesleyan Movement in the Industrial Revolution.*

JOHN WESLEY. *The Journal of the Rev. John Wesley.* 8 vols. (Ed. Curnock, 1909–16.) *The Letters of the Rev. John Wesley.* 8 vols. (Ed. Telford, 1931.) *The Standard Sermons of John Wesley.* 2 vols. (Ed. E. H. Sugden.) *The Works of the Rev. John Wesley.* 14 vols. 3rd Edn. (Ed. Jackson, 1829–31.)

H. B. WORKMAN, etc. *A New History of Methodism.* 2 vols.

BIBLICAL

A. E. BROOKE. *A Critical and Exegetical Commentary on the Johannine Epistles.* (I.C.C.)

T. K. CHEYNE. *Encyclopædia Biblica.* 4 vols.

C. H. DODD. *The Epistle of Paul to the Romans.* (Moffatt N. T. Comm.)

P. N. HARRISON. *The Problem of the Pastoral Epistles.*

J. HASTINGS. *A Dictionary of Christ and the Gospels.* 2 vols. *A Dictionary of the Bible.* 5 vols. *Encyclopædia of Religion and Ethics.* 13 vols.

H. A. A. KENNEDY. *St. Paul and the Mystery-Religions.*

ALAN H. M'NEILE. *The Gospel According to St. Matthew.* (Macmillan.)

W. MANSON. *The Gospel of Luke.* (Moffatt N. T. Comm.)

J. H. MICHAEL. *The Epistle of Paul to the Philippians.* (Moffatt N. T. Comm.)

JAMES MOFFATT. *An Introduction to the Literature of the New Testament. Love in the New Testament.*

JAMES H. MOULTON. *A Grammar of New Testament Greek.* (Vol. I. *Prolegomena.*)

J. A. ROBINSON. *St. Paul's Epistle to the Ephesians.* (Macmillan.)

T. H. ROBINSON. *The Epistle to the Hebrews.* (Moffatt N. T. Comm.)

E. F. SCOTT. *The Pastoral Epistles. The Fourth Gospel, its Purpose and Theology.*

R. H. STRACHAN. *The Second Epistle of Paul to the Corinthians.* (Moffatt N. T. Comm.)

CHARLES C. TORREY. *The Four Gospels. Our Translated Gospels.*

R. C. TRENCH. *Synonyms of the New Testament.*

J. WELLHAUSEN. *Das Evangelium Matthaei.*

HYMNOLOGY

F. J. GILLMAN. *Evolution of the English Hymn.*

J. JULIAN. *A Dictionary of Hymnology.*

G. OSBORN. *The Poetical Works of John and Charles Wesley.* 13 vols.

J. E. RATTENBURY. *The Evangelical Doctrines of Charles Wesley's Hymns.*

CHARLES WESLEY. *Short Hymns on Select Passages of the Holy Scriptures.* 2 vols. (1762.) *A Collection of Hymns for the use of the People called Methodists.* (1780.) Do. (1810.) Do. with new supplement, (1831.) Do. (1875.) *The Methodist Hymn-Book.* (1904.) Do. (1933.)

F. LUKE WISEMAN. *Charles Wesley: Evangelist and Poet.*

THEOLOGICAL

KARL ADAM. *The Spirit of Catholicism.*

F. R. BARRY. *The Relevance of Christianity.*

E. J. BICKNELL. *The Christian Idea of Sin and Original Sin.*

O. A. CURTIS. *The Christian Faith.*

GÜNTHER DEHN. *Man and Revelation.*

R. NEWTON FLEW. *Jesus and His Church. The Idea of Perfection in Christian Theology.*

P. T. FORSYTH. *Christian Perfection.*

A. E. GARVIE. *The Christian Ideal for Human Society.*

ADOLPH HARNACK. *History of Dogma.* (Trans. Wm. M'Gilchrist.) Vol. VII.

A. W. HARRISON. *The Beginnings of Arminianism to the Synod of Dort.*

BARON F. VON HÜGEL. *Essays and Addresses on the Philosophy of Religion.* (Second series.)

K. E. KIRK. *The Vision of God.*

J. H. LECKIE. *The World to Come and Final Destiny.*

WALTER MARSHALL. *The Gospel-Mystery of Sanctification.* (1819 Edn.)

C. N. MOODY. *The Mind of the Early Converts.*

R. S. MOXON. *The Doctrine of Sin.*

J. B. MOZLEY. *Lectures and Other Theological Papers. University Sermons.*

JOHN OMAN. *Grace and Personality.*

W. E. ORCHARD. *Modern Theories of Sin.*

RUDOLF OTTO. *The Idea of the Holy.*

E. ALLISON PEERS. *Studies of the Spanish Mystics.* 2 vols.

H. W. PERKINS. *The Doctrine of Christian or Evangelical Perfection.*

W. B. POPE. *A Compendium of Christian Theology.* 3 vols.

RICHARD ROLLE. *The Fire of Love.*

H. SCOUGAL. *The Life of God in the Soul of Man.* (1702 Edn.)

C. RYDER SMITH. *The Bible Doctrine of Salvation. The Bible Doctrine of Society.*

B. H. STREETER. *Immortality.*

F. R. TENNANT. *The Concept of Sin. The Origin and Propagation of Sin.*

BENJAMIN B. WARFIELD. *Perfectionism.* 2 vols.

H. WATKIN-JONES. *The Holy Spirit from Arminius to Wesley. The Westminster Confession.*

PHILOSOPHICAL

HENRI BERGSON. *Creative Evolution.*

T. H. GREEN. *Prolegomena to Ethics.*

L. T. HOBHOUSE. *Morals in Evolution.* 2 vols.

BENJAMIN RAND. *Classical Moralists.*

H. SIDGWICK. *The Methods of Ethics.*

W. R. SORLEY. *Moral Values and the Idea of God.*

E. S. WATERHOUSE. *The Philosophy of Religious Experience.*

E. WESTERMARCK. *The Origin and Development of the Moral Ideas.*
2 vols.

PSYCHOLOGICAL

G. S. BRETT. *A History of Psychology.* 3 vols.

S. G. DIMOND. *The Psychology of the Methodist Revival.*

R. SCOTT FRAYN. *Revelation and the Unconscious.*

SIGMUND FREUD. *Group Psychology and the Analysis of the Ego.
The Ego and the Id.*

T. H. HUGHES. *The New Psychology and Religious Experience. The
Philosophic Basis of Mysticism.*

WILLIAM JAMES. *Textbook on Psychology. The Varieties of Religious
Experience.*

C. G. JUNG. *Collected Papers on Analytical Psychology.*

WM. McDOUGALL. *An Introduction to Social Psychology. The Group
Mind.*

GARDNER MURPHY. *An Historical Introduction to Modern Psychology.*

J. A. C. MURRAY. *An Introduction to a Christian Psycho-Therapy.*

HANNAH W. SMITH. *Religious Fanaticism.* (Ed. Ray Strachey.)

C. H. VALENTINE. *Modern Psychology and the Validity of Christian
Experience.*

E. S. WATERHOUSE. *Psychology and Pastoral Work.*

INDEX OF NAMES AND SUBJECTS

INDEX OF TEXTS

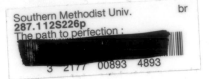